LOOK,
I MADE A BOOK

Rethinking Childhood

Joe L. Kincheloe and Janice A. Jipson
General Editors

Vol. 32

PETER LANG
New York • Washington, D.C./Baltimore • Bern
Frankfurt am Main • Berlin • Brussels • Vienna • Oxford

NINA ZARAGOZA

ERIC DWYER

LOOK,
I MADE A BOOK

Literacy in a Kindergarten
Classroom

PETER LANG
New York • Washington, D.C./Baltimore • Bern
Frankfurt am Main • Berlin • Brussels • Vienna • Oxford

Library of Congress Cataloging-in-Publication Data

Zaragoza, Nina.
Look, I made a book: literacy in a kindergarten classroom /
Nina Zaragoza, Eric Dwyer.
p. cm. — (Rethinking childhood; v. 32)
Includes bibliographical references.
1. Language arts (Kindergarten) 2. English language—
Composition and exercises—Study and teaching (Early childhood)
3. Kindergarten—Activity programs.
I. Dwyer, Eric. II. Title. III. Series.
LB1181.Z37 372.6—dc22 2004027916
ISBN 0-8204-6760-X
ISSN 1086-7155

Bibliographic information published by **Die Deutsche Bibliothek**.
Die Deutsche Bibliothek lists this publication in the "Deutsche
Nationalbibliografie"; detailed bibliographic data is available
on the Internet at http://dnb.ddb.de/.

Cover design by Joni Holst

The paper in this book meets the guidelines for permanence and durability
of the Committee on Production Guidelines for Book Longevity
of the Council of Library Resources.

© 2005 Peter Lang Publishing, Inc., New York
275 Seventh Avenue, 28th Floor, New York, NY 10001
www.peterlangusa.com

Printed in the United States of America

This book is dedicated to all the children at Little River Elementary in Miami, Florida. We thank them for enriching our learning and our lives. May they continue to stand strong and keep their heads up.

Contents

Prologue
Impressionable Artisans

Alice Chu

Some say first impressions make lasting impressions. I demur. It's the lasting impressions that are misappropriated as first impressions. On this October morning as a guest observer of room 8 at Little River Elementary, my first impression would prove too hasty, superficial, even biased. It had been over twenty years since I last walked into a kindergarten classroom. The most challenging task for one five-year-old was to find her name tag on a round piece of red construction paper taped to a nondescript wall. Five-year-olds in room 8 wrote short stories bound in books with red construction paper. Faced with tasks and responsibilities that lesser adults would need a Palm Pilot to keep track of, these students managed their projects with the ease and familiarity of master craftsmen. In this Miami kindergarten of predominantly lower-class African American children taught by a Caucasian female New Yorker, my eyes initially registered clustered desks and chairs; a macabre rug worn from contact with warm bodies; an alphabet ruler running below the windows, and words from the letter of the day hung on cabinet doors; stacks of colorful books; piles of lined brown paper; a box of musical instruments; a tape recorder; and various other classroom staples. While these details *visually* capture the kindergarten classroom, it overlooks its essence: the students. By the end of the morning, my mind was brimming with impressions of a group of artisans who were focused, animated, and ambitious. These five-year-olds were not children, young adults, or even overachievers. They represented individual artists integrated within a troupe. Together they anticipated each class day as another opportunity to create magic through the simple *art* of learning. Even now, nearly a year later, I still feel the pulse of learning that drummed through the classroom, streamed through vibrant minds and bodies, and the beat of a steady diet of knowledge.

What makes this group of twenty or so students—children of low-income housing, divorced families, crime-ridden neighborhoods, and an overpopulated school—merit recognition beyond the boundaries of their campus? Perhaps it's the thought-provoking poetry inked in bold blue letters on canary-yellow paper lining the room like posters announcing an upcoming reading at a local café. Or maybe it's the books piled high on the round table next to the door of the classroom, books wrapped in green, blue, red, and orange covers with titles like "My Day at Grandma's" or "Latisha and Me," penned by local authors in that very room. Then again, the box filled with tambourines, drums, wood blocks, and cha-cha shakers was clear evidence of the dormant reverberations that waited impatiently for musical inspiration. Their accomplishments have been great, but what truly impressed me was the students' attitudes toward learning in the classroom. At 7:55 A.M., a parade of 3-foot-10 to 4-foot-5 individuals marched deliberately into the room, gathered the tools of their trade (books, writing utensils, paper), and stationed themselves behind desks clear of clutter but full of potential. The actors carried out their roles with a striking sense of importance, with little direction and even less interference. The stars of the moment understood what was expected of them. And they were not about to disappoint. Their presence, and moreover their purpose, was etched in their posture, gleaming in their gaze, and resonating in their attitude. Learning was about to take place here.

Neither discriminating nor discouraging words emerged from anyone's lips throughout the morning. Rather, "please," "can," "may I," "let's see," and "share" echoed with repeated use, carried by sincere voices. That is not to say that disagreement and division did not rear its capricious head from time to time, for these are five-year-olds, after all, even if they seem much more mature. Through firm reminders laced with a Brooklyn accent from a facilitating figure who stood only a head taller than most of her apprentices, such lapses in attention quickly passed and were just as rapidly refocused in a new direction. Focus underlined every activity and each transition as the pace of learning never flagged. While enthusiasm and energy may be inherent in sturdy kindergarten-age bodies, empathy and encouragement require role modeling for developing personalities and maturing characters. Although the students were taught not to discriminate against others, they were tutored to discriminate against certain words. *No* and *can't*, *don't*, and *won't* were in peril of marginalization and even obliteration within this constructive learning environment. A negative shake of the head or an embarrassed, shy smile met gentle yet persistent persuasion from all fronts, apprentices and master artisan alike. Here, the quip "resistance is futile" suggested triumph rather than failure.

Whether the activity of the moment included selecting literature, gathering writing materials, marching in time to a Lauryn Hill song, composing a class play, remembering individual lines, or reciting inspired poetry, pride and purpose emanated with each artisan's gesture, strike, and vocalization. Passion throbbed through every rhyme and measure, every beat and glide, and every stroke and flourish. If passion is desire, the avid learners in room 8 at Little River Elementary exuded enough to enthrall a generation of learners. Learning may occur by happenstance through rote memorization, instruction in careful handwriting, and handed-down art projects. Deliberate learning, however, arises from shared vision, individual inspiration, and coordinated enthusiasm. The artists of room 8 list a class play, short stories, poems, recitations, and musical renditions among their achievements. Some believe there is a secret recipe for learning in which the right ingredients will rise when they reach a certain temperature. There is no secret. Learning flourishes with care and noninterference. Everyone has interests—usually several. The craftsmen in room 8 sowed their seeds of interest, let them take root, and merely watched the fruits of their labor sprout, unfurl, and blossom.

Passion is impressionable. Impassioned learning is even more so. If only all kindergartners past and present could embrace this trade.

September

Mom! I have to sit next to him! I have to help him.

When the children walked in I knew I had made the right decision. I felt right at home. I stood in a kindergarten classroom ready to practice my art fully, directly, and passionately. Even though I never distanced myself from the classroom as a university professor (most of my undergraduate classes were actually held within an elementary school classroom as philosophy and practice mixed), I knew I still missed something.

I could still hear some of my university colleagues saying, "Oh, what a change from university to kindergarten" with almost a snicker that insinuated, "Wait until you see what you've gotten into." I would just smile and say, "I started out as a kindergarten teacher." That usually quieted them down.

I have absolutely no regrets about taking a break from the adults at the university. The euphoria I felt matched that of the day before a vacation. Now as a classroom teacher I could focus on what I love best, teaching, and not worrying about dissecting what I do for others to analyze. Here's one of my first diary entries:

> The first day was so hectic that I forgot to turn on the video camera! Besides that, the day went well. We got a lot done. During writing process two children already published books. We didn't do official TAG but we did sit in a circle and I asked each child, "What is your story about?" They gave very high-level answers. It surprised me to see they didn't give every detail but got right to the main idea: "Power Rangers," "A Monster with Teeth," "A Girl."
>
> They did their diaries and decorated a bit for tomorrow so then it will be set. We did the Hello Song and read it too. We did line rules and silent reading. Silent reading went very well but I had to tell them to take more books. They definitely got the hang of it, though. Marc was so cute. He flipped through magazines and

looked just like an adult. Actually, during free time Mare chose to read most of the time.

Tomorrow we'll complete the full schedule. This will help the children feel safe. Getting down that routine is the first step. Of course, the songs and poems help too! I could tell they loved them already. How powerful, too, that we already read the song off the chart and they've already read and written! They're on their way to authorship!

ERIC: Even though I didn't like the idea of getting up at 7:00 in the morning, I was excited about spending my first full day with Nina and her kindergarten class. I had gotten a taste of Nina's work in the elementary school classroom last year when I joined her university students as they participated, taught, observed, and wrote with a group of fourth graders. During that class, her elementary school children dazzled all of us with a poetry recital, full of volume, passion, and language. There were a number of students who were learning English as a second language, and they were the ones I was most focused on. I was so moved by the music and the poetry of that fourth-grade class, though, that lines and divisions between second language learners and native speakers of English blurred. The music was of Tupac Shakur and Tracy Chapman, presumably two artists students could relate to culturally. The poetry was of Langston Hughes, José Martí, and Robert San Souci—certainly not literature of my cultural background, and I suppose not of Nina's either. Still, the children embraced it as their own. On the other hand, Nina made it her own too, even though she wasn't African American, Cuban, or Haitian. The joy and positive spirit that was evident as native English speakers and non-native speakers alike shouted, gestured, and grooved to the poetry and music made me feel like this poetry was indeed for me, a big, tall, lanky white guy from Utah.

Nina and I discussed how language arts in elementary school could be structured so that English speakers, non-English speakers, and children labeled "special education students" (whether appropriately so or not) could participate in a classroom that helped all students progress to their full capabilities. The classroom structure, as far as I was concerned, was anchored around facilitation of language. But in my conversation with Nina later, she said that the language was anchored around safety, and it was the structure of the classroom that helped all students feel safe and able to progress in spite of any widely perceived limitations.

You know, I attended a speech by poet Maya Angelou in Austin in 1996 that made a difference in my life. During her presentation, she discussed an epiphany she had as a young adult. While reading a Shakespearean play, she noticed that she could relate to the writings of an English gentleman from the sixteenth century. As a result, she decided that Shakespeare was not just writing for the sake of telling a story but for a means of communicating to people who could take in his message. In this case, it was Maya Angelou. She said that this realization made her understand that even though centuries, an ocean, and several cultures separated her from Shakespeare, Shakespeare was writing for her.

Listening to fourth graders as they belted out Hughes and Tupac, I found my eyes tearing up a bit and a lump growing in my throat. These children were speaking to me, and the words Martí and San Souci wrote became a part of me. I will always be grateful to Nina for inviting me that day.

I was to watch Nina teach every ten days or so for the next nine months, observing how she could bring poetry, culture, literacy, learning, math, science, and social studies to kindergartners. My main interest in watching Nina was to take an inventory of what she said to native English-speaking students. I wanted to start looking at the kinds of sentences a student learning English might hear from a good teacher of a class filled mostly with native speakers. I thought I was simply going to record a bunch of utterances spoken by Nina and her students. Little did I realize that I was going to observe much more than an antiseptic set of linguistic components. I got a lot more!

NINA: To set the structure in my room I get right to the learning concepts at hand. I do not lecture about rules, or expectations, but begin the teaching learning process immediately and let the structure emerge while the children are engaged in purposeful activities. For example, on the first day I give them each a diary when they come in, and say, "Here is your diary! You can decorate it and then write anything you want in it. Put your diary at your desk and go get some books so at silent reading time you'll be all ready with your books."

You'll notice that I've already begun to facilitate the procedure my students will follow every day of the school year. When they enter the room they go to the shelves to choose their silent-reading books, put them at the corner of their desks, and then begin writing in their diary. I do not wait until all children are present for this discussion but talk to each child as he or she enters. So what happens is that when subsequent children walk in they already see their peers at work, and I reinforce this by directing them to help each other: "Denise, please tell Shaquilla what she needs to do."

I also explicitly recognize children who are following our structure, and in this way we continue to create and maintain it. "Andre already has books at the corner of his desk and now he's decorating the cover on his diary. Thank you, Aaron, you're helping Virginia with remembering her books." You'll notice that even though it is the first day I am already using their names. I can do this because I have already written their name tags in bold manuscript letters and as they walk in I say, "Good morning," and then tape their names on the top corner of the desk they choose to sit in. How do you think this helps with creating a secure, safe structure? And why is such a community of paramount importance for effective teaching and learning? While you're thinking of the many answers to these questions, let me share with you some of my early diary entries. As you read these you might come up with your own questions and answers.

> First day
> Diaries
> Writing process
> Silent reading
> Reading discussion
> Free time:
>> write a story
>> read a book
>> puzzles
>> art
>
> What a fantastic day! It went so smoothly (except for Virginia crying—which has lessened, Arturo was absent). The children love the poem "Giggles" by Martin Gardner and they all know "Dreams" by Langston Hughes. Eric came to visit and he was amazed. I am too. Reading and writing went perfectly too. I can't wait until next week.

ERIC: I walked through the hallways of Little River that first morning there. I saw papers hung on the walls that read "Welcome Parents" and "Reading is cool!" The walls were white and the trim of the building was a soft, slightly lavenderish sky blue. "I guess these are the school colors," I said to myself.

Nina had told me to show up a little before 8:15 in front of room 24, wait at the door, and bring a book to read. I found the room, opened my book bag that had my notebook and my morning Spanish-language newspaper. This was Miami, after all. I leaned against the wall across from the metal room 24 door, also painted that nice blue color, and started reading my paper. At approximately 8:15, I heard Nina's voice as she led twenty-four children down the hallway. I heard her cries of:

- Beautiful!
- Wow, you're walking in such a nice way!
- You know what you need to do.
- Get ready for the day.
- You need to get focused for the day.
- What's the first thing we do in the morning?
- I think you're going to have a beautiful day.

as she monitored the children from the beginning of the line all the way to the end. She smiled at me and said, "Good morning!" and then asked the children to say "Good morning" to me in English, Spanish, and Haitian Creole. Before she opened the blue metal door, she looked at the children to make sure they understood the routine. I certainly had no idea what she was referring to, so I already felt like the children must be twice as intelligent as me. The children looked focused. Suddenly, being in bed in my apartment with the newspaper and a cup of coffee seemed much easier.

But that was a horrible thing to think! In fact, I'm almost ashamed of myself for having had that thought, because when the door opened I was in a carnival. The room was decorated with all the characters in English—twenty-six uppercase letters, twenty-six lowercase letters, and ten numerals—and these characters were all over the place! There were all colors on the walls; even the sink was streaked with pink paint. I will never forget the books and the posters and the flip charts and the signs and the magazines and the notes on the blackboard. You can see some of them in the picture. The room was covered with information. It wasn't pictures or cartoons, the kind of classroom decorations I recalled from my elementary school days. Everything in Nina's classroom was stuff that could be read.

Structure Language

There was structure in the children's routine and there was structure in Nina's language. In fact, Nina's language, the actual words she chose to use, exhibited several qualities that I saw as facilitating successful classroom discipline, especially in terms of the children's successful classroom discipline, and their understanding of the structure. She used *pivots* and *collocations*.

Pivots
When I walked in, the children started gathering books for reading and placing them on a specified corner of their desks. Their names were on their desks. There wasn't too much talking. All students collected a stack of four or five reading materials—big books, children's stories, magazines—and then went to their desks, where they each took out a folder. "I see Andre is already taking out his diary," Nina would say, referring to several different students who were doing something right. Then, as she made announcements, she included several repetitions of "Thank you," and "Thank you, for looking at me." Such repetition was common throughout the day (and indeed throughout the year). She would use the same sentence several times, changing only a single word or noun each time. Could this be a strategy for helping students learning language? Could Nina be fostering a sort of pivot language?

Pivot language? What's that? Well, as it is defined by Roger Brown (1973), it's not what a teacher or mother says to the child, but what a child says. Brown notes that two-year-old children often create language using pivots. In other words, when a child makes a two-word utterance, one of the words is often the same in the next utterance. For example, "Mommy sock" will become "Mommy cookie" and "Mommy milk." Or "Allgone cookie" will be followed by "Allgone milk" or "Allgone water."

In these cases, "Mommy" and "Allgone" become the pivots that children attach language to. They take one word and then apply the complement in the position before or after the pivot word (in each of these cases, after the pivot). But here, Nina was providing pivots for her children to attach the language of the structure and the routine of the structure to. So Nina had children gathering silent-reading books at the same time, had them placing the silent-reading books in the same corner of each child's desk, and had students write the number of the date in a calendar grid she had provided for her students' diaries. This was immediately clear. But upon hearing her directions, I realized that she used regular pivots to help structure even the language of the classroom. Why do you think she would do all this, structure in routine, structure in placement of items, and—perhaps oddly—structure in her own vocalizations?

Collocations

Particularly in the scheduling, Nina had sets of two-word phrases to describe different parts of the day. She had "writing process," "silent reading," "reading discussion," "free time," and "'Dreams,' by Langston Hughes." These are all examples of what Michael Lewis (2000) calls *collocations*. Lewis notes that most words in a language seem to hinge on the words that hang around them. When words hinge on each other to the extent that the words in the set sound wrong when one of the words is changed, that set of commonly grouped words within a phrase is known as a collocation. For example, you can have "Merry Christmas," "Happy Christmas" (if you speak forms of British English) and "Happy Birthday," but you don't generally hear "Merry Birthday." In these cases, "Merry Christmas" and "Happy Birthday" are collocations. My friend Beverly Ingram once pointed out to me that we can have a "golden opportunity" but not a "bronze opportunity." Can you think of any other collocations?

Thinking of phrases in terms of collocations is a good task to do regularly in your classroom. Researchers like Norbert Schmitt (2000) have found that when people learn collocations first, they learn the words inside those collocations faster. In other words, it's easier to learn "Happy Birthday" and then "happy" and "birthday" than it is to learn "happy" and "birthday" individually and then put them together again later to make "Happy Birthday." Nina's class is full of collocations. As we go through the year, I'll be sure to point out a number of them to you.

Structure of the Day

As mentioned earlier, the structure of the first day of class would begin the routine. This routine would be followed from the first day of the year to the last school day nine months later. Oh, on occasion there would be shifts, but this fundamental structure stayed true for the most part from the very first day. Nina even had the times of these routines listed on one of her wall posters. All the signs had collocations to define them: our schedule, our community rules, line rules, silent reading rules, TAG (part of writing process, described later in this chapter), and reading discussion rules.

On the day I visited, community rules and silent reading rules were repeated one by one. However, throughout the day, Nina referred to all sets of rules with questions or comments like:

- What are the line rules?
- What are you doing?
- You need to remember our rules.
- You already know what to do next, right?
- You don't need me to tell you.

However, Nina is also aware that having a large set of rules necessitates an acquisition process. While she helps students to keep in mind at all times that rules are essential to the structure and success of the class, she helps them get through the rules with calm but constant references to how those rules can be carried out:

- Put your homework at the corner of your desk.
- If you want a community pencil, please remember to put it back before you go.
- Let's list the things we can do during free time. Thank you!
- Put the math kits away, please.
- Put your paper in your backpack.
- Put your backpacks on.
- Do not take your writing folder or your diary home with you.
- See if there's something that needs to be cleaned or organized.
- When I come around to hug you, then you can get on line.
- Aren't you proud that you followed the rules?

What expressions would you describe as pivots or collocations there? Why would Nina choose to keep such a structure for the entire year? What would be the advantages of establishing such a rigid schedule and keeping to it all year? What would the drawbacks be?

Expectations

NINA: I'm sure you can already tell that I expect a lot from my young students. Do you notice that I do not speak to them like babies? Notice that I speak to the students clearly and directly and immediately expect them to help themselves and others. Why do you think expectations are a part of our discussion about kindergarten literacy? How do you think expectations might influence success in the classroom? How do you yourself react to the expectations that teachers might have for you?

I have noticed this year more than ever that my students meet and surpass my expectations. The more I give them, whether it is additional academic work, increased responsibility, or new projects, the more they want. Let me give you a quick example. I started to put out piles of math worksheets for the children to choose from during free learning time. I purposefully put out some first- and second-grade addition and subtraction sheets, and figured perhaps that some of the students would attempt them. Well, when word got out what was in the pile—"first-grade work!"—a stampede almost ensued. Of course, half the class could be heard reciting our rule, "Only three people in one place at one time!"

I believe that we do not expect enough from our young children. For whatever reason—readiness research, entrenched early childhood practices—we as a nation have decided not to push our youngsters to their highest potential. This is a tragedy. Our children want to learn and need to learn. Most are indeed quite capable of learning to read at five years of age. Why are we holding them back? How is it that youngsters all over the world are reading at five, and some of our children are just beginning to read in first grade? What do you think? We will explore these questions throughout this book, and you will witness the youngsters in this classroom, learning to write and read, and loving it.

ERIC: Nina wants no distraction and expects ultimate respect for the task and its demands. You will see these high expectations cut across her day and her curriculum, from getting to school on time ("You need to come early" and "Could you get him here on time, please?") to the last word of the "Goodbye Song" ("Let me hear you") to the final dismissal ("Let's see how nicely you walk down the hall"). All are expected to and do fully participate. She also holds high expectations for herself in all activities. During silent reading, she reads to herself. "Please don't interrupt me while I'm reading." During poetry and song, she recites and sings. She too follows the rules, and when she doesn't, she apologizes: "Sorry to interrupt you." Here again, you see both teacher and students equally involved in all aspects of the classroom. Why do you think this important? How will this influence student progress and their own expectations of themselves? Even in clean-up tasks, she expects the children to take joint responsibility: "Put the math kits away, please." How do you think getting chores done is related to classroom expectations and generally to teaching and learning?

Already the other kindergarten teacher has made negative remarks about two of the children she had in summer school. I just hope they're on my class list. Also these cafeteria workers are yelling at my children because they haven't learned their lunch numbers! I will not harass my children or their families about them either! (Side note: my children ended up being the ones who learned them the fastest—without my harassment.) The number of interruptions that have nothing to do with instruction is incredible. I must have had a knock on my door at least every ten minutes. The interruptions are so irritating. I think people will be getting the hint with me though soon. I ignore the knocking until I am finished with what I'm doing, or if the person comes in, I will say, "Just a minute" and finish the activity as they wait. Hopefully, this will give the hint that I see my children as the most important part of my job! How rude to interrupt the children and their work; it's basically telling them that they and their work are not important! I think the positive people really enjoy waiting for a bit and getting to see what we're doing. I enjoy people seeing it! The children are amazing. I am learning over and over again that we can expect so much more from children than we traditionally do. These children can really run the class and it is all a testament of a safe and structured community where all members know exactly what is happening, when and why. For example, children know immediately what to do after lunch—no words need to be spoken—I'll dim the lights, turn on the music, and we'll begin to read—for thirty straight minutes! Yes, no one believes that kindergartners can do it—including the other kindergarten teachers—but they are. And of course, one of the reasons is that I am reading silently too.

ERIC: Why would Nina hope to have the other kindergarten teacher's problem children in her class? Nina has one rule when she talks to other teachers or substitutes or other children: "When you're talking to me about someone, I only want to hear something positive about that person." What attitude throughout the school is she trying to generate here? Why would the cafeteria workers be so upset that five-year-olds can't remember lunch numbers? Is it that they think that five-year-olds can count so high? If so, you might think they have really high expectations of entering kindergartners. On the other hand, perhaps they just dread having to deal with children who don't know their lunch numbers. In any case, the lunch numbers and the way the cafeteria workers are treating the children is upsetting to Nina and to the children. Nina doesn't shy away from their unpleasantness. As they prepare to go to lunch, Nina helps children recite their lunch numbers and reminds them, "Now, say it loud, because I don't want the lunch lady to yell at you or me." Is she right to point out how to deal with the regular unpleasantness of the cafeteria workers? Or should she avoid the unpleasant topic? What would you do, and why?

Here's another question. Why do you think people might think it okay to interrupt a kindergarten class? Is it okay, or are we just being uppity? Nina is confident about giving her opinion to people who interrupt her class. She tells the people who knock while she is teaching that the children come first. She lets people stand outside the door, even if it takes a minute or two. She has a sign outside the door that says, "Class is in session. If you must knock, please knock only once and wait. We will answer the door as quickly as possible. Thank you!"

Expectations also entail responsibility, not just behavior modification. Nina tries to generate a sense of responsibility and pride in the students. She expects good stuff, so why shouldn't the children expect it of themselves? You can hear her own expectations in affirming comments such as:

- Remember, this is your responsibility—not your mother's.
- You really take care of your books!
- Beautiful! You're here early. Now you have time to get your silent-reading books!
- Where should you put it back? Anywhere, or in a special place?
- Almost everyone brought homework. Wow! Who didn't bring it, Marc? You need to work on that, Marc, so we can have 100 percent homework done in our community.
- I'm waiting for more hands, please. I see the same people raising their hands. I want to see more people sharing and thinking.

Why do you think Marc can take Nina's strong guidance in a positive way here? Remember how this community is set up. Children are not singled out negatively, but the community needs to know what each member needs to practice. Therefore, Marc takes Nina's advice as caring. In the meantime, while Marc might have to work on homework expectations, Nina will consciously make sure that he gets positive recognition for expectations he has met.

Families

NINA: I think it is essential that a strong positive connection be fostered and maintained with all the families of my children. This, I'm sure, is one of the reasons my children are so successful in their first year of public education. Just as I empower children with the knowledge of the structure and curriculum of the classroom, I do the same with their families. Each month, all families receive a detailed letter about the curriculum and other monthly events. In this way, they are continually connected and included in our community. My first letter, given on the first day of school, is a letter of introduction and expectations. Take a look:

September, 1999

Dear Family,

I am looking forward to working with you and your child. It will be a year of learning and high achievement. I am an experienced educator and have had 15 years' experience in both elementary school and university levels. I strongly believe in the importance of including the family in all aspects of your child's educational program.

You can expect me to provide for your child:

1. a safe, accepting, and structured learning environment;
2. high expectations for learning and behavior;
3. a classroom that values independence and cooperation among children and adults; and
4. a program that will encourage your child to express him/herself through writing, reading, and performing poetry, drama, and other literature forms.

I expect that your child will:

• do all his/her work to the best of his/her ability;
• behave in a friendly and cooperative manner toward classmates and adults;
• return completed homework on the day that it is assigned; and
• come to school with a cheerful and enthusiastic attitude.

I expect that your family will:

• make sure that your child is in school every day, on time, and ready to work;
• provide your child with sufficient supplies needed to complete work appropriately;
• provide enough time and space for your child to complete daily homework; and
• feel welcome to communicate and participate freely in all classroom activities.

Again, welcome! It is an honor to serve you and your child. Please feel free to contact me if you have any questions or suggestions.

Nina Zaragoza (305) 555-3699 home; (305) 555-9633 work

How do you think a strong relationship with the families influences the teaching and learning process? By the way, why do you think I use the word "families" instead of "parents"? Which do you think is a more inclusive term? Why do we need to be inclusive? How would such inclusivity influence the safety of the classroom?

ERIC: I noticed on my first visit that Nina spoke freely and directly to the families. As you can tell by her first letter, she expects as much from her families as she does from her children.

One of Nina's diary entries:

> Some families think it doesn't matter what time they bring their children to school. I'm already telling them make sure they are on time or they will miss a lot. I called all the families to say Hi. They seem very nice and very pleased that I called to say hello. I am looking forward to working with them and hope they come to visit regularly.

ERIC: I was watching a rerun of *I Love Lucy* the other day. Lucy's child Little Ricky comes home and has a sheet of paper pinned to his jacket. His mother says, "Uh oh! Did you come home with a note from school today?" When I was in a school play in seventh grade, I apparently acted inappropriately during a rehearsal and one of the teachers called my mom. When I got home from school, Mom said, "I got a call from Mr. Jeppesen today." Immediately my heart jumped into my throat.

Why should a message from a teacher to a child's family entail "uh oh"s or throat lumps? Why must contact from a teacher mean bad news? Doesn't that make the teacher the villain? My mother would say that if a person has only something negative to say, they don't appear to be honest because they don't seem to look at life critically. In other words, if a teacher has only negative things to say about a child, why should the child's family believe the teacher's opinion? In a sense, the same thing can be said for someone who only gives positive comments. How honest is that? How helpful is that? And is a teacher approachable if all her comments are skewed in one direction?

My first-grade teacher Mrs. Hall made regular phone calls to my mom to say Hi and to let my mom know how I was doing. Often the message was positive, but not always. On the days when it wasn't so positive, Mom didn't disbelieve or blame the teacher. There was open communication and help. In fact, they started a lifelong friendship, and now I see my first-grade teacher every time I visit my folks in New Mexico. It's been over thirty years, and now I'm on a first-name basis with my first-grade teacher, and my family has a happy and exciting relationship to brag about with her, mostly due to her honest, regular, and helpful appraisal of my progress.

Nina follows this same philosophy. She walks the children out to the bus stop in the front of the school, where families meet their children to pick them up. She greets the families and, as often as possible, says, "Your child had a beautiful day!" or "Guess what Jarrell did today! Oh, you would be so proud." I think finishing the school day this way helps everyone involved: the teacher, the child, and the family. One day, Andre had to leave early and the secretary on the intercom interrupted to call Andre to the front of the school. Nina asked Andre to tell his grandmother that the next time he had to leave early she would like his grandmother to come to the classroom to pick him up so that Nina could say Hello and see how she's doing.

It's September, and some families with their first children are bringing their children to elementary school for the first time. Some arrive late. Nina's not happy that the children are late or that the families are bringing them late, but she seems pleased that she can have a couple of moments to personally talk with the families: "Your child misses so much when she's not here, and our community is so much better when she's here. Thanks!" It is this regular sense of communication, both verbal and written, that Nina engenders. But this is not the only way Nina involves the families in the children's daily classroom activities.

Class Mascot

ERIC: An integral part of Nina's class and its connection to the families is the class mascot. In this case, it's a teddy bear called Brownie. Brownie in effect is a part of the classroom community. Brownie talks. Brownie sits next to the books. Brownie is included in reading discussion, as in this discussion of *Charlotte's Web*: "What would Brownie think about Wilbur becoming ham?" Brownie is included in TAG discussions, too, as in this question: "What suggestion might Brownie have to help Cal write his story?" Brownie's name is even on the class list. But most important, Brownie, along with Brownie's own purple diary folder, goes home with one child each day, and the child gets to write about Brownie in Brownie's diary. On the outside of the folder is a message written by Nina to the child's family:

> Your child has been given our class mascot to take home for the evening. Please have him/her write/draw about this experience! Please make sure, too, that our mascot comes to school the next day with your child! Thanks! Dr. Zaragoza

So the families diligently work with the child each night to prepare an entry for Brownie's journal. Often the child will dictate to a sister or father or grandparent or cousin. Sometimes it's a full letter. Often it's a list of sentences, usually reviewing the activities of the day, as in this example:

> 9-24-99
>
> Brownie and I were picked up after school and stayed at work with my dad until my mom picked us up. We played until it was time for my bath. Later Brownie sat by my side while I practiced writing my name. At bedtime Brownie was laying on the bed while my mom helped me read The Royal Dinner. Brownie slept with me all night.
>
> Jarrell

Sometimes, the child does invented spelling, and the family member edits the child"s words. I find this remarkable, because then the child must instruct the family member on the way editing is done during wWriting pProcess in class. Note this example:

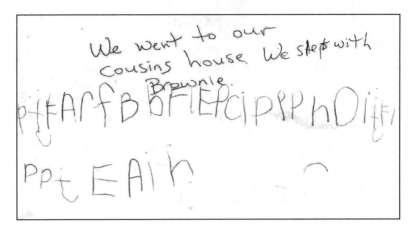

It seems that the families are very good about writing with their child and letting their child put his or her name on the work. It's also impressive to see the enthusiasm the families have over for writing Brownie. Note Aubrey's entry:

> . . . and we read a book with my mom. Brownie and I slept with my mom and sisters. We had a wonderful time together today. Thank you so much for letting Brownie come home with me. My mom enjoyed Brownie's company.

Sometimes, children write on their own, even if it's just a picture. And when it is a picture, it's usually a drawing of Brownie. Take a look at this entry:

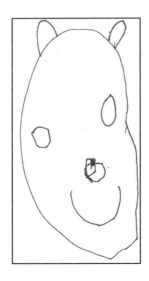

Curriculum

NINA: My curriculum is rigorous, high-level, meaningful, engaging, and flexible. All children are expected to succeed and they do succeed. A child's success does not depend on another child's failure, but all succeed at their own rate in their own time. Children are pushed and push each other within a writer's workshop that honors all children's stories and writing and reading levels. All children are taught in full community, and absolutely no child is ever denied any access to the curriculum. While all children might not use the skills under discussion at the same time, they have the right to listen and begin to connect.

Interestingly, when most educators in the United States talk about kindergarten curriculum, writing is not included in the discussion. In fact, when I proposed this book to an editor, she replied, "I didn't know much writing was going on in kindergarten." But in the kindergarten class you will connect to in this book, five-year-olds do write, and they write every day. They are involved in many forms of writing: diary writing, pen pal letters, thank you notes, drama productions, and family-facilitated writing centered around a class mascot. Most notably, they progress through the writing process and bring their own individual narrative pieces to final publication. These young authors also read and discuss the work of other writers and poets such as E. B. White, Langston Hughes, and Gwendolyn Brookes during daily literacy conversations. Because of their emerging self-perception of authorship, they begin almost immediately to connect other authors' work to their own writing. Why do you think these children begin to connect in this way? What do you think it is about writing that enables children to more actively respond to other forms of literacy? Have you ever thought that writing can be taught even before children begin to read? Think about your answers to these questions, and you'll hear our answers as we go through the year. Do you remember what Piaget said about learning and proceeding from concrete to abstract? What do you think is more concrete—writing or reading? Bear this question in mind for now, and we'll look into it more deeply as the months progress.

> We have at least 100 empty book covers done and already the room is surrounded with literacy—just think when we start creating the charts! Very exciting. I expect these children to read in no time! I can't wait!
>
> There are books surrounding us! I can't wait until the children come!
>
> The instructional time went great! I integrated Math with Attendance and it was so much fun for me and the children—counting—making faces on the board for each child, etc., etc. They loved it!

ERIC: As you can probably tell, Nina's classroom is pretty complex. In many ways, each of the components of the day is connected to others. So how does

Nina address curriculum? You've seen the structure and rules. You've seen how the family is at the forefront of thinking. You've seen that asking children to challenge themselves is part of the expectations. Now, how does the content that needs to be learned, the supposed reason children go to school, get put in the spotlight? For Nina, there is one word that transcends all learning done in the classroom: *author*. The children are authors and they speak to each other as fellow writers. The word *author* is found in the word *authority*. Therefore, the children are authorities of their own learning that they relate to the families when doing homework or writing for Brownie. They are also authorities for each other as they work in community. Finally, as authors, they work as researchers of their next novel by looking into other authors as they work their way through the world. These authors help them understand not only writing and reading, but also science, math, and social studies.

As you already know, structure and curriculum are in many ways synonymous in Nina's room. Therefore, because structure was immediately set, so was curriculum. Children immediately got a sense of what they needed to do and learn in this classroom. Let's give you a sense of what's happening by presenting a brief overview. In October, we'll give you more details about the curriculum and the exact rules children followed as they progressed.

Diaries, Attendance, Poetry, and Morning Discussion

First, children write in their diaries. As you may remember, Nina tells the children that they may write whatever they would like. She encourages self-expression and the daily habit of writing. As you can see from the diary entries on the following pages some children draw pictures. Others will actually start attempting to make letters.

After the children write in their diaries, listen to the morning announcements, take attendance (Nina does this by asking them to share something; one day it was their favorite food or their favorite animal), the children do poetry. The first poem of the year is "Dreams," by Langston Hughes (see *The Collected Poems of Langston Hughes*, 1995). Why would Nina choose this poem for this class?

As they recite "Dreams," complete with gestures and rhythm, Nina highlights some vocabulary and underlines words. In their discussion, the words "puppy" and "New York City" come up. Those words are on the wall, so Nina asks, "Where is 'New York City' found in this room?" and "Can anyone find the word 'puppy' in this room?"

Nina also introduces them to the sounds of the language and how these sounds can correspond to written symbols. For example, Nina received a box from a friend, which had a surprise in it. She brings out the box and says, "What do you think is in the box?" Students guess. At first, they ask Nina to tell them what's in the box, but she doesn't know. Still she asks them to guess. Why do you think she would do that?

After they have guessed, she asks them to guess one more thing, the name of the person who sent it. She says, "The name of my friend begins with the sound /sh/. Can you guess her name?" Many children guess Cheryl or Shane or Sean, but it's really Shauna. Each time a child guesses, she says, "That's a pretty good guess. That name does begin with /sh/, but it's not the name," and she makes a sad face over the student's being wrong. But quickly she reemphasizes, "But that's a good guess. It does begin with /sh/." Nina then opens the box a little and gasps. A couple of students shout out, "What's in there, Dr. Zaragoza?" whereupon Nina looks at a student who has not called out and says, "Thank you, Denise, for not calling out," in the pivot way described earlier. She then says, "Oh wow! There are some things in here that start with /m/. What do you think they are? I'll give you a hint. It starts like mmmmmoney. It starts like mmmmmarshmmmallows. Let me see some hands of people who think they know what might be in here."

The hands go up, and Nina starts to call on them.

"They're meatballs!"

"Meatballs begins with /m/, but there aren't any meatballs in here. Good try, though! Cal?"

"Cherries!"

"Mmm! Cherries! But cherries don't begin with /m/. That word begins with /ch/."

This goes on for a while, until Nina pulls out a set of magazines. "Look! They're mmmmagazines." At this point, Nina notices that a bunch of the magazines have pictures of wild animals on them. "Oh look! These have pictures of wild animals on them. We can use them during silent reading and while we're learning about living things."

Writing Process

After poetry and the surprise, the children engage in writing process. In our October chapter, you'll get the full details on writing process. However, we know you must be excited to know at least a little about writing process, so here's a quick sample of one young author's first piece.

Already, Aubrey is attempting to write letters. The letters seem to be capital *A* and *D*. In both cases, they're letters that start on the left bottom side and then go up and curve on the top. Aubrey also has an illustration of a mom and a dad. On her story side, she keeps the picture in lead-colored pencil, but she illustrates the people again on the front cover with colored crayons.

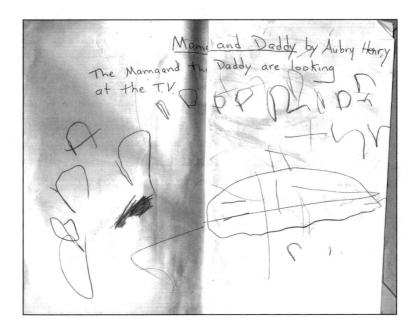

When writing process is finished, Nina cries out, "We have a bunch of cool new books. Perhaps you can look at them during silent reading." Indeed, children do take these publications and look at them during silent reading, treating them with the same respect as the other books and magazines that come from the library or outside the school.

Later, the class listens to each child as he or she shares a story he or she has authored. The author first recognizes which children are sitting nicely. Nina encourages this by saying, "Thank you for waiting until everyone is listening. Wow, good listening, Jamal!" The child then announces, one by one, three tasks and waits for classmates' hands to go up. The announcements are:

> T—Tell what you like
> A—Ask questions
> G—Give suggestions

The children do contribute in TAG sessions, but some have trouble distinguishing between "Tell what you like" and "Ask questions," particularly during the latter. Nina often says, "That was nice that you liked that, but that's not a question. Can you think of a question for Larry?" If the child can, Nina lets the question go. If not, she then asks, "Do you want me to come back to you?" During the discussion, you can hear Nina guide the children in their conversations:

- Any ideas for Larry and his story?
- Should he add anything to his story?
- What part of his story do you like?

Probably the biggest problem during this phase in early September is the volume of the children while working through TAG. They speak softly, both when reading their story and when asking and answering questions. As a result, we often hear Nina say, "Say it louder, please!"

Reading Aloud

The first book Nina shares with the class this year is E. B. White's *Charlotte's Web* (1952). Do you think this is a good book to start off the year with? Why or why not? For the children here, having Nina read *Charlotte's Web* aloud serves several purposes. First, it gives the child authors yet one more shot at discussing creative writing. While reading the chapter of the day out loud, Nina interrupts the story to ask the children some questions. For example, she says,

- Why do you think the author wrote ___ in that way?
- What would you do if you were the author?
- Have you ever written a story with animals that talk? Do you think you might one day? Why?

What other questions related to authorship can you think of while doing reading aloud? Furthermore, why would reading aloud be an important activity in a kindergarten class and how does it connect to the children's writing development? The answers to these questions could be long lists, and we'll touch on them throughout the year. Still, give it a first go, then we'll look at it further in October.

Silent Reading

For silent reading, lunch is over, the lights are dim, children have their stack of books on the same corner of each desk, Sade is singing softly on a cassette tape, and Nina takes out her book and sits at one of the desks with the children. I have my newspaper, so I'm busy looking at it. However, I can't help notice what's going on with the children. They're looking at the pictures, they're noticing the script, they're trying to put the book in the right-side-up position with the binding on the left, they're humming words to themselves, and they're pointing to things. The children are on task, and the thirty minutes whiz by, as far as I'm concerned. I actually did read a number of articles in my newspaper. Occasionally I hear Nina saying, "What beautiful silent reading!" She allows the humming and the occasional rustling of books, but she doesn't allow the hum to become raucous. Perhaps she's using Sade as a volume gauge; I don't know. It seemed to me that when we couldn't hear the soft music, Nina asked children to lower the volume a bit. But she never stifled it. Silent reading is the goal, and she respects the acquisition process in achieving that goal.

Reading Discussion

After silent reading, children are given the opportunity to discuss their reading material in small discussion groups. Children often meet in groups of two or three people, and Nina directs them with comments such as "Help your friends find a group," "Make sure there are only two or three in a group," "Make sure everybody gets a chance to speak," "What are some things we can talk about in reading discussion group?" Children respond with "our books, our favorite characters, why we picked our book, what our books are about," and so forth. Note here again that children are actively connecting to the work of other authors. In this way, children begin to understand that reading and communication with each other are linked. Just as we as readers want to talk about books we read with our friends, children do as well. Reading in this classroom, then, not only is an academic pursuit, but also helps to build social relationships. So why do you think Nina's children are so successful with silent reading? Most kindergarten teachers will complain that their children cannot successfully read silently for thirty minutes. So why can Nina's children? As you're thinking about answers to this question, think about why reading discussion always follows silent reading in this community. We'll give you a hint:

the answers have something to do with reading discussion and also what Nina is doing during these activities.

Interdependence

NINA: All children have the responsibility to help all others in the community, including me. Again, you've already seen, even in some of my first interactions with the students, that I begin to lay the foundation for interdependence early: "Thank you, Aaron, for helping Virginia remember her books." Do you see how that immediately lets the children know that they are expected to depend on each other? I am not the only one directing the community. Each and every child is too. We are all involved in helping each other succeed. How do you think this influences our classroom? Think about issues of power, competition, and the roles of the teacher and the students when you begin to develop answers to this question. As the story of this classroom unfolds, you'll get a clear vision of children and their teacher working with each other and for each other. They are united in the common purpose of ensuring success for all.

ERIC: I remember that during my first visit to Nina's classroom, a child came to me for help on work and Nina quickly admonished me, "Don't let them come up to you. I don't want to set that pattern." When I listened closely to her conversations, I understood what she meant. Nina peppers her talk with questions such as

- Are you helping her look at the words?
- What do you need to tell Jamal?

to quickly set the pattern that she is not the only teacher in the room. And while she exudes a strict authority over all that happens in the room, she also consciously steps back with directions such as "Don't look at me! Look at your friends," allowing children to express their own authority. That she allows children this authority doesn't mean that it diminishes hers at all. Indeed, in Nina's view, authority is a renewable resource that all people and children have the right to experience. When everyone has the right and responsibility to teach and learn, all people gain. Notice that Nina did not have to deal with the lunch numbers on her own. She had her children help her and each other. They help her with curricular decisions, remembering assembly times, what poem to type up next, and finding the pen she just lost. Think about how the children must think about themselves when they're active authorities in their room. Why do you think this would be important in the literacy process?

One of Nina's diary entries:

I have two children crying for a while—Virginia and KeAndre—it should die out soon. The children are so patient with noise and they continue their work as I say "Thank you for being patient with Virginia and KeAndre. That will show them that we care."

After just one week, Virginia is a different child! Oh it gives me the chills just to think about it. Now she runs to class—her face radiant, her eyes beaming. I am so serious and I have a picture to prove it! She has a certain glow about her that is almost tangible. She feels safe and loved! And she is! To help her learn to write her name I wrote it letter by letter for the whole class to learn it with her. Powerful. To help her, Aubrey, Denise, and KeAndre to learn their lunch numbers we all recited it for a few days like we do our poems. Now, they, and all of us, know our lunch numbers. God! Isn't that what a community should do for each other? Yes! And we do!

KeAndre has turned the corner too. His mother said one morning he woke up and said, "Hurry! I have to get to school!" After this he hasn't cried since. So much love surrounds him! Shaquilla especially has taken him under her wing and watches over him. She makes sure she sits next to him in circle time and reminds him to look at the pictures when we read. I can hardly describe it. His eyes hurt him and so he doesn't open them fully sometimes and so walks with his head down if it's too early or too sunny. Somehow, Shaquilla makes sure he is behind her on line and lets him hold her backpack as they walk. It brings me to tears.

Shaquilla's mother came and asked whether KeAndre's condition was contagious. I said no, but if she wanted me to get a note from KeAndre's mother, I would be happy to. I also suggested moving Shaquilla's seat away from KeAndre's. Her mother said, "Oh no! I already suggested that to Shaquilla, and Shaquilla refused. She told me, 'Mom! I have to sit next to him! I have to help him.'" They truly take care about each other.

My little crisis today had nothing to do with the children—I thought I lost the empty attendance envelope (horrors!) and wasted a lot of time looking for it! Turns out the office never gave it back to me!

ERIC: How can a teacher follow twenty-four children at the same time? When there are twenty-four children in a classroom, how can a teacher ensure that each child gets an even distribution of personalized attention? And finally, are the goals of school exclusively to learn the subject matter, or are there certain life lessons that can be generated here?

The problems that Nina encountered in this first month—lunch numbers, outside interruptions, missing attendance envelopes—have little to do with reading, math, or science. Or do they? They do, because those problems are obstacles to overcome if we want reading, math, and science to happen and happen successfully for every child. When presented in these terms, I often feel overwhelmed, like teaching's a job I would never want. But then, when success and learning happen as a result of children helping each other, I can't imagine being in some other place.

You'll often hear Nina proclaim,

- Remind me where my chalk is.
- Remind me that we have to have the forms in tomorrow.
- Thank you for reminding me.

With Nina's showing the children how they help her, she can model how children can help each other. The children of the classroom community pitch in to do the chores together. Nina doesn't trail children around to pick up after them. Instead, she gives them responsibility. She asks long sets of questions concerning this responsibility. We often hear:

- Good, Tommesha, you're keeping it in control.
- It's very respectful to allow everybody to do it.
- Make sure your friends are doing it.
- Let's give Virginia a hand for being on time.
- I need to hear "thank you."
- Thank you for being understanding about the instrument you get during music time.
- Help the person next to you with the number.
- Are you helping her to look at the words?
- Please listen to what Andre just said.
- We help our friends follow the rules.
- We're all friends and we have to help everyone in the classroom feel safe.
- What do you need to tell them? Does someone need help?

When a child is late or has missed a day, that child can expect to hear:

- We missed you yesterday. It's great that you're here.
- Tell your family you can't be absent. We need you here.

But also you will see Nina laud the students who have followed the routines and rules:

- Let's give Virginia a hand for being on time.
- Give yourself a hand. You all brought your homework.
- Thank you for looking at your friends when they're presenting.

This design of a classroom centered around interdependence is not new, although it isn't discussed much in the United States. In Asia, particularly Japan and Korea, this type of setup is the rule, not the exception. The ministry of education in each of these countries has specific standards that dictate that such structure be a principal part of a school's makeup. In these schools, the first item on the agenda for education is that children learn to get along with each other. This ideal is extended with the notion that getting along is most effectively fostered by teamwork. As a result, schools and grades are divided up into *kumis*, or groups. Each kumi gets a nickname, and each kumi selects a leader for the week. Every child has a kumi, and every child has a chance to be kumi leader. Decisions are made by kumi; therefore, if a kumi leader doesn't agree with an answer, the leader has an obligation to say so, but must represent the kumi's answer in front of the class regardless of his or her own opinion. The kumi then has chores to do. These chores could include making lunch for the grade, serving lunch, cleaning the school, or a number of other daily projects. There is no custodial staff, so the children understand that if they mess up the school, they have more to clean up or more to apologize for in front of other kumis.

Such is the makeup of Nina's class. The groups may not necessarily have nicknames, but they do communicate. There seems to be three groups of students in Nina's classroom, delineated by three clusters of desks. Groups get applause if all members have homework ready. The members of a group help one another edit and gather books. Groups share in the cleaning of the class and the organization of the books and children's publications on the bookshelves. So what do you think? Is it fair to ask kindergartners to have such a number of responsibilities? Is it reasonable to ask kindergartners to take care of each other and their teacher?

We think so. Not just because asking them helps them become better members of our community, but also because it gives the children a sense of pride and self-worth. But perhaps there's a more pertinent question you should ponder here, one that you should pinpoint each day of your study here and throughout your career: To what extent can you set up a safe environment where children's responsibility and caring, as well as the consequences of giving children that level of responsibility, are extended to their fullest? Connecting to and maintaining the community is of utmost importance, and Nina and her children know it. After all, part of the children's daily responsibility is to make sure that Brownie arrives on time and is safe and sound upon arrival. Believe me, if a child hasn't done this with Brownie, they will hear about it, and Nina won't have to say a word.

October
But how? Last year he wouldn't even sit up. Now he looks like a normal child.

NINA: So now we're in October and I already adore all my children. I know that might sound corny to some, but I can't deny this love I have. Furthermore, it's clear that the children love each other. In fact, I know this is a big part of the success of our classroom community. We appreciate each other for who we are, and because of this we naturally encourage growth in each other. As I write this, I think about Shaquilla's caring for KeAndre, and I see our little Virginia. Remember how she cried in September? She also wouldn't speak and would slip under her desk, thinking we wouldn't miss her. But we did, and she soon learned that we did, so she emerged to become an active member of our community. Why wouldn't a child emerge from under a desk in a loving community?

This year in my special education class, Matt also decided to sit in his chair and not under his desk. I heard that he had spent most of the kindergarten year under his desk. When the aide who worked with him last year asked how I did it—when anyone asks me "But how? Last year he wouldn't even sit up. Now he looks like a normal child!"—I mention all the pedagogical elements like implementation of an engaging, purposeful curriculum, allowing children to move physically throughout the day, and so forth. But really, it is all about a teacher's love for each of the students.

I know a common response to this is, "But come on, Nina! That's impossible. How can we love every student?" Yes, I know that we actually condone or accept that teachers will always have their favorites, but I strongly challenge you to question these kinds of assumptions. You *can* love each child. You *can* see the uniqueness of each child. It is a decision you need to make if you want all your children to feel safe and be successful in your classroom. Now, I am not talking about that general way that some people use the word *love*: "Oh, I love children! They're so cute." It's love that is not based on whether you are in a good mood or not, a love that is not emotional. It is a love not based on the system's label but based on the inherent preciousness of each child.

Would it be easier if we change the word *love* to *respect*? Could you respect every student for who they are and who they are meant to become? What if we change the word *love* to *care*? Could you care about every one of your students enough to fully support them in their growth? Use whatever word that might help you move toward this kind of connection with all of your students. It is this connection—this love—that enables the success you will continue to read about in this book. It is a love that is illustrated in our actions and encompasses the discipline and work that will enable the realization of a vision for each of your students. So, when I have high expectations for my students and hold them accountable for appropriate interactions, I am loving them. Let's talk some more about how my structure allows me to have these expectations.

ERIC: Nina challenges you to love every child. This means to love every kind of child, no matter what. Let's look for a moment at Nina's contention that to love each and every child is a decision that a teacher must make. She suggests that to do so or to say so might sound "corny." I suppose to some extent it does sound corny, but there is plenty of evidence suggesting that doing so helps all students. However, more important, there is evidence of student failure, with dire consequences, when teachers actively choose *not* to love or care for every child.

To understand that children have the capacity to embrace one another in a school situation is to understand what children bring to the learning process. A child upon arrival to kindergarten brings five years or so of human interaction grounded in language. These children have already gone through stages of language learning, stages that Jean Piaget (1970) describes as a scientific inquiry into the environment in which children find themselves. At first, they may draw similar conclusions regarding items such as hunger and cookies, suggesting to them that to utter the word "cookie" is to relay both the sense of being hungry and that eating a cookie would alleviate hunger. Michael McCloskey (2002) notes that children often skew their thinking toward the concrete words, in this case *cookie*, as opposed to the more abstract *hunger*. However, by the time students reach kindergarten, children have well parsed an abundance of these experiences and can display expertise in their categorizations. In sum, they don't come to kindergarten a blank slate.

It's very nice to spout ideas like establishing love in the classroom. Our saying such may even appeal to your sense of goodness and humanity. But we also hope you see that with our goal of establishing the most effective environment for learning we're suggesting ideas that are entrenched in research and pedagogy. In other words, if students were somehow learning in an environment where hatred and admonishment were the key ingredients, we would be suggesting that as the vehicle for success. Hatred is, fortunately, a vehicle for failure, as demonstrated in various scientific inquiries. The ingredient we speak of here—the research variable of consequence—with which we see tremendous growth in children is in fact a simple concept with a long description: the establishment of mutual respect among children in an environment where the teacher's respect for the children plays a vital role. A vibrant example of the degree to which this ingredient or lack thereof is of value may be observed in bilingual education and teaching English to new learners.

Vera Collier and Wayne Thomas (2001) have studied several different formats for teaching immigrants in schools and, for more than fifteen years now, they have looked at the effectiveness of the following types of programs:

Mainstream: Students are immediately placed in regular classes regardless of their English ability.

Pull-out: Students are taken from mainstream classes for a supplementary lesson.

Transitional English as a Second Language (ESL): Students attend English classes until they reach an acceptable proficiency level and then join native English-speaking students in mainstream classes.

One-way bilingual: New language learners are taught in their home language half the day and English the rest of the day, while native English speakers have instruction in English all day long.

Two-way bilingual: All students at the school study all subject matter in English half the time and in the second language, most likely the one that suits the community most logically, the other half of the time.

According to Collier and Thomas (2001), the two-way programs yield more students who do better on all kinds of college entrance exams and high-stakes exams, and have better graduation rates than do students in the other kinds of programs. Additionally, immigrants and new English learners tend to make up ground on their native English-speaking counterparts, catching up to them and working comparably in their schoolwork. New English learners do pretty well in the one-way bilingual system as well, but not quite to the degree of those in the two-way system. For all other systems, success is not nearly as evident. Ultimately, in many cases, students going through these nonbilingual systems may not ever expect to catch up to their native English-speaking peers or even to graduate.

Why would the two-way bilingual system show such high rates of success? And why would a two-way system yield more notably favorable results than those of the one-way system? It appears that when all variables common to the five systems are removed, the difference that remains between the one-way bilingual system and the two-way bilingual system is *empathy*. In other words, in a two-way system, all students are in the same boat. They must all learn a new language, they must work in culturally challenging situations where no one culture stands out, they must look at the world from differing points of view, and they are required to get along within this atmosphere—this community. In the one-way system, the native speakers spend the entire day in that dominant language while the non-native speakers spend time in two languages. Hence, the language majority people don't spend equal time experiencing what language minority people do. If this is the case, aren't some clear issues of power eliminated by going to a two-way system? For students in two-way programs, where power is less a concern for both teacher and student, success is strong, while for students and teachers in other programs, where native English speakers have much more power than language minority students, dichotomy and failure are evident.

Unfortunately, most school systems in the United States consider two-way bilingualism a financial hardship and logistical challenge, thereby choosing not to go to this format. This, however, does not mean that a well-trained teacher can't find ways to distribute power evenly in class. Candace Harper and Elizabeth Platt (1998) found evidence that most mainstream teachers in Florida preferred *not* to deal with language minority students or students with varying exceptionalities, often choosing to place these students at the back of the room, hardly ever calling on them, and often leaving them to do handout sheets that might consist of activities not related to the curriculum (for example, coloring or connect-the-dots). What kind of outcome might you expect for these students—children for whom these teachers have overtly decided not to love?

And if it's this way for non-native English speakers, how might it be for students with other needs? How will the children react to the people who are different in any setting? And in which setting do you see students being most accepting of children from different backgrounds or circumstances? Do you see immediately the consequences of choosing not to try to love every student?

In sum, to love students is to understand their backgrounds, whether similar to or different from yours, in concert with those of all the participants in the classroom, to create a harmony from which comfortable learning can take place.

Structure

NINA: You saw how I set up the structure in September, right? The students now in October are comfortably working within this structure with little interference from me. While I still positively recognize students who are following our structure, it is not to maintain it. It's to truly appreciate it. At this point, though, I don't do it often because my artisans are deep in thought and action. Remember the prologue, by Alice? It is a perfect window into our community in October. Now, all learners know exactly what they need to do and get for their work of the day. They know what role they play; they know their purpose: to continue to create and support themselves and each other. When I do need to help them refocus, it takes little time because everyone shares a clear vision of what is expected and what needs to be accomplished. This shared vision was created on the first day as the structure and curriculum emerged. Remember how the children became immediately involved in the curriculum from the first time they entered the classroom? Well, now this structure or our plan for the day is written on the board to solidify the vision:

Things to Do Today

- Diaries
- Pledge/song/poetry
- Go over homework
- Writing process/TAG
- Reading aloud
- Lunch
- Silent reading
- Reading discussion
- Practice play
- Free learning time
- Poetry/music/reading aloud

Notice that this kind of planning reinforces the pivot language Eric spoke about in September. This language continues in October both verbally and through writing. Now my students also participate in this language by sometimes deciding the order or a detail of our plans. For example, I might ask if they'd like silent reading before writing process, or what poem they would like to recite. Since by October they are confidently working within the structure, I allow a certain amount of flexibility. What never changes is the fact that there is purposeful work to do and it needs to get done. This foundational principle is what has helped our community achieve so much in such little time. It helps them remain focused and on task. It also continues to increase the children's sense of authority over the teaching/learning process. The plans aren't secretly placed in my plan book for only visiting administrators to glance at but are open for the whole community to see and use.

Do you see how this is connected to children being independent and interdependent? They know what is expected of them and are confident that they can achieve these expectations in our supportive community and also feel competent to help others achieve these goals.

Let's look at the structure of the day for a minute and think about how and why curriculum activities are ordered in the way that they are. Why do you think children are writing in their diaries first? What message are they immediately receiving as they walk into the room? Well, of course, the first message is, "Okay, let's get writing!" Some might say, "Oh, Nina, can't they just relax for a minute before they have to get to work?" But for my children, writing in their diary *is* relaxing! To love to write and to write first thing in the morning is joyful for people who are authors, and my children are authors.

Do you see?

So what I am saying to them first thing in the morning is, "I respect you as an author." I am also allowing them to collect their thoughts individually before requiring them to participate in full class activities. I see this as a soft, smooth transition from home to school. They do get to relax and take a few breaths as they think about their diary entries. Because they have total choice over what they write in their diaries they are free to think and write about whatever they choose. We'll talk more about the diary writing process later in this chapter when we focus on curriculum.

ERIC: How might you feel if someone said to you, "The first thing you can do every single day is spend time expressing yourself, and no one will criticize it?" What would that be like? And what if that were done in the form of writing every day from your very first day of class?

Many teachers feel they must correct a student's diary, but if we're fostering writing fluency and opportunity to use writing as the most sophisticated form of expression, why would we stifle the advancement of a child (or anyone, for that matter) in this aspect by marking up their papers, their creations, and their artwork? I have also seen teachers take a rubber stamp with the teacher's name on it and stamp the diary work of the student, as if to say, "I approve." Who then has ownership of that work? Some teachers ask their students to write their name on the front of the paper and write the teacher's name immediately below it. Usually students will write both names with characters that are the same size, but usually students write their first name and last name on the paper while the teacher receives the respectful "Miss," "Mrs.," or "Mr."

title. Yes, I understand that if the paper gets lost it's easier for other teachers to bring you that paper. But what message is conveyed through these kinds of labeling activities? What messages do these choices send students? Could it be possible that some teachers recall how they felt when their teachers did these things to them? And is it possible that there's another place (for example, the back of the paper) where the teacher's name could be kept so that it doesn't detract from the student's ownership of his or her creativity?

Yes, I think titles and respect for teachers have their place. I am not suggesting that addressing teachers as Miss, Mrs., or Mr. be abandoned. But we're talking about the ownership of creativity and the morals and ethics behind the labeling of such. If you paint a watercolor or carve a sculpture or compose a symphony, do you put your teacher's name on it? Clearly, Nina and I would like you to constantly think about power and about directing it appropriately and in a timely manner. It seems that when power is placed in the students' hands at the proper times, their learning and positive experiences can flourish. Getting the day started on the right foot through self-expression through writing is clearly a point of departure in Nina's system.

NINA: After diary writing is the Pledge of Allegiance and "The Star-Spangled Banner." As you can probably imagine, my young students are as involved in this activity as in any other. We stand and recite and sing as we look at the words displayed on chart paper. In fact, every day a child is chosen to take the pointer and point to the words that we need to say and sing. Can you guess how we decide which child will do that? Think about what you already know about my philosophy. Is there any competition among children in my room? No, there isn't, so the way we choose children to perform certain tasks is through the use of the class list. Our class list is a major tool to structure responses in our room. The names are listed in alphabetical order, and even Brownie's name is on it—though he never did learn how to hold the pointer! Think about how this activity is connected to writing and reading in kindergarten. What skills are being used during this "pointing" activity? We'll talk more about it in the "Curriculum" section later in this chapter.

Why do you think we have poetry or song after the Pledge? Think about where the children are in the room, about transition time, and about pace. Since the children are standing in a group already, many times right after the Pledge and announcements we go into poetry and music. It is a natural transition because poetry and music are group activities and the children are already standing in a group around the chart. Also, going right into poetry and music allows us to waste no time transitioning into another activity and keeps up a fast pace. Giving children opportunities to stand enables them a variety of movement and lessens the time they are required to sit for uncomfortably long periods of time. How else do you think poetry and music influence daily living and learning in the classroom? Why do you think it might be important to include those in our morning activities? Choral activities give community members an opportunity to warm up. We are not yet asked to perform individually but can work within a group and feel successful immediately. And, perhaps most important, we can hear our voices within the community and feel the connection that will carry us through the day. I also think that our poetry and music generates excitement and passion that will help carry us through our day. What do you think?

ERIC: What came first historically, writing or song? Is this a chicken-and-egg question? Actually, I don't think so. If we look at the history of writing, it's not very old. Humans have been talking, walking, and singing for thousands of years. Really, writing has only been developed in the last two thousand years.

It may not be necessary to look at how music and song progressed anthropologically. You can just look at your own life. What happened first, your writing or your singing? Notice that in academia we have fields like the anthropology of music, and ethnomusicology. Many academics in these fields (see, for example, Nettl 1983) study societies whose languages are not written down; but the music is a viable, integral, and basic human means of communication, and that holds true worldwide.

Think about the number of songs you know and how you know them. For some songs, you probably know the melody. For others, you may just know the words. For many, you know both. For those songs for which you know both, can you recite the words without singing them? Think of a favorite current song, and sing it. Now hum the tune. The tune probably isn't too hard to recall, right? Now start just saying the words. For some people, this is difficult. Try reciting your national anthem without using the melody. Was it just as easy as singing the song? For those of you who know "The Star-Spangled Banner," try this! Start reciting, not using music, with this line:

O'er the ramparts we watch'd

What happened? Could you start there and keep going? Did you have to go back and repeat the lines before it in order? And if you did, did you find yourself using the music to help you? And what did you do when you wanted to hang that long note out on the line "yet wave"? Did you feel compelled to say the word long, just as it is in the song, or were you okay with just saying it normally? And even if you said it normally, did you take a deep breath after saying it, just as you would have while singing it, preparing yourself for the next line?

So, you see how music and language go hand in hand, and how poetry, music, and song are really critical precursors to literacy.

One of Nina's diary entries:

> I expect the children to be on time and with their own homework! I hear from D'Andre's (a new child in our community) grandmother that he said he loved school, and every morning he says, "I have to be on time!" Most days, too, they all bring in their homework!

NINA: You can see from the above entry that homework is important to our community, so the next thing on the list is usually going over the homework. Why do you think we address the homework first thing in the morning? Again, what message do I send about homework when it is one of the first things we look at? It might be hard to believe, but all of my children complete all of their homework most of the time. One of the reasons is because it is important in our room, and its importance is illustrated in a number of ways. First, it is given a prominent place in our daily plan. We don't do it first to get it over with but because it is important. Homework is done consistently, too, because what is assigned or chosen is purposeful and is an integral part of the curriculum. It actually helps to drive curriculum. For example, if some of the homework focuses on *Charlotte's Web*, we will begin reading aloud so that the connection to homework is strengthened. And yes, you did hear the word *chosen* in regards to homework! Many times my students get to choose what they want to do. Isn't that cool? Don't you think that might be a reason they almost always do their homework?

The next activity is usually writing process. Although, as I've already mentioned, we might adjust the order once in a while, especially as the year goes on, writing process generally happens after homework review. Why, do you think? Look again at our order. Do you notice a pattern? First there are diaries. What kind of activity is this, individual or group? Next are the Pledge, songs, poetry. What kind of activities are these? Do you see what I'm getting at? I try to order things not only so that there is less transition time, but also so that children are enabled to interact in a variety of ways both physically and mentally. Writing process is a mixture of individual, small-group, and large-group sharing. That balance among individual, full-group, small-group activities in different areas of the room gives the room that certain rhythm that Alice mentioned in her prologue. It's an exciting feeling and sound as we dance and weave through our structure. And by the time we get to writing process, we are warmed up and connected to each other. Now, we are ready to roll up our sleeves and work individually or as coauthors on our writing pieces. Children have a choice to move around the room and work on their pieces together or stay in their seats and write individually. Many children are in different parts of the process, since by October children are not publishing all their pieces but are choosing only their best pieces to publish. Yes, I will give you the details soon, in this chapter.

ERIC: As children develop their October publications, a number of phenomena begin to become evident. First, children bring with them the immediate ability to create different kinds of writing. In the Brownie diary, produced in tandem by family and child, we see almost exclusively sequential storytelling. However, in the published books from Nina's classroom, there are other rhetorical styles evident in the children's narratives, including:

- sequences (sixty-three instances);
- descriptive stories (forty-four instances);
- cause-and-effect stories (sixteen instances); and
- quotes (eleven instances).

Sequences
The most common type of story Nina's students expressed when they started writing process is a sequence of events. Look at these prototypical examples:

Me and My Sister by Denise
Me and my sister went to the pool. Then we played jump rope. Then we went inside.
Me and Roderick and Shaquilla went to the pool. We jumped in the pool. Then we went to Roderick's house and went to bed.

Of note in these sequence stories is the use of the transition word "then," as well as the connecting word "and." In the first example here, the three sentences are all simple sentences, but the second example shows that some children can make compound sentences as well.

Often the sequences have a quick last sentence. Two common endings to stories are the conclusion that a set of activities was entertaining:

My Birthday by Denise
We played. We played catching. We had fun.

The Skateboard by Jamal
Me and Shaquilla went to the beach. We skateboarded on the sidewalk near the beach. Nobody fell. We had fun.

Other examples of closing sentences include the following:

- I was sad.
- We stopped playing.
- I took a nap.
- We went back into the house.
- He went to the hospital.
- He drove away.
- We got away.
- It was over.
- We won the game.

Remarkably, as we will see later when we look at Brownie's diary, the results of family writing almost always include sequences of events. Thus, episodic reporting of events must be a linguistic skill children bring with them to kindergarten, due at least in part to the children's families' regular use of sequences in their reports. To suggest that families develop their own text frame patterns or skeletons (Kossack et al. 2003) is not out of the realm of imagination:

Family member: Hey!
Child: Hi!
Family member: Guess what we did today!
Child: What?
Family member: Well, we . . . and we . . . and then we . . .

Descriptive stories

The second most common type of storytelling observed in the first couple of months is a description. In other words, the children prefer to describe a scene rather than give us a play-by-play listing of events. Here is an example:

The Party by Marc
It was Dr. Zaragoza's birthday. I gave Dr. Zaragoza a present. Balloons, flowers, and I bought her a cake. It was fun. We also had pizza.

In this story, the order in which events occur is far less important than in a sequencing story, but the description of the event is still valid, and certainly of interest to its author.

Additionally, to a great extent children clearly bring the ability to describe a setting, either observed or imagined, with them to kindergarten. In Marc's example here, he describes what he does at Nina's birthday party. In Andre's example below, we see an imagined situation, though the vision he shares is quite clear:

> *The Fish* by Andre
> The fish were jumping in the water. All the fish were happy. They made good friends.

For now, that is Andre's complete story. But ultimately, can you see how this description may someday become a setting or introduction to a longer piece?

Cause-and-effect stories

Among the stories published, a number indicate cause and effect. To observe such storytelling skill may surprise a number of us, particularly since research has shown cause and effect to be one of the harder styles to master (see Kossack et al., 2003). Nevertheless, in these published stories, we see children creating such works on their own. Here is an example:

> *The Dragon* by Marc
> The dragon came to my room. He was hungry. His fire burned all my room. I went downstairs and we got a new house.

Here, we not only see the cause of the fire burning the house, but we also see the effect: Marc's getting a replacement.

In some stories, children will combine these writing styles to create a more sophisticated story. Often they naturally establish a conflict and end the story with a resolution. Note the following examples:

> *The Man with Bleeding Feet* by Larry
> A man lived far so he had to walk a long way. His feet bleeding. He got a napkin with alcohol and wiped the blood off his feet. Then he felt better.

> *The Monster* by Christian
> The monster came in my Nana's room. Then it walked into my room. I let him in my bed to sleep with me.

The content of the stories is significant. In many cases, the stories reflect a retrospective of occurrences in students' daily lives. And in the majority of cases, the stories reflect a matter-of-fact relaying of what happened the previous day or a short time before the time of writing.

Basketball by Denise

Everybody was sleeping. They woke up and they ate. They went outside to play basketball.

However, on occasion, as in Christian's story about a monster, the children's stories refer to fears they may be having.

The Man by Denise

Her mama came outside. A man had came. He was trying to get the girl. The police came. They got the mail and put him in jail.

The Shark by Darrius

One day my Daddy took me to the beach. The shark came and ate me. I crawled out of his mouth. I was afraid of the shark. I almost got ate by a shark. I don't want to go to the beach anymore.

It's not surprising that children often place classmates in their stories as characters. What you may be interested to know is that a number of stories also allude to classroom activities. Note the following examples:

Books by D'Andre

I read a book. I like to read a book. I like books about alligators. I like to read a dinosaur book.

NINA: After writing process we usually read aloud from a "chapter book." In October, we are still reading *Charlotte's Web*, and the characters have become a living part of our community. Why do you think reading aloud is after writing process? Why do you think I usually don't start with reading aloud? How might reading aloud actually hinder my children's writing, especially in the first months of school? Because they are such young authors, presenting another author's work too early might block a child's own writing. It's analogous to me telling a child what to write about. For young children, giving them the topic does not make it easier. In the long run, it makes it more difficult because we are sending the message that we are the authority and we will give them the ideas and the form. So you see, I wait until they've written before reading aloud so that they do not get the idea that they must write like E. B. White. I can hear you say, "Oh come on, Nina, aren't you carrying it a little too far?" No, I don't think so. Teachers must reflect on every decision we make and base each decision on our philosophy of teaching and learning. It is this reflection that helps our classroom foundation remain strong and consistent and helps us maintain the structure we are discussing.

ERIC: You recall that in September we noted that Nina reads stories aloud but interrupts the story often, usually to ask questions of authorship. These questions during reading aloud are an integral part of effective teaching, particularly in the advancement of the children's critical thinking skills. Some questions include: "Why do you think the author wrote the story this way?" and "If you were the author what would you change? Why? If you were the author what would you keep the same? Why? In this way children are actively thinking as authors even as they are being read to.

If we're trying to get children to read, why would we read to them? Don't we want them to look at letters and move their eyes, linking the messages of each letter to the subsequent one, creating a word, and linking each word to the subsequent one, ultimately creating a sentence, and linking each sentence to the subsequent one, ultimately creating a paragraph, and so on? To a degree, this is true, and this is really what we do during silent reading. But to do only that would limit a look at reading to the nuts and bolts of the reading machine. And like a machine, nuts and bolts can either stand as individual parts, in which case they wouldn't work, or they may work in concert as an entity amid other elements. Here letters, words, sentences, and paragraphs are indeed nuts and bolts. But someone has to put them together, and the order and linkages they ultimately make create a machine called reading. And like a machine, one must look at the entire entity, often overlooking where the nuts and bolts are. Nevertheless, if we take away the nuts and bolts of a machine, even if we're not even noticing them, the machine couldn't work.

To limit reading to an activity of moving eyes across letters is to describe only the reading skeleton. As a machine, it is more, and throughout this book we'll be discussing a number of reading's other elements.

First and foremost, reading is a public and community-edifying experience. It is a constant direct connection to the human species and information flowing around the world. And yet, we can enjoy this experience in the privacy of our own bedrooms, under apple trees, or on a rowboat in the middle of the ocean. All you need is something to read. However, someone had to write it. Hence, when you read, you're interacting and engaging with another human. If it's a magazine, most likely it's many more people. Lev Vygotsky's principle of scaffolding is directly linked to the idea that people cannot learn without other people, no matter what. Hence, to leave out the human connection and all the emotions that go with it is to leave out vital nuts and bolts of the reading machine.

In research, we have seen the variable of human connection appear. Stephen Krashen (1993) found that when students are enjoying themselves during reading activities, including even readers who are just learning English, their vocabulary development soars. His graduate student Kyung-Sook Cho

(Cho and Krashen 1995) found that when teenage Korean girls were working through the *Sweet Valley* series (in English), two primary phenomena were observable. First, their vocabulary development increased dramatically, but more important, second, they were having an absolutely joyful time. Both Cho and Krashen note that upon reflection on their students' love and interest in constant reading it seemed unrealistic to consider that an equal development of vocabulary and new English language skills would have occurred if the students were having less fun.

Krashen wanted to find out if this was true or not. He and another student then studied two groups of students as they read through Anthony Burgess's *A Clockwork Orange* (1962). No, these were not kindergartners or even high schoolers reading this material (probably would not be the most appropriate text in the world), but the results are still applicable. In this book, as in other books, such as Frank Herbert's *Dune* (1965), there is a glossary at the end of the book to which readers may refer so they may understand the vocabulary the author is making up and using as regular language in the story. Krashen tore out the glossary of the book, giving one group of students the book to read, sans glossary, and giving the other group the glossary to read, without allowing the second group to read the book itself. After the read-the-book group had finished reading the book, and after the glossary group had studied the glossary for three days, the researchers gave the two groups a vocabulary test on the glossary words. Which group do you think did better on the test? Right! It was the read-the-book group. Even though the glossary folks had the specific definitions in front of them to work from and the read-the-book group didn't, the read-the-book group had the context from which to operate, thus enabling them to internalize the language. Finally, Krashen noted that the read-the-book group reported that they really enjoyed the activity of reading the book (I guess they liked it), and the glossary-studying folks didn't report such fun. Clearly, just working off a set of definitions was considered a more sterile and less interesting activity by a majority of the glossary folks. (I probably would have enjoyed the glossary activity and might have done better, since, unlike the majority of people, I like reading the dictionary.)

Well, all this leads to the amount of vocabulary building that is elicited from enjoyable reading practices. Doesn't it make sense, then, to connect positive reading experiences with books or other forms of literature? That's what Nina is trying to do here: to connect the positivity of a fun story through reading aloud with the book itself, thereby showing that students will ultimately be able to enjoy reading on their own, and thereby encouraging students to inadvertently learn new and critical vocabulary.

NINA: Usually after lunch we go into silent reading. I bet you can guess why. They need a little silence after the noise in the lunchroom. I need some silent time too. (I choose to eat with my children and not in the teachers' lounge, partly because I want to strengthen our bond—but really because I love them!) So we all read, the way Eric described in September. As you can see, I am a full participant in our community and actively take part in all activities. Do you see what message I send my students? I am telling them that everything we do is so important that I do it too. I am also showing them my real love for literacy. They know how much I love to write and read. They see it in my actions, they see it in my eyes, and I see it in theirs. Many people question how successful young kindergartners can really be during silent reading. You have already read how successful these children are. Why do you think they're successful? Well, I'm reading with them, and that helps them see that reading is a worthwhile endeavor. Also, my definition of *silent* is not a strict definition, and I allow young children to read and talk aloud to themselves, since most young children are unable to read totally "in their heads." What also keeps silent reading successful is high interest. Remember, my children have chosen their books in the morning, so they look forward to reading them. Also notice what is scheduled after silent reading. Reading discussion groups follow, so the children know that they will soon have an opportunity to talk. I can guarantee you that silent reading sessions will not be successful unless you consistently allow your children to talk about their books after (not during!) silent reading is over.

Don't you think that discussion after silent reading is a natural progression? When you read a good book, don't you want to talk about it to a friend? I do. Our children do too. When we give children a regular time to talk about their reading we shape their view of reading. They learn that reading does not just encompass word calling but is a complex process that includes connections and relationships to other people (both in the classroom and the book) and the author. The discussion groups are very flexible and are either chosen by me or the children. I'll give you more details soon. Let me first make a few more remarks about our structure.

I'm sure you will notice when you look over our plan for the day that I have left out some areas like social studies, math, and science. Actually, I do teach these things, but usually they are integrated within the literacy block. For example, this month we discussed and wrote a play about the city and the country, since it was a natural offshoot of *Charlotte's Web*. We integrate math within various parts of our day, such as literature and attendance. If I am introducing a new mathematical concept, I do this first thing in the morning (after poetry and music) and then reinforce that concept at various times during that day and week. Math also becomes part of writing process when children work on writing number stories. Many times children have math homework, so going over the homework in the morning becomes a math lesson.

Let's take a final look at the order of our activities after lunch. Notice that it is similar to our morning rhythm. Silent reading is an individual activity—allowing children to take a breath and make individual connections before they are required to interact in a group. Then we follow with small-group work in which all children are responsible for helping their group to run smoothly. When discussion groups are finished, the books are put away either in our class library or in the children's backpacks to read at home.

After this we switch to the full-group activity of practicing our play. By this time, we have done a good amount of connecting as we've been carried along by our common vision. Now toward the end of the day the children can do whatever they want as long as they can answer the question I ask during free learning time: "What are you learning right now?" It is here where I might do some extra facilitation with individual children. It is very interesting to see what children choose to do during free learning time. It is also quite telling to hear what they say and how they speak to each other. They so clearly mirror the kind of teaching and learning that is happening in the classroom. How rewarding it is to hear comments like "Oh, today in free learning time, I'm going to help Virginia in math!"

To bring us together as a full group again, we end the day reciting poetry or singing a closing song. It is a beautiful ending as we join our voices together and rejoice in each other and the work we have created and completed.

I bet you can see how, as Eric said, my structure and curriculum are almost synonymous. Do you sense how difficult it is for me to separate the two? It really is a false separation, at least in our classroom. The curriculum really is the structure. Do you see? I can hardly imagine how a classroom structure could be developed without that connection to curriculum. Often I am asked, "But what do you do about children who don't behave? They're not going to learn how to read unless they learn how to behave first." I don't see how this is a hierarchical relationship. We help children learn appropriate interactions within the teaching/learning environment. So positive small-group interactions are encouraged during small-group work. Let's look at why my children exhibit appropriate interactions within our community.

As Eric mentioned, we do have rules, and they are posted clearly all over the room:

Classroom Rules

- We try our best.
- We listen and look when others talk.
- We are kind and helpful to others.
- We help others to remember our rules.

Line Rules

- We stand with hands at our sides.
- We stand directly behind the person in front of us.
- We look straight ahead.
- We walk silently so we don't bother other classes.
- We help the person in front of us follow the line rules.

The children and I create these rules, and as you can see they are worded in a positive way and begin with the word *We*. This, of course, reinforces the way we speak to each other and strengthens our community identity. The children are invested in these rules because they helped create them, and because they value our community they generally adhere to all our rules. Why else do you think there are no real behavior problems once the structure and curriculum of our room are set?

You already know that in my room children are spoken to respectfully and are given an enormous amount of positive attention. They begin to feel safe and cared for, and they learn that they need not act out negatively to get recognition. They get so much positive recognition they have no reason to seek any other kind. Don't we all need this? Don't we all want to be noticed, to be valued? In my class this need is met. What other needs are met for the members in my community? I'll start the list for you. We all need to:

- feel important or significant;
- have a sense of belonging;
- have a purpose;
- feel connected to others;
- tell our story; and
- feel successful.

ERIC: What are some of the lines Nina uses to foster this atmosphere? Here is an analysis of a fifteen-minute stretch of comments Nina uses while directing an October class where we see the kinds of comments Nina makes to her children. In the following chart, we will see the following trends: 1) the purpose of Nina's comments, 2) an example of a comment referring directly to purpose, 3) the number of occasions such statements were made, and 4) the mean length of statements made for this purpose.

You may find it useful to (a) pay attention to the kind of language you use regularly in order to foster your own atmosphere and (b) write down some key sentences and commands in ways you feel enhance your classroom. You might find in doing so that some of the sentences you use may usurp power

Purpose of Sentence	Example	Number of Occasions	Mean Sentence Length (words)
Direction to children to help others in class	What do you need to tell them?	14	7.86
Correction in the name of a child's importance	We need you here.	3	5.00
Reference to your own modeling of good academic behavior	I'm sorry I interrupted.	2	4.50
Reference to students' own appropriate academic behavior	Excellent, you're talking to Jamal about writing!	3	5.25
Promotion for children's self-approval	Give yourselves a hand!	2	4.00

from students rather than unleashing it. You might find that some of your comments are too strong or not strong enough. Are your sentences too long or too short for the students you direct them to? Are you considering language issues related to students with special needs or language barriers? You might also find that some of the sentences you write are skeletons of nice pivot language that will help all students, much like the "Excellent, you're talking to Jamal about writing!" You can substitute "Excellent" with "Super" or any other interjection. You will substitute the names of the students, obviously. You can substitute "writing" with "editing" or any other gerund. In sum, you may find that by editing your list of regular commands you can actually coach students more effectively.

NINA: So children like Virginia and Matthew soon emerge from under their desks to become active participants. They want to sing and recite poetry with us. They want to write and hear stories. They want to be part of the play and talk about Wilbur and Charlotte. So you see how it is all connected to curriculum? When curriculum is truly purposeful and there is real work to create and complete, all children become involved. All children become the artisans they are meant to be.

Curriculum

Eric did a pretty thorough job of describing the curriculum in the preceding chapter, and, as you see, even when I talk about structure I get into curriculum. So you already have a grasp of what we do and what the children produce in writing process. What I'll do here is fill in some of the details for you. You can see that we work intensely and passionately from the minute we enter our room until the minute we leave. We are artisans involved in our craft and are eager to connect and create. We are constantly communicating and connecting in various forms, whether we're writing diaries, responding to attendance questions, reciting poetry, or writing and reading stories.

Diaries

In October diary entries become longer and the children continue to have total choice in what they write. The only requirement is that they must make an entry every day, and they meet this requirement happily. They bend over their papers in total concentration as they write. I do sometimes ask for volunteers to read an entry to the class, and many are eager to share. I do not edit these entries because these are personal pieces of writing that will never reach publication. Children just write for the sheer joy of it. What are children learning as they write daily diary entries? Think about what they are doing and thinking in the process. Let me just give you a few ideas:

- physical manipulation of writing materials such as pencils, papers—connection between talking or thinking and writing down;
- connections between writing down, reading aloud, and remembering events;
- there are different forms of writing;
- left to right progression;
- sound-to-letter correspondence; and
- writing is important.
- What else can you think of?

Poetry and music

Poetry and music are such a part of my room I can't imagine a day without at least one poem and/or song. I am sure my passion for using these vehicles is a major reason why my children are so successful with them. They are successful, too, because we work with this kind of literature so consistently and so deeply. Poetry and music also allow all children to be successful, because it is a choral activity that usually includes movements. Do you see that when children are reciting or singing together they have the support of the community and so missing a word or two is not a big deal? The repetition of poetry also enables language-delayed children and ESL students consistent, purposeful opportunities for success.

Reciting and singing is enjoyable for our community, is filled with learning opportunities, and is purposeful because we always have a poetry or song recital planned for February. This gives us added incentive to learn our chosen pieces well. How do you think I choose the pieces we will perform? Remember Eric asked you why I use "Dreams" as my first poem?

One of the most important reasons I pick this poem is because I love it and I want my children to hear how much I love it. I want to immediately inspire this passion in them. This is also a poem that is easy to create movements for, as it is rhythmic and very visual. It is really very easy for children to memorize, too, and so it brings them almost immediate success. This poem also fosters a very deep conversation about personal dreams ("What do you dream of being when you grow up?"), and not giving up until you achieve them. And, of course, in this conversation there is much vocabulary building. Finally, because the recital usually happens in February, African American History Month, I choose a lot of African American poets for my children to learn. You'll hear much more about the specific pieces of poetry and music as the months go on and I will also talk to you about how I first present poems and songs and how they continue to be used throughout the year in our community.

ERIC: Here are some other songs and poems that Nina has used in October:

- "The Giggles," by Martin Gardner;
- "Hope," by Langston Hughes;
- "Rudolph Is Tired of the City," by Gwendolyn Brooks; and
- "Two Friends," by Nikki Giovanni.

Do you know these poems? Which ones are traditional classics? Are any new to you? Notice that Nina seems to make two choices: those poems, stories, and songs that belong to her culture, and those that don't.

Benjamin Alire Saenz (1999), a teacher and children's author in El Paso, tells an important story. As a fourth grader growing up in New Mexico, a teacher one day had all the children recite and read the poem "Birches," by Robert Frost. Clearly this was one of the teacher's favorite poems, and it's certainly respected across the United States as a classic poem. She let the students read the poem and then asked them for their initial reaction. No one in the class raised their hand or volunteered any opinion—just silence. The teacher became a bit cross and asked the students to read the poem again. This time, she asked them to read the poem, knowing that they would be asked to reveal an opinion of some sort. The students read the poem. Again the teacher asked for immediate reactions; however, the class remained motionless and silent. A bit exasperated, the teacher raised her voice slightly, indicating her disdain in the lack of participation. Finally, according to Saenz, a brave soul raised her hand and asked, "Teacher, what's a birch?"

How many birch trees are in southern New Mexico? Where are most of the students from? What concrete aspects, as well as attitudinal aspects, of any piece of art are these students going to relate to most easily? Robert Frost?

Nina asks similar questions regarding her students from this section of Miami. What concrete and attitudinal aspects of art are most easily conveyed to her students? Nina has made a choice: Langston Hughes. But notice something even more important. Even though Langston Hughes is not necessarily of her culture, she has made his work a vital part of her life. It's not a novelty.

Writing Process

NINA: By October we really identify ourselves as authors and are immersed in the craft of writing. I treat my children like the authors they are. They are authors in their own right. I often say that an author is an author whether they are four years old or eighty years old. All authors go through the same process as they write No, and that is why we call this part of the curriculum writing process. Writing is exactly that—a process that includes a number of steps all the way to the publication of a written piece. Let's look at the steps we use in our classroom:

1.   Write three different stories.
2.   Pick one draft to publish.
3.   Self-revise/edit your draft.
4.   Get a friend to revise/edit your draft.
5.   Sign up to have an adult revise/edit your draft.
6.   Write your final copy.
7.   Proofread your final copy and make corrections.
8.   Give a friend your final copy to proofread.
9.   Give an adult your final copy to proofread.
10. Put your final copy in a cover.
11. Illustrate, help others, share your book, and go back to step 1.

In September the children did not write three different stories before publication but were able to publish their piece immediately after it was edited. Why do you think this happened in September but changed on October? In September I wanted my children to learn the writing process and identify themselves as authors. To do this they needed to actively participate in the process all the way to publication. Remember, I don't lecture about what we're doing or what we will be doing; the children learn while they are actively involved in the activity. So in the beginning they needed to publish more quickly so that they could understand the purpose of this kind of writing: connecting to an audience through publication. Why else do you think quickly getting to publication is important?

Let me tell you a little bit about how publication happens in our room. You already know about the one hundred empty book covers I had ready for the first day. These covers are so exciting and add to the passion about writing for both the children and me. Doesn't that make sense, though? The job of a writer is to publish. To see a story you created yourself in a hardcover book placed in the library is an amazing event. And the minute my children see the first book published they desire to do the same. I believe that as human beings we all have a desire to tell our stories and we all have stories to tell. So what we do in this program is build on this innate desire and use the vehicle of writing and publication to tell and share these stories.

Now, publishing in our room is not stapling a piece of handwriting paper onto a piece of construction paper. Children know those aren't real books! We make actual hardcover books. While over time I will teach the children how to make these covers, in the beginning I have covers ready so publishing happens quickly:

Making Book Covers

Materials
17-by-12-inch piece of contact paper or regular construction paper
Two 6-by-9-inch pieces of cardboard
Scissors
Glue (a glue stick is easiest and neatest)
Writing paper (8½ by 11 inches)

Procedure
1. Place construction paper/contact paper sticky side up and glue the two pieces of cardboard side by side in the center, leaving approximately ½ inch between the two pieces of cardboard.
2. Cut the corners of the construction paper/contact paper off and fold sides over onto the cardboard (just like wrapping a present).

Paper for inside cover
1. Put one piece of blank white paper under three sheets of writing paper.
2. Fold papers in half and staple together at the fold.

Putting paper inside cover
1. Put glue on the back cover and adhere last sheet of stapled paper.

2. Adjust papers for opening and closing the book.
3. Add any other personal touches you like (pockets for cards to borrow, binding tape on spine to add more color, and so on).

Now back to the question I asked you to think about. Why is it so important to get children published immediately? We've already spoken about the excitement that these covers engender and how this really gets students to write. It also allows them to complete the purpose of authors. When authors finish publication they have gone through the entire system and have worked through all the major skills needed to be successful. In fact, the inclusion of publication allows us to teach these skills within the context of purposeful activity and at the time each individual skill is most important. What are these skills? Let's look at each stage of the process and the corresponding skills.

Draft writing

Writing drafts is just that. We just write to get our thoughts down. The only important aspect of this stage is idea gathering and getting it written down. Are you wondering about where our young authors get their ideas? Do you think I assign topics? Remember, I treat these children like real authors because they are real authors and they all have stories to tell. My stories are not theirs and I have no right to give them a topic I think is important. All authors need to struggle through getting their own ideas. You already know one way that ideas are generated in my room. Eric mentioned TAG previously and the G signifies "give suggestions." So our authors aren't just sitting there staring into space (though sometimes this is good!), they are given a lot of support as they decide on their topic. They are allowed to talk, move around, and so on. By October they are overflowing with ideas because of all the writing and reading we have already done. Spelling and handwriting are never spoken about in this stage. Notice that I said "in this stage." Spelling and handwriting will, of course, be addressed but not during draft writing. When do you think we will speak about these things? In what part(s) of the writing process is spelling and handwriting important? Think about it while we talk a little more about what our young authors are doing in drafting.

Eric: As children improve, we see elements from the TAG emerge in children's stories, most commonly in terms of incidental descriptive sentences. For example, we might see a story about a child's mother. However, after talking about what happened to the mother, the writer will say something like "Mother is very pretty," thereby adding a piece of more descriptive language.

One can easily observe progress in the student's storytelling abilities, just in these two months. Stories at the beginning in September may be no more than one or two sentences. Further, the sentences may be no more than five words long. Of the 126 stories examined in September and October, only 9 were one-sentence stories, ranging from 5 to 24 words (the latter using an "and" to construct a long compound sentence), averaging 10.8 words. By the end of October, 12 stories are 5 sentences long, ranging from 24 to 46 words long, averaging 32.2 words per story and 6.4 words per sentence. Two stories are 6 sentences long—one 27 words long and the other 44 words long. Four stories are 7 sentences long, ranging from 34 to 45 words, and averaging 5.7 words per sentence. As a result, we see that the more sophisticated stories are those with the five-sentence structure, since they yield more complex sentences than those with more sentences, which generally are assemblies of shorter sentences.

NINA: To draft stories children have a writer's notebook. As the writing session opens children take out their writing process notebook and begin to write. I used to use writing folders to contain loose drafts. This proved very unruly, as many drafts littered the floor or were crumpled in desks. So now I use stiff-covered composition notebooks that are neater and also are an excellent way to immediately see each author's progress over time. How amazing to see in October the random lines written all over the page change to meticulously placed letters! I'm sure you've noticed that my definition of writing is broad. As soon as the author marks the paper I call it writing. In fact, I'll even carry it a little further: as soon as the author begins thinking or talking about a story it is writing. So not only do children physically write during the twenty-minute session, they also sit and think or get up and talk to their friends about ideas. Do I allow them to talk about spelling? No, because we are not worried about spelling here. If they ask about spelling I show them how to put a blank line so that we can go over it during editing. Do I let them worry about handwriting? No, because handwriting is not important here. They talk about ideas. It is here where we start talking about characters, setting, problem, and solution. As you saw in sample September stories, all of these elements have not yet emerged—but they will!

Revising/Editing

After three different stories are written, authors pick their favorite to publish. Remember that in September all children published even their first stories, but now that they know the full process through publication I am slowing them down and teaching them that authors don't publish everything they write. This also is a great help to me, since I don't end up having to revise/edit each piece of writing. I only revise/edit what will be published. Doesn't that make sense? I've seen teachers going crazy trying to edit each piece of writing. I realized, though, that they tended to do this because publication was not a consistent part of their writing program. I find that many teachers see publishing as a big project that happens two or three times a year. Well, for young authors this is not consistent enough and because publication gives purpose to all the skills, without it children will not truly internalize the skills needed by all authors.

Notice here that I have combined revision and editing. As children grow in writing, revision and editing become two different steps, but for our youngest authors they are merged. As the year goes on you'll see how I slowly begin to work with revision by asking them to add things such as detail, dialogue, and description. Right now in this stage children are reading their story to me and I am writing it for them in standard writing. Yes! This is where we begin to talk about spelling.

Nina:	Listen: So I see you signed up for an adult to edit.
Aubrey:	Yeah.
Nina:	Which one of your friends edited?
Aubrey:	Marc
Nina:	Oh! Everybody goes to Marc for editing! I hope you said thank you to him. Thanks for editing, Marc. Okay, Aubrey, read me your story.
Aubrey:	I was in the car and Mommy let me read a book.
Nina:	Wait, honey, go a little slower, so I can edit what you're reading.
Aubrey:	(Repeats slowly.)
Nina:	Oh, I see you put the /m/ sound for "Mommy." Good! Watch how I spell "Mommy." (I make the sound of each letter as I write.) Now, what sound do you hear in the beginning of "book"?
Aubrey:	/b/
Nina:	What other words have the same first sound as "book"?
Aubrey:	Barney.
Nina:	Yes! So did this really happen? Did your Mom let you read a book to her?
Aubrey:	Yeah.
Nina:	What book was it?
Aubrey:	*Playtime*.
Nina:	I know you love that book. What did your mother say when you finished?
Aubrey:	"Very good."
Nina:	Would you like to write what she said?
Aubrey:	Yeah.
Nina:	Okay, say it to me and I'll edit.
Aubrey:	"My Mom said, 'Very good.'"

Nina:	Great, Aubrey. Can I show the class how you have talking in your story?
Aubrey:	Okay.
Nina:	Listen for a minute, please. Thank you for looking at me right away, Denel. Thank you, Roderick, you're ready to listen. Guess what? Aubrey has talking in her story. Aubrey, do you want to read what your mom said or do you want me to read it?
Aubrey:	Me. "My Mom said, 'Very good.'"
Nina:	Did she say, "My mom said," or did she just say, "Very good"?
All:	"Very good."
Nina:	Okay, everyone, let's say what Aubrey's mom said. Aubrey, how did your Mom say, "Very good"? Did she say it loud like she was happy, or soft?
Aubrey:	Loud.
Nina:	I know she was so excited to hear you read! So everyone, let's say "Very good" like we are happy and excited.
All:	"Very good!"
Nina:	Very good to all of you! Let's give Aubrey a hand. She's ready to publish. (Most children clap.) Everyone needs to clap. Let's do that again and show Aubrey we are proud of her. (Now everyone claps.) Okay, go back to your writing. Thank you for listening. Congratulations, Aubrey, go get the publishing paper and pick your cover.

You see? Isn't it cool that Aubrey's in publication? And you see that because of publication I can teach all the skills? Look how much I covered with Aubrey in a conference that took about five minutes. Do you see the seeds I am sowing? Do you see what will later come to fruition? There are so many seeds it's difficult for me to know where to begin.

Well, first of all, I am reinforcing the role of writer and editor here. I never say I am writing but always use the word "edit" in relation to what I'm doing. Aubrey is the writer of her piece, no matter what she wrote or didn't write. Aubrey is always kept in power by my questions and suggestions because she is the author and I am only the editor.

Oh, the tears I have seen children shed because their teacher forced them to make unwanted changes to a piece the students initially loved. We do not have a right to change an author's piece to make it look the way we want it to. We can suggest but we must respect the author's final decision.

A perfectionistic attitude during the writing process is deadly and will kill your children's desire to write. It is this power that is part of the fire that keeps children writing. Notice, too, that I ask Aubrey permission to share some of her piece with the class and give her a choice about who would read it. I am glad that she feels safe enough to read it, but I give her the opportunity to decline if she doesn't.

Do you see how easily spelling and phonics can be addressed during editing? It's easy because this is the most natural and purposeful time to talk about it. Why would we talk about these things during the first draft, when the idea is what is being focused on? In fact, talking about spelling while the children are drafting is counterproductive and will block the flow of the ideas so vital to creative writing. This discussion during editing is perfect and totally purposeful because during editing spelling is important. Why? In publication we must use standard spelling so that our readers understand our story. Yep, there it is again, that relationship to publication. When children publish they come to understand why spelling is important and they want to spell correctly because they want their friends to read their stories.

Look at where I talk about the /m/ sound and the /b/ sound. Why do you think I ask Aubrey about the sound and not the letter? When you say the name of the letter, does it help you with its sound? The name of the sound /m/ is "em." The name of the letter that makes the /b/ sound is "bee." Does that help Aubrey with writing and reading? It really doesn't. Learning the names of the letters is actually very confusing to our beginning writers and readers and hinders their literacy learning. So many children are held back because they don't remember some of these names. Sadly, some children are even referred to special education if they don't know their letter names by the end of kindergarten. I teach the sounds of these letters and the formation of these letters but try not to name them. It really does help clear up the confusion about how to sound out for many children.

ERIC: Why would Nina balk at naming the letters of the alphabet and just go for the sound? She's right! I too have seen teachers fail students for not knowing the names of the alphabet characters just when the students are starting to read. Such a decision does concern us, because we think there are a couple of other steps that should come before alphabet learning. First, there's phonemic awareness and phonics. Let's make certain we're clear on the distinctions.

Phonemic awareness only eventually has anything to do with reading, but that in my mind is an outcome of the funkiness of the phenomenon. The skill we speak of here is exclusively aural. Just take the word *phoneme*, and use its linguistic definition. It is all about listening. Philip Gough once explained that the difference between a child's knowing that the first sound of "fish" is /f/ and "glub glub" (the sound a fish makes with its mouth) is phonemic awareness. Likewise, phonemic awareness is a child's understanding that the first sound in "fish" is the same first sound in "photo." Ultimately spelling has nothing to do with phonemic awareness.

You may see, in your classes and curricula, handouts that prescribe and tout phonemic awareness. Often these entail several pictures, some of which have the same first sound and some of which do not. The child's task is to circle the objects that have the same first sound. For example, you may see four pictures: a dog, a doll, a house, and a hat. The instructions would have the teacher direct students toward circling the dog and the doll. Such a task has merit only if all the children in the class can agree on the names of the pictures. In other words, we're sunk if the child looks at the dog and says "puppy," or looks at the doll and says "baby." I hope we'll be careful when we look at phonemic awareness tasks; to assess progress in a child's phonemic awareness by *looking* at a visual and asking all students to refer in their heads to the exact same word may be an unrealistic goal.

To be sure we're keeping track of a child's parsing of sounds, we must keep the word "sound" at the heart of our activity. Nina noted in her dialogue with Aubrey how she does this during editing. I have also seen Nina use guesswork as a means of eliciting phonemes. My favorite of Nina's activities is the following one.

A present from one of Nina's friends arrives in the mail. Nina looks at the return address and says, "Wow, look! I got a present from my friend in Minnesota. What do you think the name of my friend is?" Yes, it's an extremely open question, but it has purpose. She adds, "I'll give you a hint. Her name begins with /sh/. I want to see a lot of hands." Nina waits for a moment until the bulk of the children have demonstrated that they're thinking, ultimately raising their hands with a guess. From there, students start stating names like Sherry, Cheryl, Sean, Sibhon, and Xica. Note that all these names begin with different letters, but they all begin with the /sh/. Hence, regardless of the name, so long as it begins with /sh/, it would be a reasonable guess. In fact, I suppose they could even come up with names I had never heard of, just so long as it begins with /sh/.

Some of my other favorite in-class tasks are "I spy with my little eye something that begins with /sh/." Traditionally, this has been a spelling game, but it can be used for phonemic awareness tasks. In this case, you simply say /sh/, rather than spelling out SH.

Next, there's phonics. Yes, in the study and acquisition of English literacy, phonics is necessary, but this doesn't mean that phonics is necessary to read just any language. There are many languages, for example Russian, Greek and Thai, in which the sound-to-character correspondence is almost always one to one. (There are a couple of exceptions to this rule in Greek, but generally it is so.) English orthography is borrowed from Latin; hence, not all the sounds of English are appropriately accounted for in the Roman orthographic system. For starters, Latin only has five vowels, and English has far more. Why do you think we make the distinction between long vowels and short vowels, or the "oo" in "good" being different from the "oo" in "food"? The reason is because English has so many vowel sounds but only five characters, which must be used in a variety of ways to assert their written representation. Thus, as we look at the /sh/ names above, we see that the sound can be expressed in a number of ways. Fortunately, the number of ways is finite and somewhat predictable. For example, the letter *p* isn't going to be used for the /sh/ sound. The subset of character representations for any sound is the art of phonics.

Hence, for kindergarten, you can see that the role of phonics is a bit early in the game. It's not unreasonable to get started, but it's not the precursor to phonemic awareness, it's the result of it.

Even more complicated, then, is the alphabet. Nina and I are advocating that the names of the letters in the alphabet and their order derive from the sounds and their orthographic correspondence, not the other way around. Notice the difference in the names of "em" and "bee." Where is the sound of the letter in these names? "For "em" it's at the end of the name, and for "bee" it's at the beginning. Do we ever tell our kindergartners such things? Most likely we don't. Therefore, we have to ask if it's necessarily intuitive for a child to immediately understand that the emphasis sound of the name is "m" rather than "e." And if it's at the end of the letter name of *m*, then why wouldn't it be at the end of the name for *b*? And how would it be for students learning letters like *c, g, h, q, w, x,* and *y*, where the phonetic sounds of the letters are not even included in the name of the letters? Is it therefore intuitive for teachers to teach the alphabet first? We think not. We maintain that logically, to do so is out of order.

But even as I write this, I feel myself starting to get bogged down in the nuts and bolts of writing, and I want to guide myself away from that. Let's look at how Nina keeps the big picture as the center of attention.

NINA: Do you notice that I ask Aubrey to read slowly and to watch while I'm editing? I do that for a very specific reason: I want Aubrey to continue to develop that connection between speech and writing. Young writers and readers are trying to figure out what in the world all those letters on the page mean. When Aubrey looks at me and sees that what she says becomes an image on the page, she is broadening her definitions of writing and reading. She is also continuing to work on the idea that in English we write and read from left to right.

When we revise we focus on the content of the story and think about things that we could adjust to help us tell the story more clearly, in a more interesting way, and so on. In this conversation with Aubrey you get a clear picture of how I combine revision and editing with young authors. My questions about whether her story is true, about the book she read to her mother, and about what her mother said all have to do with revision. I am planting the seeds of detail, dialogue, and genre. I love when I do that. The trick is to remember the seeds I plant so that I can water them and allow them to grow in the child and in our community. This isn't really hard, though, because since we are always writing and reading in our community the same concepts come up consistently and I connect to them across the curriculum. I also write down the concepts I am planting or want to plant in my daily or weekly plans. We'll talk more about skills lessons in the November chapter.

Do you see how I begin planting within the full community when we share the dialogue in the story? I don't bog them down with the vocabulary, but I give them a sense of the concept. It's that same "name" issue we spoke about in relationship to letter sounds. We don't need to know the name of something to be able to use it. We can have talking in our stories whether we know it's called dialogue or not. Don't worry, my children do learn all of the names, and they learn them well, because they already have experienced that "name" in action and have a concept to hang it on. Here I also planted the "exclamation point" seed—my favorite one! They begin to love it too. Once they learn how to write it they begin using many at the end of one sentence!!

Before we talk a little bit about Aubrey in publication, let's look briefly at my general interaction with Aubrey and the community. I am doing a number of things to reinforce our rules and hold children accountable to these rules. I don't edit Aubrey's draft until I ask her which of her friends edited it. This is reinforcing the rule "Get a friend to revise/edit your draft." I positively recognize Marc's expertise as an editor and at the same time reinforce the need to say "thank you" in our community. When we come together I thank people who are ready and involve them immediately in the conversation. When we clap for Aubrey I make sure that all children clap so that our identity as a community is strengthened. I also thank them for listening. Our authors are successful because they are:

- positively recognized—engaged and involved;
- not singled out negatively;
- excited; and
- respected.

Do you see how curriculum, structure, and positive interactions and behavior are all related?

Now that Aubrey is in publication, she will concentrate on handwriting. It is now when handwriting is important because this book will be placed in the class library, will be read aloud by a classmate or me, and will also be taken home to be read by Aubrey and her family. In October most of the children are still publishing their story on a piece of handwriting paper, since they need practice with letter formation. By this time, though, some children's handwriting is so legible they don't need practice and move to publishing on the computer. But even children who need handwriting work get to publish at least every other story on the computer to add variety and to build computer skills.

So, we started at publishing and now end at publishing. But actually I want to encourage you to see it as a cycle or circle, because for an author it's never-ending. Whenever I hear one of my students say, "I'm finished" during writing, I usually answer, "We're never finished in writing!" And it's true. Remember, the last step on our list of rules includes "start a new story." It's a complex process to explain, but when you see it in action it becomes very clear. You know one of the best ways to understand writing process is to become an author yourself if you aren't already. You have a story to tell. I'm sure you have many—like we all do. The easiest way to start is to write about your experiences. My young authors usually start with themselves, their family, their pets, and so on. It's a perfect place to start. You will be a better teacher if you work through this process just like you ask your students to do. My students write every single day and so do I. Just like anything else, the more you do it the better you become at it. To learn how to play basketball you need to play basketball often. To learn how to write you need to write often.

We're not finished with describing the whole process yet. Part of my program is sharing the writing piece in front of the whole class. As you know, we use a system that I created called TAG (Zaragoza, 2002; Zaragoza and Cruz 2001; Zaragoza 1987) to help us respond to each other's work. Let's listen to Aubrey and the class right after she read her whole piece to the class:

Aubrey:	Tell what you like. (Hands go up.) Denise.
Denise:	I like how you read to your mother.
Nina:	Aubrey, ask Denise why that's her favorite part.
Aubrey:	Why?
Denise:	Because I like to read to my mother too.
Aubrey:	Ask questions.
Nina:	Wait a minute, Aubrey. What do you need to say to Denise for telling you what she liked?
Aubrey:	Thank you.
Nina:	Okay. Go on.
Aubrey:	Ask questions.
Virginia:	I like books.

Nina:	Good, Virginia, but now you need to ask a question about Aubrey's story. (No response.) What else do you want to know about the book that Aubrey read? Denel.
Denel:	The color.
Nina:	Okay, so ask her about the color.
Denel:	What color is your book?
Aubrey:	Red.
Nina:	What else can we ask about the book? Shaquilla.
Shaquilla:	The name.
Nina:	Okay, so ask her that question now. What's the name of your book?
Aubrey:	"Playtime."
Nina:	Oh, I have another question, Aubrey. Where were you going in the car?
Aubrey:	To Pizza Hut.
Nina:	Mmmmm, I love pizza. Raise your hand if you love pizza. (Hands go up.) Raise your hand if you don't like pizza. (Other hands go up.) Okay, Aubrey, go on to G.
Aubrey:	Give ideas or suggestions. Danielle.
Danielle:	Maybe next time you can write about your little sister.
Aubrey:	Thank you.
Nina:	Oh, you remembered to say thank you. Let's give Aubrey a hand for sharing.

This is how a sharing session would sound in the beginning of October. I am giving a lot of support as they work through TAG. This support is critical so that in the future children can implement the system with no interference. Notice how I am raising my expectations by directing Aubrey to ask Denise "why." This pushed Denise to think more deeply by making other connections to the text. This is also supporting Aubrey to take more charge of the conversation. You will see that soon the author will automatically ask "why," and over some more time the responder will not even wait for the prompt but will immediately defend his or her statement using a "because" clause.

Here the children are still working on formulating questions, and now in October I am intervening with questions like "What do you want to know about?" Then in my own question to Aubrey I model the "where" form of questioning. This, too, is a building block for later discussion of setting in a story. If I saw that the children weren't ready to form the question after my directives "Ask her about the color" and "Ask her that question now," I would have formed the question and asked them to repeat it after me. Often in September and October we need to do this for our second-language learners or language-delayed students. Because Denel and Shaquilla formed the question appropriately, they modeled it for the children and I didn't need to. In this last transcript we are discussing Aubrey's finished piece—her publication—but it is very important to remember that young authors need to use TAG during all stages of their writing. It is very necessary that children and their teachers see sharing as part of the process and not an ending to the process. What message would we be sending if we only allowed children to share after they published their piece? It actually wouldn't be a process program but one based on product. We want children to enjoy and be reinforced by the whole process, not just one aspect of it. If we only focus on publication, only certain skills can be purposely addressed. When each stage of the process is validated, young authors learn the full spectrum of skills and responses all authors need. You'll see as the year goes on that TAG plays a major role in helping children talk about and work through revision. "Ask questions" and "Give ideas" are powerful vehicles that encourage and enable our young authors to revise.

Here, too, I am reinforcing the courteous behavior I expect from every member of our community. Again I am directing Aubrey to say thank you and then positively recognizing her when she does it on her own at the end of the session. As you can see, I consistently work on maintaining the structure that I laid out in September. You will see in the months to come how our TAG sessions become more advanced and complex as we connect to our writing, reading, other pieces of literacy and the world.

I'm sure you realize I am not at all finished with writing process, and I'm not. In the November chapter I'll show you how I organize the sign-up books, and how I help children self-edit/revise. You'll also hear more advanced TAG sessions and some of my skills lessons. You'll, of course, see more of the children's pieces, too.

Reading Aloud

You already know that we are reading *Charlotte's Web* and that as we read this book together we discuss it as authors. Remember the questions Eric shared in the September chapter? Most were connected to authorship—for example, "Have you ever written a story with talking animals?" As I help children with these questions I am strengthening their identity as authors, and by October they really are beginning to see themselves as authors—just like E. B. White. Did you have a chance to come up with other questions related to authorship? Let's think of some together:

• Why do you think E. B. White chose a farm as the setting? What are some of the settings you have chosen for your stories?

- How do you know that E. B. White likes animals? Who are your favorite characters? Why?
- What is Wilbur's big problem? How do you think it will be solved? What are some of the problems you have in your stories?
- What does E. B. White do to make us want to read more? What can you write in your stories to make them even more interesting?

Each of these questions builds on critical areas that every author needs to develop: setting, characters, problem, solution, and details, and, in fact, during writing process we will bring these questions up again as I help them develop and revise their stories.

Nina: I see you have a talking dog in your story. Were you thinking of Wilbur when you wrote this?
Aaron: Yep.
Nina: I also learn from other authors. So what will the problem be in your story? (No response.) What was one of Wilbur's problems?
Aaron: The father was going to kill him.
Nina: Yes, that was one, and what was the solution?
Aaron: Fern cried, and he gave her Wilbur.
Nina: Okay, so is something going to happen to your dog? (No response.) Think about something that could happen to your dog. He could get hit by a car. That is definitely a problem. So, will a car hit him?
Aaron: Yes.
Nina: Oh! Will he die?
Aaron: No, they'll take him to the hospital.
Nina: Okay! So you have a problem and a solution.

Reading aloud is an incredible way to connect to all areas of the curriculum. In October we begin writing and practicing a play called "Living Things around the World"; *Charlotte's Web*, along with our science curriculum, serves as the foundation of this play. We'll examine this play more closely in November, and you will see how music and poetry also become an integral part of our production.

Silent Reading

You actually got a pretty good picture of how silent reading works in our community when Eric described it in September and as I talked about it in this chapter during our discussion on scheduling. So let me show you the rules we use, and as you read them think about why these rules might be important.

Silent Reading Rules

- We read silently.
- We remain in our seats.
- We have our own books.
- We only read during silent reading.
- Children and adults all read at the same time.

Of course, these rules are important because they allow the members of the community to know exactly what is expected of them. So often teachers assume that children know what a term means and forget that many need an explanation to be successful. So with these rules children all learn a common definition that is added to our growing shared vision.

We've talked about inspiring children to read, the value of reading as a full community, including adults, but why do you think we are all reading silently in the first place? Why am I spending at least twenty to thirty minutes on this instead of other kinds of work like worksheets, fill-in-the-blank activities, and so on? If you look at my program I have a variety of reading and writing forms (reading aloud, discussion groups, poetry, music, playwriting, letter writing) that are very interactive. Within these forms my students fully develop the sense that reading and writing has to do with relationships and connections within the community. Silent reading, on the other hand, allows them to enjoy the individual pleasures of reading, reading totally for joy, and connecting individually to their own inner thoughts with the text and author.

As I'm sure I've already mentioned, we become better at something when we practice it: you play basketball to get better at basketball, you jump rope to get better at jumping rope, you read to get better at reading. Think about what kind of reading we do the most as literate adults. Yes, we usually read silently, and we need to help our children to do the same so that they continue to read as adults.

ERIC: Up to now, you've seen various sets of rules: line rules, silent reading rules, and rules for our community. You may need to make variations or differentiations on rules that suit your classroom and/or activity, some of which might be noticeably different from Nina's class yet appropriate to your own. What are some guidelines you might follow in the construction of those rules? Here are some rules Nina and I consider as we—and our students—create and write:

- We keep our rules short.
- We make our rules positive, avoiding the words *don't* and *not*.

- We avoid commands and directives from a single power figure.
- We include the word *we*.
- We start with a small number of rules and gradually build up as we need to.
- We have students agree on the rules, giving them responsible roles in the creation and maintenance of them.
- We assert that rules reflect student success, kindness, helpfulness, community, progress, and concrete activities.
- We regularly reflect on our rules.
- We edit our rules if they have adverse effects on our community.

You need to be clear that rules have reasons for existing, that they're not haphazard, and that the consequences of not following them have effects on all people. Therefore, the rules must regularly be discussed. You may even find rule writing and development to be a part of writing process or homework, including any edit or rewrite phases. You'll find that you're helping students follow rules by giving indirect commands regarding them. Often Nina uses language like:

- What rules do you need to follow during edit time?
- Are you sitting next to someone who is following the rules?

Reading Discussion

NINA: I also have clear and concise rules for our reading discussion groups so that my young communicators know exactly what is expected of them. Here they are:

Reading Discussion Rules

- We take the book(s) we were reading during silent reading.
- Two, three, or four people make up a group.
- All groups are mixed (each group needs to have boys and girls).
- We talk about reading and other subjects connected to what we're reading.
- We help our friends form our groups.

Some educators have questioned why I use the word *rules* instead of *guidelines*. Well, simply because they are not guidelines and are not suggestions but are required rules. My children do have a choice of what questions they can use while they discuss their books:

Some Questions to Ask during Reading Discussion Groups

- Do you like your book? Why or why not?
- Who is your favorite character? Why?
- What's your favorite part of the book and why?
- Why did you choose this book?
- Why do you think the author wrote this book?
- Where do you think the author got his or her ideas?
- What is the problem of the story?
- What is the solution of the story?
- Where does the story take place? (setting)
- What genre is your story? (fiction, nonfiction, science fiction, horror, adventure, and so on)
- What character would you like to be? Why?
- What would you do if that were your problem?
- If you were the author, what would you change? Why?
- What part of the story connects to the title?
- What ideas would you use from the book to write your own story? Why?

Why do you think my children very easily learn to question in this style? Remember that we are a community of writers: analyzing literature is a natural part of our discourse, as we look at books through the eyes of authors. It is so incredible to be able to do this! The whole literacy process becomes alive and vibrant because my young readers are also published authors and hold a stake in whatever they read and discuss. These active members of the larger literate community have a deep reason for reading—to continue writing.

Families

My heart fills with gratitude that I have been given the opportunity to spend my days with these children. I tell the families this and I know they appreciate it. I've written a family letter once a month and keep them informed on all aspects of our classroom. They can tell that I am a professional and that their children are in good hands. So many teachers here have trouble with families. Already there have been two negative incidents concerning parents and teachers. This is sad, but I do understand the family's point of view. When a teacher is negative about my child I'm defensive too. One thing I do, too, is call the families at least once a month just to say Hi. I can hear it in all of their voices how appreciative they are. It really doesn't take much time, either. These little caring touches are so important. I am strong and strict with their children and I know that is appreciated too, because it shows I take my job seriously.

Let me show you the letter I sent to my families on October 12. I think it serves as a good condensed version of what happens in October.

Dear Families,

We have had a busy month! You should be *very* proud of your children. They are doing well and learning every day. I want to thank you for all your help with making sure your children do their homework and return their homework books. Please continue reading with them every night. I'm sure you can tell that they are already beginning to read!

During the next few weeks I will be sending home a script of the play we have written together. Your children have worked very hard on learning their lines and we hope to present the play to you and the rest of the school at the end of October or the beginning of November. Please help them with their lines as you encourage them to speak loudly and clearly.

We have also learned some new poems during this past month. Ask your children to recite: "Dreams," by Langston Hughes; "The Giggles," by Martin Gardner; "Hope," by Langston Hughes; "Rudolph Is Tired of the City," by Gwendolyn Brooks; and "Two Friends," by Nikki Giovanni.

Please continue helping your children with their first and last names. I will send home lined paper so that they can practice writing within the lines. We are also practicing to write the letters *Mm, Tt, Pp, Aa, Ss,* and *Nn*. Ask them about words that begin with these letter sounds. For example, "What sound does Mommy begin with?" "What other words begin with the same sound that 'Mommy' does?"

In Math your children are learning to recognize numbers 0–10 and to draw sets for each number. For example, 1 = 0; 2 = 00; 3 = 000; etc. Please help them with this up to the number 10. We are also doing simple addition and learning our right hand from our left.

In Science and Social Studies we are talking and reading about living things and community helpers. Ask them to categorize what is living and not living. In connection to this we are reading *Charlotte's Web* aloud. Ask your children about Charlotte and Wilbur!

As you can see, your children are getting many types of learning experiences. Please make sure they are in school every day and on time (8:15). We start our learning immediately and learn straight through the entire day. When your children miss a day of school they miss a lot!

Let me share our daily schedule:

8:15–8:30	Get silent reading books, write diary entry
8:30–8:40	School announcements
8:40–9:20	Good morning song, collecting homework, schedule
9:00–9:20	Circle discussion time: attendance/reading aloud/sci/SS
9:20–9:30	Writing process including sharing
9:30–10:15	Choral poetry/sci/SS
10:15	Prepare for lunch
10:20–10:50	Lunch
10:50–11:20	Silent reading
11:20–11:50	Reading discussion

11:50–11:55	Put silent reading books away, choose homework book
11:55–12:00	Reading aloud
12:00–12:25	Outside play
12:30–1:15	Math
1:15–1:45	Individual learning time
1:45–2:00	Review assigned homework; ending discussion; poetry; reading aloud; goodbye song

Remember, you are always invited to come and learn with us!
Sincerely,

Dr. Zaragoza

We talked a bit in September about why I use the words "families" instead of "parents" and how the former is much more inclusive. Many of our students do not live with their parents but maybe with grandparents, aunts, uncles, or even older siblings, so using "families" shows respect to these different family situations. I strive to show my families how much I need and appreciate their help. I really do think it is an honor to be able to work with their children and I want the family to know this. I also want them to know that I believe that working together is an important element in their children's success.

It is great to see how seriously the families take their role in their children's school success. It is especially evident in the Brownie entries. Families are really involved in helping their children with these entries and seem as excited as their children to have Brownie as a guest!

ERIC: What would you prefer to do first, talk about the potential headaches you might face as a kindergarten teacher or little caring touches?

In a small way, you might think that Nina looks at small monthly phone calls and updates on their children as a means of preventing problems down the road. She considers this an integral part of the job, a piece of the children's learning puzzle that is critical to their success. Hence, if she doesn't do it, she's not doing her job well in her mind. She tries to look at the children through the eyes of the families. And while incidents such as Roderick hitting Virginia pop up, Nina states that she has far fewer problems than do her counterparts who don't add this aspect of their work into their daily plans.

So what are some of the little caring touches Nina implements? Not surprisingly, you'll see that a positive interaction with families in light of problems is a point of emphasis. Note here Nina's diary entry regarding Roderick's hitting Virginia:

Roderick is hitting Virginia. I think he is having trouble because he sees her as a bit slow. I spoke to his mother about this, and she says he's the same with children who don't catch the ball well, etc. We agreed that we'd work on this with Roderick.

You see how the issue is addressed and that the result of the conversation is a positive goal that occurs over time? Of course, they hope for good behavior overnight, but they agree that together they'll work on this on an ongoing basis.

In contrast, you also see the families interacting with children in terms of their authorship, especially in terms of keeping Brownie's diary. The families are clearly willing to be their children's voice in the writing. They also write a sequential narrative, usually a timeline of what the child and Brownie did after school. Occasionally, there is a "thank you" or "I love you, Brownie!" statement thrown in, but it's clearly a sequence of events in just about every single missive.

Step 11 of Nina's writing process is "Illustrate, help others, share your book, and go back to step 1." The children offer only a few illustrations, often just a handful of attempted circles that resemble Brownie. However, overwhelmingly children are choosing to illustrate with letters. The letters are well formed and recognizable. I decided to do an analysis on the letter chosen, since they do appear to be arbitrary, without regard to upper- or lowercase.

I went back and looked at the illustrations of students' publications, as well. Again, while students elected to draw pictures of things in September, they more often preferred to illustrate their stories by practicing letters. In fact, of the 126 stories we looked at, 69 of them had letters as part of their illustrations. Of these 69 illustrations, 1,563 characters were attempted with the following breakdown:

Character	Number of Appearances	Comments
O/0/zero	170	Circles are the most practiced character.
S/s	100	Some are correct; some are backward; squiggles are interpreted as important; in that this is the most common letter in English.
I/1/l	89	Three characters seen as lines.
E	81	The most commonly used vowel.
R	79	Coupled with *L* and 7, this type of character accounts for 119 examples of long lines with an adjacent hat or bottom.
P/p	66	Grouped with *b*, *d*, *g*, these tries account for 139 examples of a circle with a down- or upturned line.

Table continued on next page.

Character	Number of Appearances	Comments
N	65	Most popular of the line and hump letters, including *m* and *u*.
A	64	Could be confused with *d*. When coupled with *d*, accounts for 88 characters.
D	60	*P, B, D* the most commonly practiced capital letters, all with a line and half-circles to the right, accounting for 179 characters.
B	63	
A	49	
g/9	49	
I	47	
T	46	
B	44	
X/x	38	
L	36	
T	34	
H	31	
C/c	30	
M	30	
H	25	
R	25	
E	24	
D	24	
M	21	
U/u	16	
W/w	13	
K/k	12	
J	11	
N	10	
6	9	
F	8	*E* and *F* account for only 32 examples, *E* three times as common.
G	8	
2	8	
V/v	6	*N, V,* and *w* seldom practiced.
Y	6	
4	6	Angle-lined characters such as *K* and *4* rarely practiced.
Q	5	

Table continued on next page.

Character	Number of Appearances	Comments
3	5	
5	4	
7	4	
Z/z	3	Zigzags rarely practiced, much like angle-lined characters; 2 and z rarely practiced.
8	3	
G	2	
F	2	Line-plus +-curl letters, g, f, j hardly ever practiced.
J	2	

Interdependence

NINA:

> I guess this says it all: Shaquilla was sick today but she sent her mother to bring in her homework! Wow! (Diary entry 10/22)

Shaquilla seems to have learned that many can share responsibility. If she can't get to school at least her mother can get the homework there. As we saw in September, Shaquilla has also taken responsibility for KeAndre's care. What a testimony to this type of classroom that encourages cooperation not competition. I, too, allow the children to take on responsibility so that we do really carry the community together. Children never want to be absent because they help create and maintain the community and have a personal stake in keeping it running. It is amazing to see and hear. Of course, I encourage this as I direct all children to help each other. In my classroom helping is not a choice or a special prize. As a member of our community it is our honor to be helpful to all. In fact, instead of separating children who are having difficulty with each other I have them sit together and work it out. So, now Roderick sits next to Virginia:

> I changed Roderick's seat so that he sits next to Virginia and told him that he needed to help her and let her help him. He smiled with pride that he would be "in charge" of helping Virginia. We'll see how it goes. (Diary entry 10/22)

Expectations

NINA:

> I laugh sometimes and say, "Oh no, I've created monsters!" They are so independent that on our way to the library or cafeteria they get in line and just go without waiting for my directions! I guess they figure they know the directions, so why do they have to wait for me? I love it but at times I do say (after a child has already told another what to do) "Can you let me tell them please?" (Diary entry, 10/22)

Actually, I wouldn't call my students monsters, but other teachers have. When my children need to interact with other teachers, such as their music teacher, PE teacher, and so on, their independence sometimes seems scary to the other teachers. Some teachers complain that my children call out too much and try to tell them how to teach. I have actually heard them say, "We don't do it this way!" or "Dr. Zaragoza doesn't do that!" or "You're supposed to recognize our good work and say 'thank you.'" In the end, though, the teachers come to appreciate these children because of the children's desire to learn.

I started this month of October talking about expectations, didn't I? I think you have a good idea about what I expect from myself, my students, and their families. I expect a lot, but I don't usually get what I expect. I get much, much more! In a living, connected, and vibrant community, everyone's energy helps inspire all participants to reach goals that they never thought were possible. It's an exhilarating experience, and I wouldn't change it for the world.

Talk to you in November!

November

Please write again. Love, Darrin.

NINA: November is an exciting month for me because my young authors are more and more comfortable with authorship and they deepen their understanding of the craft of writing. We also begin to explore different kinds of writing as we add letter writing to our repertoire. Our diary writing has become more fluent and our drama production/poetry recital is almost ready to perform. Our entries about Brownie are more elaborate, with much help from the families. In fact, by November the families and children are so excited about Brownie they even give him baths! Why don't we look at the November letter to families so that you get an overview of what we're doing this month?

November 18, 1999

Dear Families,

We have had a fantastic month! Your children are doing so well and progressing rapidly! Thank you for all your help. Almost every child brings in homework each day. Thank you for helping with this important responsibility. Our play practice is going very well. We have started practicing on stage and will be ready to perform for you soon! We are already talking about our next play. We have also learned some new poems during this past month. The newest include "My Little Sister," by William Wise, "Sun Song," by Langston Hughes, and "My People," by Langston Hughes. I know they would love to recite them for you! Ask!

Please continue helping your children with reading as you allow them to read their homework books and their word list each night. Please let me know if you do not have the word list I sent home.

As you know, in Math your children are learning addition up to the number 10. Please continue to help them as you allow them to count on their fingers or draw corresponding circles for each number. Most children recognize their numbers but make sure if your child needs practice that you work on this at home. We have also started counting with pennies and measuring with rulers. Next month we will begin working on telling time.

In Science and Social Studies we are talking about the body and keeping ourselves healthy. We are also growing our very own flowers and talking about taking care of our trees. We finished reading *Charlotte's Web* and have already started a new book called *James and the Giant Peach*. Ask your children to tell you about James's two aunts.

As always, please make sure your child is in school every day and on time (8:15). Your children are a pleasure to work with! Thank you!

Sincerely,
Dr. Zaragoza

I love writing these family letters because I know the families appreciate them. These letters help me to regularly connect to the families and also help to strengthen our collaborative relationship. Writing these letters helps me to review what we've done and to decide on what we will do in the future. They really do help me monitor my curriculum and make sure that important connections are created and continued. The connections I speak about here are not only curriculum-related but are also familial. I cannot overstate how important it is to connect with your families throughout the school year and allow them to be a part of your classroom community. Doesn't this make sense to you? Just think: you are with the children of these families for six to seven hours a day. Those are a lot of hours! I feel a certain comfort knowing that my families and I feel at ease with each other and are both working to help the children progress. It helps to know that I am not in this alone and that I can depend on families for their help. I think, too, that families feel relieved that their children have a teacher that really cares and sets up a classroom where students are safe and learning.

ERIC: Clearly Nina and I feel responsibility on our shoulders. It's a good responsibility, but it's important to underscore what that responsibility is. These children spend approximately one third of their lives with us. One third is spent with their families, and the other third is spent sleeping. Often we hear on TV, usually with respect to issues concerning controversial topics and when they're presented to children, comments like, "I feel that should be taken care of at home" or "it's the parents' responsibility" or "that topic doesn't belong in school." What subjects have you heard those comments refer to before?

Still, these controversial subjects are only a minute portion of the issues students encounter, and Nina seems to begin with social justice and responsibility in terms of community. If we look at the next chart we can see how the ideas of community and curriculum intertwine with social responsibility:

COMMUNITY	
Taking care of oneself	Taking care of each other
We write about how we live our lives and share our stories.	We read about how people take care of each other.
We write our own books.	We read each others' books.
We grow our own plants.	We read about how people grow food and animals.
We love books.	We love trees.

Here the community is first and foremost the leading element. From there we take two perspectives simultaneously: first, that we help one another, and second that we learn to take care of ourselves in responsible ways. From there we look to resources: first, what other people are saying, for example in books like *Charlotte's Web*, and then take the opportunity to tell the world what we do in our own lives during writing process. Language arts becomes a content lesson as we then employ science by growing our own plants. We check out books and do our best to read them, including the books written by our peers in the class. All books, those written by other authors and those written by us, are kept on the same shelves and are treated with equal respect. And then we overtly state that we love books and we love nature.

Expectations and Structure

NINA: In November we are off and running. The foundation of our classroom community has been laid down and has definitely solidified. The children and I have a structure to work within and we all know what is expected of us and what needs to be accomplished. It is, in fact, this foundation and this structure that allow us to be creative and ever growing. Does that sound paradoxical to you? Let's think about it. Why do you think our type of structure ultimately allows for greater freedom? Why do my students and, in fact, I feel so free in our community? Meaningful structure enables community members to feel safe because they know exactly what to expect and what is expected of them. Why is this sense of safety so important? When we feel safe we are willing to take more risks, right? This risk taking is crucial to the learning process. As a matter of fact, it is crucial to the teaching process as well. Both my students and I feel strong and empowered and know that we will be supported in any new teaching/learning endeavor. There is no danger of ridicule or negativity because our structure (for example, in TAG, and in the overall principle of noncompetition) doesn't allow it. It is amazing how cooperative children are when their community fully supports this cooperation. Let's talk a little bit more about how my community fosters only positive interactions.

Did you notice that there is absolutely no competition among children? I believe that this kind of competition in the classroom is deadly. Children are pitted against children and they are continually vying for position, whether it be door holder, office monitor, or star of the month. I have systematically obliterated all of these positions in my room because I see them as manipulative and unkind. I wonder if some of you are thinking, "But, Nina, don't we want to build responsibility in our students?" Yes, of course we do, but I don't want to do it for one child at the expense of another. All our children deserve the honor to serve others whether they meet your behavioral expectations or not. Many teachers use these positions as rewards for compliant behavior and not as a requirement for all children. Do you see why there are fights on the lines in school? It's all about power and recognition. Children have learned that the esteemed position is line leader so they fight to get to the front. Somehow by the time they get to kindergarten this is an already entrenched rule and it takes a while to eliminate:

Roderick: I'm first!
Denise: I was here and I want to hold the door! (Pushing ensues.)
Andre: He pushed me! (Andre pushes back.)
Nina: What's happening?
Roderick: I want to be line leader!
Nina: There are no line leaders in our class. We just all go on line to get where we're going.
Denise: Can I be first?
Nina: Roderick and Denise, both of you get to the end somewhere else on the line. You need to learn that it isn't important where you are on line.

I have to have these types of conversations for a while before I am able to extinguish this type of bickering. At other times I might say things like:

- Do you think you are better than someone else because you're first on line?
- Does it make you a good person to be first on line? Of course not! You don't need to be first on line.
- We love you no matter where you are on line!
- Good! Larry's not running to the line. He knows it doesn't matter where he is on line.
- I see Danielle's not first on line. She knows it's not important where you are on line.

After a few weeks in our classroom the children realize that they needn't seek attention through classroom jobs or line positions because they get enough attention in other areas and they know that they are loved for who they are and not for what they do.

Of course, that doesn't mean they don't do anything—you know already that they do a lot, and all the time. They are expected to be helpers in the community, and this expectation holds for everyone and is not dependent on compliant behavior. What a tragedy to deprive children from helping. What a disservice. Have you ever been of service to someone? How do you feel when you help someone? Don't you get an incredible sense of fulfillment? I want all my children to feel this and so I make sure that all children help each other all the time. It really isn't a choice—it's an obligation.

In our community this obligation is usually embraced wholeheartedly. Shaquilla can't bear to be absent because of KeAndre, and Roderick learns to help and appreciate Virginia. They are also all convinced they have to be in school to help me—and they're right! I'm always losing my pens, my chalk; I need help in choosing books and giving ideas for writing and helping other children with math. You see, they don't need to feel powerful as a line leader because they have real power in the classroom. And by November it doesn't matter who's first because we're all going to the same place.

When we do need to pick people (a schoolwide student of the month program or office monitors), we use our class list and select names in order. If we have started at the top for a number of decisions then we will switch to the bottom for a while. I actually use the class list often throughout the day for a number of activities. If I want a response from everyone, or I want to collect the homework in order (for easy filing), I'll use the list. So for example:

NINA: I want you to choose something from your book to read to us. So take a few minutes to look and then I'll use our class list to call on you. (A few minutes pass.) Okay, Danielle, you're first on the list. Are you ready or do you need another minute?

Danielle: I'm ready.
Nina: Oh, let me just go down the list and make sure everyone is ready before we begin. Andre, are you ready?
Andre: Yep.
Nina: Aaron, did you pick something to read to us?
Aaron: Not yet.
Nina: Okay, keep looking and raise your hand when you're ready.

How does the use of this list help to maintain a noncompetitive environment and enable children to feel safe? Well, everyone knows they will be called on so there is no uncertainty. And while it initially might seem that the first person on the list would feel more pressure, this isn't the case because I ask the child if he or she is ready to respond. If he or she isn't ready, we wait. As a matter of fact, we don't begin responding until the whole community is ready. I circulate around the room helping those who need help, and the other children read while they wait. Using the list also helps me to make sure that I am not calling on the same students all the time and allows all children sufficient opportunities to connect.

ERIC: Up to this point, now a little more than two months into our year, how many stickers or lollipops do you think Nina has handed out to students? Why do teachers tend to give out treats to students? And why hasn't Nina followed suit thus far? Do you think she ever will?

It will come as no surprise that Nina and I will actively choose to err on the side of promoting intrinsic motivation. I know: I can just hear people shouting out, "When the child is screaming and you just need to shut them up, what do you do?" I understand. Some people reach for the quick fix, occasionally that lollipop, and the child stops crying. I can understand why someone would be motivated to do so and continue doing so. It's just easier sometimes. But by doing so, what signal are you perpetuating, as Pavlov did with his dogs? Nina and I constantly ask ourselves that question. Edward Deci (1975) describes intrinsic motivation like this: "Intrinsically motivated activities are the ones for which there is no apparent reward except the activity itself. People seem to engage in the activities for their own sake and not because they lead to an extrinsic reward. . . . Intrinsically motivated behaviors are aimed at bringing about certain internally rewarding consequences, namely, feelings of competence and self-determination" (p. 23).

Abraham Maslow (1970) found that extrinsic rewards led to less superior results in learning and supported a system of "self-actualization." Mark Lepper and Melinda Hoddell (1989) found that children tend to look for the easiest ways toward completing projects when awards like grades or candy were evident. In other words, students were less likely to spend time contemplating and examining issues from a critical standpoint if the outside rewards were waiting for them upon completion. And in support of Maslow's suggestion of fostering a "self-actualization" process in students, Lepper and Hodell suggest the following, particularly in cases where a child's natural inborn motivation has already been doused for some reason: challenge, curiosity, control. Based on what you've seen so far, how does Nina look toward these three elements in her structure? There is an abundance of reasons I'm sure you can come up with, but these three strike me immediately:

Challenge
Children are asked to look toward their achievement, striving to perform in the sophisticated way many adults do.

Curiosity
Children are asked "why" and are encouraged to ask "why" at almost any opportunity.

Control
Children are encouraged to offer their own ideas as they engage in discussion and composition. Nina does not restrict their creativity with the nuts and bolts of language.

H. Douglas Brown (1994) also suggests consulting the following checklist in order to ensure that intrinsic motivation is a key feature of one's class:

- Appeals to the interests of the students; relevant to their lives
- Presented in a positive manner
- Students aware of the purpose of the technique
- Students have choice in choosing some aspect of technique
- Encourages students to discover for themselves
- Contributes to students' autonomy and independence from teacher
- Fosters negotiation with other students
- Students receive feedback from other students

If you'd like, you can look to the attributes of Nina's class that work with Brown's checklist. You may even wish to keep it in mind as you read this book. Meanwhile, you can ask yourself how your class activities relate to the checklist.

One last point on this subject is worth mentioning. Earlier, I wrote that Lepper and Hodell hold that intrinsic motivation is inborn; in other words, it is a trait of human existence that every child comes with. As Nina and I have worked with these children, we have seen no evidence to the contrary. Those children want to be there and they are ready to soak up any information they can get their hands on. As I said earlier in the book, the first day I arrived to work on this project, I was initially regretting having to get up so early. But then I saw the children and how the time of day was so little a problem and how eager they were to get going. My attitude changed immediately, and I found myself looking toward their example and readjusting my own attitude and motivation. Getting up was never again a problem.

Curriculum

Nina: We also use the class list to help us with organization of our drama productions and poetry recitals. Because there is no competition among my children in our classroom, there are, of course, no auditions. But because we write our own plays children usually write their own lines, so there is no need for auditions. Let me share our first play with you.

Living Things around the World

Scene 1: In the Park

Child: Let's go visit the places so we can see all different living things.
Child: Okay. Where should we go first?
Child: Let's go to the beach because it's not so far away.
Child: Okay! I'll ask my uncle so we can all go in his truck.
Children: Let's go!!

Scene 2: At the Beach

Child: Look at the ocean!
Child: It's beautiful!
Child: A lot of living things are in the ocean.
Child: I know. There are fish.
Child: They are pretty and they're all different colors.
Child: Like red, green, blue, yellow, orange, black, and brown.

Child: I see white fish, too.

Child: Yeah, fish eat other fish and also eat the living plants in the ocean.

Child: That's how all living things grow and stay alive. They eat.

Child: Oh, look. I see a dolphin.

Child: I see it too!

Child: Dolphins are friendly. If someone is lost in the ocean they will try and help them.

Child: Hey! Look at that pelican! It just caught a fish to eat!

Child: Oh no! I see a shark! We better get out of here!

Child: Let's go to the Everglades.

Scene 3: The Everglades

Child: Look, I see an alligator!

Child: Look at that big old mouth.

Child: Yeah, look at those big teeth.

Child: They look a little like a dinosaur.

Child: There's a bird near the alligator.

Child: I hope the bird flies away so the alligator won't kill it!

Child: Oh, I see another living thing—a panther!

Child: Look, it's running really fast!

Child: It must be looking for food.

Child: Let's get out of here! It might eat us!

Child: We can go to the jungle next.

Child: That's really far.

Child: I know. We better take an airplane.

Scene 4: The Jungle

Child: I hear the monkeys in the tree.

Child: I see them too.

Child: They're eating bananas.

Child: That's one of the things monkeys eat to stay alive!

Child: I love bananas too!

Child: Gorillas eat bananas and other fruits too.

Child: I know! They grow really big!

Child: Oh no! Here comes a lion!

Child: Run, monkeys, run! The lion will eat you!

Child: I miss my family. Let's fly back to my family's farm.

Scene 5: The Farm

Child: This is a nice farm!
Child: There's the farmer. Let's ask him if we can help.
Child: Can I ride the horse?
Farmer: Sure! You can feed him too.
Child: What does he eat?
Farmer: He eats hay and carrots.
Child: There's a pig!
Child: Like Wilbur in our story!
Child: How many ducks do you have?
Farmer: We have 10. Let's count them.
Children: 1, 2, 3, 4, 5, 6, 7, 8, 9, 10.
Farmer: Very good!
Child: Oh there's a cow!
Farmer: We get all our milk from that cow.
Child: We know a song about a cow. We'll sing it for you.
(All children sing "Did You Feed My Cow?")
Farmer: Thank you! Let's milk the cow and then you can drink some of the milk.
Children: Yummy!
Child: I hear a rooster.
Child: Me too. I think it's early in the morning.
Child: The rooster sings in the morning like we sing our good morning song.
Child: Let's sing "Jambo."
(All children sing "Jambo.")
Child: We saw a lot of living things!
Child: Let's go back home and tell our families about everything!

Usually the order of the parts is the order of the class list we have already spoken about. In this way whoever goes first, second, or last is never an issue. This also helps the children remember the order in which they need to say their lines, since they really do know the order of the list because we use it for so many things. Every child has a part and no child is ever, ever denied a part. Being in our drama production is not an extra activity but is a requirement of our language arts program. Can you see that the play actually is a cohesive element that connects the various pieces of my curriculum into a unified whole? The theme is social studies–based, poetry and music are involved, and there is even a little math! Of course, we are reading the play we have written ourselves. Very cool! Let me tell you how we write our plays.

No matter what grade I taught I always included drama in my classroom, but in my earlier years of teaching I would use already-written pieces of literature like *Sleeping Beauty*, *Peter Pan*, and *The Wizard of Oz*. While those final performances turned out well, it was actually very difficult to adapt in the beginning stages. We had to write enough parts for everybody, and put the story into our own words. This, very often, was like pulling teeth and took an enormous amount of time and patience. One day, though, I realized that what I was doing was counterproductive to my writing process program, in which I give children total choice of topic in writing. After this realization my class and I started to write a play with a blank piece of paper, and it is so much easier now. Here's how we start:

Nina:	We're going to write a play now. Has anyone gone to a play before?
Shaquilla:	Like *Disney on Ice*?
Nina:	Yeah, kind of like that. What other plays can you think of?
Larry:	*Scooby Doo*?
Nina:	Well, a cartoon is a little like a play because there are characters that we're watching.
Roderick:	Oh, I saw a play with my aunt on the stage.
Nina:	Do you remember the name?
Roderick:	It was about a bear in the forest.
Danielle:	I saw that one too.
Nina:	Okay, so we are going to write a play. What should we write about?
Virginia:	A cat?
Nina:	Great idea, Virginia. What else can we write about?
Aaron:	A dog.
Nina:	Good! So maybe we can write about animals since we've been talking about living things. Where do some of the living things we talked about live?
Anthony:	The farm.
KeAndre:	The beach.
Denise:	The city.
Nina:	Yes! So let's start writing. I'll write our ideas on this pad and then I'll go home and type up the script for us to read. Now, let's see, where should we go first? Maybe let's start in the city because that's where we live and then we can travel around. Where do we see animals in our city?
Aubrey:	The beach.

Nina: Oh, my favorite place! Who else loves the beach? Raise your hand
           if you love the beach. Raise your hand if you don't love the beach.
           Well, let's start at the beach, since we do live in Miami! What ani-
           mals do we see at the beach?
Latisha: Fish.
Nina: Okay, what do you say when you see a beautiful fish?
Latisha: Wow!
Nina: What color fish do you see at the beach?

Do you see how the play is already emerging? As the children talk I jot
down the lines and thoughts they contribute. By the end of this first session,
which usually takes about ten minutes, I have enough to type the initial first
script. I bring it in the next day and the children and I add and make changes to
it. I, of course, guide them to include songs and other elements with questions
like, "What morning song do we sing that a rooster would like?" or "What farm
song or poem can we sing or say in the farm section?" The songs and poetry we
include are pieces we already know and are not an extra burden on the children.
Remember, I use the play to bring my curriculum into a unified whole.

You can see that I use the vocabulary of a playwright (script, scene) immediately in our initial conversations. Just as in writing my children learn new
vocabulary as they use it. They definitely learn what a script is because they
use it almost every day at school and at home. As a matter of fact, once we have
finalized the script each child gets two copies of it: one for home and one for
school. This way, there is no hassle about children forgetting their scripts. I
do the same thing with poetry and music. Once it is written down children get
two copies. We'll talk more about how I teach poetry after this discussion on
our productions.

Because our play usually includes major elements of the curriculum, we
practice the play either within the language arts block or within the content
area (science, social studies, math) time. I find that short consistent periods of
practice are more effective than practicing for a longer time fewer times during the week. Therefore, I try to include play practice for a short time every
day. Our beginning plays are short anyway, so ten to fifteen minutes a day
is sufficient—and fun! Memorization happens gradually, as children are assigned "study play" each night for homework and as we chorally read the play
as a whole class for the first week or so. When most of the children know their
lines, we start practicing on the stage and the children help with the direction
as I teach them with stage directions like:

- Very good.
- Louder.

- More expression.
- Try again.

If the stage is not available, we invite classes into our room to see our play. Classes sign up for certain times during the day over a week, and we have the opportunity to show our work many times. The invited classes sit in our seats and we surround them when we perform. This actually works out very well, and when we perform our poetry recital this roundtable format is very comfortable and inviting.

ERIC: You can see the details Nina takes you through in developing the play. You can also bear a few more things in mind as guidelines, mostly from a language-use point of view. Note that this play has 72 lines, 464 words, and is about four pages double-spaced for the twenty-three students in the class. That entails an average line of about 6.4 words in length. The play has 15 sentences of 10 or more words, meaning that not quite one fifth of the play has some challenging line lengths. The longest line is 16 words long, and 7 lines have 13 words or more. These figures don't include the songs or the poems. When the songs and poems are included, the play itself lasts approximately fifteen minutes.

Now let's look at Brown's intrinsic motivation checklist. With the elements named here, can you account for features, descriptions, and/or examples of the play—its development, preparation, and/or performance—that incorporate aspects of the checklist? See if you can fill them into the following chart:

- Appeals to the interests of the students; relevant to their lives

- Presented in a positive manner

- Students aware of the purpose of the technique

- Students have choice in choosing some aspect of technique

- Encourages students to discover for themselves

- Contributes to students' autonomy and independence from teacher

- Fosters negotiation with other students

- Students receive feedback from other students

Next, where does Nina incorporate the following attitudes into the construct of the play development?

- Challenge
- Curiosity
- Control

Poetry and Music

NINA: Now let's talk a little bit about how I teach poetry and song. When I introduce a poem or a song I first sing or recite it fully to the children. Let's listen for a moment:

Nina: Today we're going to learn a new poem by, oh, who do you think it's by?

Andre: Langston Hughes.

Nina: Why do you think that?

Andre: Because almost every poem we know is by him.

Nina: That's right. It is by Langston Hughes! Listen. "Sun Song," by Langston Hughes. Sun and softness, sun and the beaten hardness of the earth, sun and all the sun stars, gathered together, dark ones of Africa, I bring you my songs to sing on the Georgia roads. (Children clap.) I'm glad you like it. Let's say it together, now. I'll say the each line and then you repeat it. Ready? "Sun Song," by Langston Hughes.

Children: "Sun Song," by Langston Hughes.

Nina: Sun and softness

Children: Sun and softness . . .

We practice the poem for a few days in this manner as we add movements and vocal variations to each major concept. For example, the first word "Sun" is very loud and the word "softness" is said as softly as possible. This sets up the rhythm of the poem and immediately enables the children to become actively involved. When we say "Sun and the beaten hardness of the earth" the children stomp one foot to the beat like this: "sun [stomp on the word *sun*] and the [stomp on the word *the*] beaten hardness [stomp on *beat* and *hard*] of the earth [stomp on *of* and *earth*]." When we get to "sun stars" we lift our hands up and use them to show twinkling stars. As I mentioned in October, in this way we match the words to physical movements that help children memorize, and with two or three days' practice (usually five minutes in the morning) they've gotten it. And have you noticed the children haven't even seen the poem in writing yet? I do this purposely so that by the time I write the poem on chart paper all children can successfully read it because of their memorization. Do you see how this helps all children be successful?

In October we spoke about why I use many of Langston Hughes's poems. Remember? Notice that the poems of his that I use for my children, "Dreams," "Sun Song," "Merry Go Round," "Hope," have a definite rhythm, the words are concrete enough to move to, and discussion of the meaning of the poems can easily be adapted to people of any age. I think my students are very successful with poetry because of these reasons, and they are very passionate about poetry because of my own passion for it. As you probably can guess, we are always working on poetry and we always revisit the poetry we know. It's not hard to do, because eventually all our poems are on our walls and surround us. If you walk in during free learning time you will probably see children with pointers going from one poem or song to the next, reading or singing each word.

Songs are treated the same way as poetry—don't you think poetry and music are similar? We move to our songs as we sing and when we master them we read them from our charts and take them home to readjust them, just as we do with our scripts. It's such an exciting way to learn, don't you think? The songs I choose for kindergarten are morning songs, farm songs ("Did You Feed My Cow?"), and contemporary songs like "I Believe I Can Fly." They usually find their way into our plays, too, and are sung at our poetry recitals. Can you see another reason why my children successfully learn our poems and songs? There is a purpose for memorization: they will be performing them. You see? It's actually connected to why they are successful authors, too. They have a purpose for writing: publication.

ERIC: Now let's look again at Brown's intrinsic motivation checklist above. With the elements named, can you account for features, descriptions, and/or examples of the songs and plays—their learning, practice, and/or mastery that incorporate these aspects? See if you can fill them into the same chart. Also, note where Nina incorporates those same elements of challenge, curiosity, and control into the construct of the song and poem mastery.

Now that you've been through this consideration a couple of times, I won't subject you to it formally again. However, I hope as you work with us through the year, you'll still look through these intrinsic motivational lenses as you examine our work, as well as your own.

Writing Process

NINA: The children continue to develop as writers in November as they continue to write every day, publish their best work, and make connections to other pieces of literature. Because the structure is very consistent, our writing sessions run smoothly with little adult intervention. Now my energy during writing is not spent on solidifying or maintaining the structure but on expanding lessons and discussions around literacy. In November, too, the children are given more responsibility for themselves and each other. They are pushed in all areas of the process, including the writing of their drafts, revising and editing the pieces they will publish, and sharing what they have written.

Nina:	Let's listen, everyone, for a minute. Sorry to interrupt, but I want to hear what some of you are doing. What are you working on, Andre?
Andre:	About my grandmother?
Nina:	Tell me more.
Andre:	She bought me a Spiderman.
Nina:	Oh, so where did she buy it?
Andre:	Toys Я Us.
Nina:	So, you can write where it happened. Who remembers the word we use when we talk about where our story is?
Aubrey:	Setting.
Nina:	Yes, so the setting of Andre's story is Toys Я Us. Raise your hand and tell me about your setting. Shaquilla?
Shaquilla:	In McDonald's.
Nina:	Oh, what happened in McDonald's?
Shaquilla:	A monster ate up all my fries.
Nina:	Wow, that is a problem! Do you have a solution in the story? Are you going to have more fries?
Shaquilla:	I'm gonna cry, and the monster is going to buy me more fries.
Nina:	So you have a plan already for your story. Who else has a plan in their head?
Denise:	My sister's birthday party.
Nina:	What's going to happen at the party?
Denise:	The cake is going to fall.
Nina:	So you already have your problem. Who will the characters be? What people are in your story?
Denise:	Me, my sister, my mom, my cousin, and my aunt.
Nina:	I see you do have a plan. So, Andre, what's the problem in your story?
Andre:	Spiderman breaks.
Nina:	And the solution?
Andre:	My grandma gets me another one.
Nina:	What will you say when she gives you the new one?

Andre:	Thank you.
Nina:	Oh, very polite! Will you put that dialogue in your story?
Andre:	Yes.
Nina:	What mark will you put after you say "thank you"? (No response.) Are you excited when your grandmother gives you the toy?
Andre:	Yeah.
Nina:	So how do you say thank you? Loudly or softly?
Andre:	Loud.
Nina:	Okay, so what mark would you put at the end: a period, a question mark, or an exclamation point? Let's all make those marks in the air with our fingers, and don't forget to do the sounds with your mouths! (Children make the marks in the air and make sounds we created for each mark.) So, which mark tells us the character is talking loudly or with excitement, Andre?
Andre:	Exclamation point.
Nina:	Okay! So raise your hand if you have people talking loudly in your story. Thanks for letting me interrupt you. Go on to what you were doing.

You see that I am continuing to nurture the seeds planted in October. I am also planting some new seeds that children will be responsible for using and developing in November and beyond. I am pushing them toward planning before writing, including setting, problem, and solution in their pieces. Actually, by November all pieces need to contain these basic elements before they can be brought to publication. The depth of each element might differ according to each author's skills, but they are required of all authors. So even though Virginia is still writing short sentences I will question her in revision to draw out what her story needs. Here is an example of an individual conference:

Nina:	Hi Virginia! Is that the draft you want to publish?
Virginia:	Yep.
Nina:	Okay, so let's revise it. Read it to me.
Virginia:	I have a balloon. It is red.
Nina:	Oh, I like how you say what color. What's the problem with the balloon? (No response.) What can happen to a balloon?
Virginia:	It can fly away.
Nina:	Yes, what else can happen to a balloon?
Virginia:	It can break.
Nina:	Okay, so what do you want to happen to this balloon in your story?

Virginia:	To break.
Nina:	Say the sentence you want to write. (No response.) The balloon what?
Virginia:	The balloon breaks.
Nina:	Listen. What sounds better: "The balloon breaks" or "The balloon broke"?
Virginia:	The balloon broke.
Nina:	Did you get another one?
Virginia:	Yeah.
Nina:	Say it. "I got . . ."
Virginia:	I got another one.
Nina:	Good! Now write down those two sentences and then get someone to edit it for you. What will you write now?
Virginia:	I got another one.
Nina:	But before that. What happened to the balloon?
Virginia:	It broke.
Nina:	Okay. So write that now. Let me watch. (Virginia writes random letters and stops.) Now write the next sentence, "It broke." (She writes.) Good! Now find someone to edit. (Virginia goes to Marc, who is writing a draft.) Excuse me, everyone. Let's listen for a minute. Thank you, Andre, you stopped writing and look ready to listen. Thank you, Larry. Thank you, Denel. Give Virginia a hand. She finished a story and is ready to get it edited. (Everyone claps.) Now, who do we go to for editing?
Denel:	Marc.
Nina:	Yes, everyone tries to go to Marc for editing, but who else can we go to?
Roderick:	Danielle.
Nina:	Okay, who else?
Denise:	You.
Nina:	Yes, after you go to a friend you sign up for an adult, but what other friends can you go to?
Denise:	Larry.
Nina:	That's right. We can go to all of our friends, not just Marc. We are all editors, so make sure you go to other children. Is that okay with you, Marc?
Marc:	Yes.
Nina:	I know you like to edit, but you also have to have time to write your own drafts, right? So who would like to edit Virginia's story? (A number of children raise their hands.) Pick someone else, Virginia.

There are many things happening in the above discussion. You can see that while I do much of my teaching in full-group sessions, I also conference individually. Notice that Virginia is expected to use the same elements as the other authors, and I give her the amount of support she needs to meet this expectation. This kind of support is necessary for many of our young authors and authors just learning to speak English.

I worked with Virginia on revision but for editing I sent her to the greater community. This is the way that I consciously begin to separate the revision and editing stages. In September and October this division is blurred because children are still internalizing the identity of authorship and learning the whole process. Now, with two months of experience, they are ready to learn some of the refinements of the craft. They also have the vocabulary necessary to talk effectively about revision. Remember that revision addresses the content of the piece and not the form, so children need to be able to deal with concepts such as setting, characters, problem, solution, and dialogue. In November they can do this, some with adult support, comfortably.

Do you remember that in October Marc was the editor of choice? Now I am pushing others to take up that role. Poor Marc became overloaded with editing work and needed more time to develop his own pieces. Also, other children need to develop editing skills, and in November I push them to do so. Of course, all children will not be editing at the same level, but they can edit at whatever level they are at. Yes, I could easily edit all the pieces first and it would probably be easier for me from a management perspective, but doing this would be detrimental to my students. Whether they are editing the way I am or not is not the point. What is important is that they are internalizing the process and through their own actions are beginning to understand the steps of the writing process.

ERIC: You've seen how Nina interacts with the children during the editing parts of writing process. But what goes on around the room when Nina is spending time with an individual child? Are the children engaged and working? And if so, what exactly are they saying to one another? During one November writing process session, I took notes on interactions among students during the writing process.

Immediately, it was clear that students were excited to be working through the writing process. When Nina announced, "Writing process!" a couple of children yelled, "Hooray!" Next, just as Nina follows the class list and sign-up sheets for various activities, she has a sign-up sheet for editing during writing process. The discipline issue Nina faced here was that the students actually wanted to argue a bit in order to get on the list. Still, the arguments were very short-lived and mild in nature, leaving Nina without having to spend any time asking students to check their behavior.

Jamal signed up for editing, and two students nearby—Shaquilla and Larry—helped him edit. As Jamal began telling his story, Shaquilla suggested to Larry that during editing he "try to write as many letters as possible."

Jamal: Me, Eric, and Dr. Zaragoza are . . .
Shaquilla: (Interrupting.) Who's the author?

Jamal spelled his own name, and Shaquilla tried to write it. Jamal interrupted her as she wrote, exclaiming, "You got the 'm' wrong!" Nina heard this and responded directly to the group from the other side of the room, "Give instructions to Shaquilla nicely, please!" Denel, who was working with other children at a nearby table, was attracted by the conversation and joined the group, examining the incorrect "m."

Denel: (Looking at the error.) You ain't gonna do my name. I know how to do an "s" (seemingly referring to Shaquilla's name).
Shaquilla: No, you don't.
Denel: Yes, I do.
Shaquilla: "S" is in my name.
Larry: Can I use your pen?

With three boys now in a group, Shaquilla seemed to tire and joined Andre at a different table. Nina stopped by briefly to be sure that Shaquilla and Andre were clear on the editing rules.

Andre: I put words in my picture in the clouds. (He had indeed. He wrote the word "pig.")
Andre: Pig, P-I-G. How do you spell "Shaquilla"?
Shaquilla: (Begins to spell her name.)
Andre: Wrong!
Shaquilla: (Protesting.) Um-mm!
Andre: Put an "R" right here. That's right. Shaquilla! Write in here in the clouds. (Shaquilla begins writing arbitrary letters—not Andre's name.) No, you got it all wrong. You put it there.

Meanwhile, at another table, Alex and Jamal were working with one another, also discussing the writing of names.

Alex: The "a" has too long a tail.

Jamal: That's the same name?

    Larry and Shaquilla quickly walked to other tables, leaving Andre alone to organize his papers. Shaquilla walked to Darrius's table and picked up a pencil. As I arrived, they were laughing.

Shaquilla: What else?
Darrius: (Says something under his breath.)
Shaquilla: He did what?
Darrius: The monster said he was going to the zoo.
Shaquilla: (While writing letters, repeats slowly.) Going to the zoo.

At this moment, Nina interrupted the class to remind them what they should be focusing on.

Nina: What's the main story, editors?

Shaquilla then looked at Darrius and asked the same question:

Shaquilla: Darrius, what's the main story?

    In another section of the room, Danielle and Jamal were working together.

Danielle: Someone edited him already.
Jamal: (Writes the letters "p," "b," "d," "g," and "h" throughout the paper.)
Danielle: Jamal, it's too late. I edited him already.
Jamal: I can edit him some more on the back. (Jamal turns the paper over and writes "a," "t," and "d.")

Nina stopped the class here and announced,

Nina: "Spanking!" What letter does "spanking" begin with?
Danielle: "C."
Nina: Yes, but . . .
Marc: (Interrupting.) "S."

Cal and Marc got together. Marc said each word slowly, as if to ensure that Cal had enough time to accurately write each word; however, on the lined paper, Cal wrote, "MALrccMjY."

By all accounts, one could look at the editing process from one of two perspectives. First, one may suggest that since the accuracy of the letters and characters isn't correct, no editing or writing or composing is taking place. However, if we look from a broader perspective, we see that this is the only component of the writing process that is not similar to that of older folks. The conversation about authorship exists, and exists in a focused manner. Students are strict with the spelling of their own names, but look upon spelling of other items more loosely. Yes, students are engaged in a communal activity, and talk about stories. Students gleefully help the others work toward creating a piece of material that goes between two book covers. Most of the letters are accurately drawn, and all letters drawn are clearly identifiable, even if they are backward or of varying sizes. Oh, the letters may not be in the right order, but they do belong exclusively to the subset of characters in the universe that represent English writing. And, for the time being, to the satisfaction of both the editor and the storyteller, those characters do indeed define the author's story.

As Nina and I decided to look at this subsection of class, we wondered to what degree the students were talking about writing. This day, I did not even once come across a group that was not on task. In fact, if there were any behavioral problems, as may be examined in some of the dialogue above, it was that a person wasn't telling the story in a way that pleased the editor or that the editor wasn't transcribing the storyteller's message accurately, usually in terms of writing the storyteller's name.

NINA: Children continue sharing their written pieces with TAG, but in November they need much less support and the technique is expanded a bit. Listen to the TAG response to Virginia's story:

Virginia:	T: Tell what you like.
Roderick:	I like the way you read the story.
Virginia:	Why?
Roderick:	Because you improved in your reading.
Virginia:	Thank you. A: Ask questions.
Aaron:	Do you like balloons?
Virginia:	Yeah.
Aaron:	Why?
Virginia:	They're pretty. G: Give ideas, suggestions.
Nina:	What else, Virginia? What did we add to G? (No response.) Can anyone help her?
Shaquilla:	Connections.
Nina:	Yes, what does that mean?

Larry: Like we think of other things.

Nina: Okay, someone else?

Danielle: We remember things.

Nina: Yes, we think of things connected to the story and we can say, "Your story reminds me of . . . ." So someone connect to Virginia's story.

Marc: It reminds me of that book about the red balloon.

Nina: Yes, I remember that book. Did you make a connection to yourself, the world, or another story?

Marc: Another story.

Nina: Can someone make another connection?

Aubrey: I had a red balloon too.

Nina: Okay, that's a connection to you. Where did you get that balloon?

Aubrey: At the youth fair.

Here I used Virginia's simple story to illustrate how we begin to make genuine connections to any piece of writing. Here I didn't need to guide Virginia with T and A, but because of the addition of "connections" she needed a little more support with G. These connections flow smoothly by November because of all the modeling and practice the students had in September and October. Remember all the connections we made to *Charlotte's Web* and E. B. White? Look at our play: filled with connections across the curriculum. It is through these connections, too, that I teach the skills young authors need to develop.

ERIC: So how can we describe the development of the children in their authorship? If we analyze stories students have published over the course of the last three months, we can look at their actual publications and see what kind of figures come up.

As we look at these data, we see that a typical story over the last three months is about three to four sentences long. Some are even one sentence long. It seems that a typical sentence runs just shy of seven words long, but some sentences are shorter, though usually no shorter than three words long, while a handful are just over ten words long. The length of the shortest sentences may be a bit of a surprise, but it does indicate that the students are not using many two-word sentences in their stories such as "I do," contractions such as "She can't," or even one-word commands like "Go!" These are not part of the children's stories as yet.

It is also worth observing that there was a spike this month when lined paper was introduced into the curriculum. Perhaps the children see this graduation to lined paper as a step into adult writing.

Name	Number of Stories Submitted	Average Numer of Sentences	Average Sentence Length (words)	Sentence Length Range (low)	Sentence Length Range (high)
Larry	8	3.50	6.86	3	15
Shaquilla	6	4.00	4.79	3	11
Christian	7	3.43	8.46	3	24
Jamal	7	3.00	5.62	2	10
Cal	6	4.00	7.67	2	10
Latisha	5	4.67	5.79	3	9
D'Andre	6	3.33	8.30	4	15
Andre	9	3.67	6.09	3	15
Denise	12	4.17	5.50	3	17
Marc	8	3.88	6.06	3	10
Virginia	7	2.43	4.65	3	11
Tommesha	5	3.60	8.28	3	18
Jarrell	5	3.00	7.87	3	14
Darrius	7	4.70	7.51	4	17
Darrin	6	3.00	6.36	3	10
Aaron	2	2.50	7.67	3	11
Roderick	8	4.33	7.35	3	12
Danielle	2	4.00	7.54	4	13
Alexander	4	3.00	7.00	3	11
Typical	**6.24**	**3.59**	**6.81**	**3.41**	**12.97**

Publication

NINA: With all this talking during writing and with the development and deepening of skills, publication has slowed down a bit by November. That's okay, though, because my children have internalized the identity of an author and they needn't publish so frequently anymore. They are more content to work on their pieces longer and do not rush off to publish as in the first months of authorship. When children are ready to publish they now are responsible for making their own book covers at the publishing table. This table has everything the children need to construct the covers:

- pieces of construction paper or contact paper;
- cut pieces of cardboard;

- glue or glue sticks; and
- paper for final copy.

Now the children have control of the entire writing process, and this control enables them to internalize it even more deeply and helps them to truly see themselves as authors.

Sign-up books

What also helps keep the whole process organized and keeps children in control are the sign-up books. Children need to sign up for adult help for revision, editing, and proofreading. They also need to sign up when they want to share in front of the community for TAG. Let's look at how the TAG book is set up:

Monday, November 8, 1999

_____   _____   _____

Tuesday, November 9, 1999

_____   _____   _____

Wednesday, November 10, 1999

_____   _____   _____

Thursday, November 11, 1999

_____   _____   _____

Friday, November 12, 1999

_____   _____   _____

I set up the book with the day and date and lines for three children to sign their names for each day. This gives me a say on how many children share a day. Also it enables children to share in front of the class once a week. The children need to follow two rules when using this book: they cannot erase anybody's name, and they can only sign up once a week. In the beginning some children are so eager to share that they erase a name to make room for their own! It might be a good idea to use pen for this book. If over time I see the same children sign up to share over and over again and others not sharing at all, I will encourage the children not sharing to do so:

Nina: KeAndre, I notice you haven't shared in front of the class for a
           while. When do you want to share?

KeAndre:	I don't know.
Nina:	If you're a little afraid you can read with someone. Would you like that?
KeAndre:	Okay.
Nina:	Who would you like to share with?
KeAndre:	Shaquilla.
Nina:	Okay, go ask Shaquilla now to practice your story with you and you both can sign up for tomorrow.

So KeAndre will share but will feel safer with Shaquilla next to his side. This is fine because we are here to help each other and to give each author the support needed to succeed.

The other sign-up book combines revision, editing, and proofreading in list form. It needn't be organized by date, just by name. Whenever children are ready for an adult to work with them they sign their name on the next available line. I go to the book and go to each child in order of the list. When I finish I cross off the child's name and go to the next. This helps me stay organized and also helps me to visually see who is working consistently through pieces and who might need more encouragement to complete pieces.

Contextualized Lessons

The way I teach skills is through the children's own writing and reading. You already have a sense of this as you read through most of the discussions I have shared. Do you notice that whenever I touch on a skill—for example, problem, solution, or exclamation point—it is connected to someone's work? I only teach skills within the context of a piece of work. It might be within a child's work, a book we're reading aloud, or a poem we're learning, but it is never in isolation. That doesn't mean I don't know what I want to teach; it means that I look for what I want to teach within the work we are focusing on. So, for example, if I want to work on dialogue I will look for it in a child's piece using this piece as the vehicle of instruction for the whole community. If I don't see it in a child's work and think some of my children are ready to use something new in their work I will look for it in something we are reading aloud. Let me give you an example, using *James and the Giant Peach*, by Roald Dahl (2000).

Nina:	Did you hear that word Roald Dahl just used again?
Andre:	Yeah, "suddenly."
Nina:	He really uses that word a lot.
Larry:	I think about a hundred times.

Nina:	Oh, did you count?
Larry:	I tried.
Nina:	I did too, because I noticed he used it so much. Raise your hand if you've ever used "suddenly" in your writing. (No hands go up.) Oh, so it's new to everyone. When do authors use this word? Let's listen to how Dahl uses it again. (Reads the sentence with "suddenly.") So when do you think authors decide to use "suddenly"?
Shaquilla:	When something scary is going to happen.
Nina:	Okay, anyone else?
Roderick:	When it's exciting.
Nina:	Yes, maybe to make it sound exciting or scary or to make us want to read what will happen next! Raise your hand if you will use the word "suddenly" in your writing. (All hands go up.) Okay, I can't wait to read how you use it.

So you see, I connect to Dahl's writing in the same way I talk about the writings of my young authors, so that we learn from each other and from the other authors we read. This is such an incredible way to learn for me because the characters and authors of the books we read aloud together become real, live members of our community. It's not uncommon for us to talk about one of these characters just as if they were present.

Nina:	So what do you think Aunt Sponge would say about you sharing?
Denise:	She wouldn't like it.
Nina:	Why not?
Denise:	Because she's greedy.
Nina:	Ha! Ha! That's true. She's very greedy and selfish. So what would she say to you if she saw you sharing with Virginia?
Denise:	"You silly beast."
Nina:	Ha! Ha! I love how you used the word "beast" because that is exactly the word Aunt Sponge would use. Do you think you might have a greedy character in one of your stories?
Denise:	Maybe.

So Aunt Sponge is spoken about and will be spoken about throughout the year whenever we make connections to the concepts of selfishness or greediness. Isn't that cool? I couldn't let the opportunity go without connecting to Denise's future writing, either! We'll talk more about lessons in December, when I'll show you how I contextualize one skill across the entire curriculum.

Critical Thinking and Questions

ERIC: Why do you think Nina regularly asks her students "why"? You notice that two elements of classroom interaction between Nina and the students are based on asking questions. Have you been following the kinds of questions Nina has been asking? In November, here is a list of quotes she made from various classes, but all questions:

- What change did you see?
- What looks a little bit different?
- How do you feel, Aaron?
- What Skittle colors do you think are going to be in there?
- What do you do with a book you hate?
- Whose feet are bigger?
- Are you proud of yourself? (Follow-up: You should be!)
- What could I do to try and remember what those green things are?
- What can I do?
- Would you touch the giant peach? Why?
- You know what you're doing, right?
- Who do you want to help you follow rules?
- Do horses love people? Why?
- So what's the main story about?
- Why do we try to do our best?
- Whose name begins with "V" in the classroom?
- You're writing about a cake?

Of these questions, how many can you answer using either "yes" or "no"? How many of them have predictably only one single answer? How many of them have more than one possible answer? You'll notice that Nina tries to ask questions that elicit possibilities as often as possible, though she doesn't necessarily depend on it constantly. Why might we want to direct our language in such a way?

When we think about advancing our learning, we find that the language used to foster learning and elicit critical thinking is actually rather difficult. For example, if I ask you a question, using the word *what*—for example, "What is the capital of Zimbabwe?"—how many answers are there most likely to be? Often in the world, regardless of whether the calculation is easy or simple, there is only one answer.

- What are 2 and 5?
- What is the volume of that glass?

Regardless of whether you can count on your fingers or implement calculus, for either of these questions there is but one answer to be expected. Such questions are usually elicited using words like *what*, *where*, *when*, and *who*. But if I ask you, "Why do you think the artist made the wineglass into that shape or that size?" and you're asked to speculate, how many answers might there be? The key ingredients to such a question are the words *why*, *how*, and *if*.

James Cummins (1981) found that when students are engaging in the *why*, they're more likely to advance. A combination of linguistics and addition can bring such a conclusion into light. If the teacher asks questions that elicit a single answer, what then would be the total number of words used by students in order to answer the question? Obviously, there would be many times when an accurate and well-judged response could be but one word long. However, the problem then lies in the amount of language that is being practiced. If the teacher can come up with a big long question, but the answer is only one word long, then how much is the student practicing language and thinking?

The practicality of producing questions that elicit an abundance of possible answers was demonstrated by Vera Woloshyn, Allan Paivio, and Michael Pressley (1994) in the "why-question" study. They asked young learners to always pose the question "why" when referring to material they were about to study. They found that students who regularly question reasons for phenomena generally understood any new material to a deeper degree. Often in TV shows, usually silly comedies, we see children portrayed as obnoxious if they constantly ask "why, why, why." However, it appears that science would support their doing so, since it would generate a plethora of probabilities and possibilities for them to examine on a regular basis.

As I was growing up, I recall vividly my friend Paul always asking me "why, why, why," up until the point I thought I was going to shout. When I got older, I finally realized that his mother constantly asked him to look at issues from various viewpoints. Jokingly one afternoon, I was conversing with Paul's mom about the idea of looking at things from different perspectives. I commented to her, "Yep, there are two sides to every story." She smiled, looked at me, and said, "Actually, I think there are nine, and you're fortunate if you find two."

So Nina is looking to promote this kind of critical inquiry, even in her young authors. However, in one of our conversations about the children, Nina and I observed during November that we were making most of the questions and children were merely answering them. Yes, they were answering hard questions, and we were proud of them, but they weren't practicing the making of these questions at all. As a result, we decided to invite guests into the class and let students interview them.

One day, we asked the children to interview me. Here is the list of questions the students generated for me:

- What's your favorite poem?
- Where do you work?
- What's your last name?
- What's your favorite car?
- What's your favorite color?
- Do you read?
- What are your sisters' and brothers' names?
- Where do you live?
- What's your mama's name?
- What shoes do you like?
- What store do you go to?
- What's your favorite food?
- What do you eat to get healthy?
- What's your favorite TV show?
- What's your dad's name?
- What's your favorite number?
- What's your favorite pet?

We were pleasantly surprised by the number of questions students could come up with so quickly. Sure, very few of them offered me chances to elaborate very much, though I did so when I could. As you can guess, the most evocative question is the one regarding food that helps me get healthy. Great question! The hardest one to answer, though, was my favorite TV show. I finally answered the news and MTV videos, but Nina appropriately mentioned that sometimes MTV OK programming isn't so suitable for children. I felt a little bad about my answer, but felt I would be more prepared next time and that I could come up with an answer that would be more helpful. Finally, though, I realized that the actual problem with the question was that it really did have only one answer. I do love the news and music videos, but since the answer's being unhelpful or potentially harmful made me realize that the merit of the more critical questions may lie in the fact that when we have more nebulous answers we're not boxed into the limitations that a *what*, *where*, *who*, or *when* question might lead us to.

So, I'll ask you this: Why do you think Nina and I intersperse our writing with questions to you?

During the children's interview of me, they asked me, "What shoes do you like?" To answer the question, I lifted up my own shoes and said that I liked them. However, Nina interrupted and asked, "Does Eric have big feet?" Some of the children raised their hands and said, "Yes!" Then Nina asked, "Are they bigger than my feet?" Some children again said yes, but Nina asked, "How do you know? Do you know Eric's shoe size? Do you know my shoe size?" Nina and the children exchanged a few comments on how they could judge someone's shoe size. Finally, someone mentioned that a number could be found on the bottom of a shoe.

Nina: Eric, do you have a number on the bottom of your shoe?
Eric: I don't know. Let's look.

I took off my shoes and looked at the bottom. There was indeed a number.

Eric: Well, there is a number. It's a . . .
Nina: (Interrupting.) What number will Eric have on his shoe?

The children started guessing some numbers.

Eric: But Nina, what size is your shoe?
Nina: I don't know. Should we look?
All: Yes!
Nina: What number do you think will be on my shoe?
Denise: Six.
Nina: You think I wear a size six?
Denise: Yes.
Nina: Why do you think I wear a size six?
Denise: Because Eric will have a bigger number?
Nina: Why will Eric have a bigger number?
Denise: Because his feet are bigger!

All the children laughed. We did too, but you can see how at the very moment during the interview, it became a perfect opportunity to have a quick lesson on comparatives. The interview became a brief but appropriate math lesson. You saw how the visit to the farm during the play also became an impromptu math lesson as the children counted the ducks.

Interdependence with Families and Friends

NINA: November is a month filled with all kinds of writing. While children continue to work on writing process every day, they are also involved with writing letters to pen pals and visitors. Here's Darrin's letter to his fourth-grade pen pal:

> Hi,
> I am six years old. For Thanksgiving I'm going to eat turkey. Then
> I'm going to my friend's house. What is your favorite food? What is
> your favorite pet? Please write again.
> Love, Darrin

Here's D'Andre's letter to Tiara:

> Dear Tiara,
> Yes, I like kindergarten. It is not hard. I get turkey on Thanksgiving.
> Do you like Math? I like Math. What do you like to eat? What's your
> favorite drink? I want you to write back soon.
> Love, D'Andre

My children also wrote letters of thanks to Eric for an Everglades calendar and for bringing his friend Alice to visit. Here's Darryl's letter:

> I thank you for the pictures of the pelican, alligator and panther.
> Thank you Eric for bringing Alice.
> Love, Darryl

My students are eager to write and receive letters. Letter writing adds variety to our work, is purposeful, fun, and polite. Our pen pals this year are fourth-grade children in another Miami public school. As the students write these letters we talk about categorizing, asking questions, and answering questions. For example, we guide them to ask personal questions (about family), school questions (about favorite subjects, favorite books, and so on), and questions in other such categories. These lessons will be reinforced later on in the year when children begin to interview classmates, school personnel, and community members.

After children write their letters and an adult helps edit, they are sent out. You can see even from these few examples that children are working on telling about themselves, asking questions, and thanking their friends. Of course, they end with a form of the classic "Write back soon!" And it is like a celebration when we receive responses from our pen pals. The writing and reading of these letters are integrated into our literacy block: they are written during writing time and read during silent reading and reading discussion groups.

And guess what? At the end of the year we will get to meet our pen pals! You will too!

We started this chapter with a letter to the families, so let's end it with some of the writing families wrote in Brownie's diary this month:

11-1-99

Brownie and I went to Burger King after school today and we came back to school to pick up my sister Tamara. Brownie and I came home and we went to see my friends. Last night me and Brownie went to my friend's house when my mother went to church. Brownie and I had fun all day and night together. I hope Brownie and I can spend some more time together on another day!

Love, Aubrey

God bless you, Brownie and many more visits to come in other children's homes.

11-2-99

Brownie and I had fun with my dad and my sister. Mom picked us up after work. We went home and watched Sesame Street on TV then ate dinner. After my bath I did homework with my mom while Brownie watched. Mom read us A Day with Grandpa before bedtime.

Jarrell

11-3-99

When me and Brownie got home from school me and Brownie watched a movie with my big cousin. After the movie me and Brownie played outside. Later me and Brownie and my two brothers ate burgers, chips, and juice. Then my mother gave us a bath and we all went to sleep for school the next day.

Tommesha

Reading these letters bring tears to my eyes because they touch me so deeply. My children and their families take such great care with writing in Brownie's diary. Even though most work full time, have other young children to care for, and speak English as a second language, they take this time for their child and Brownie. Can't you just see them sitting next to their child asking them what they want to say about Brownie? What a powerful illustration of home-school connections and what a blessing!

December
Dear Daniela . . . You missed our play! It was fantastic!

ERIC: It's rehearsal time. Students are standing in a row on stage. Nina stands at the midpoint of the cafeteria, where the audience would sit. Students begin reciting their play, "Living Things around the World." The first two voices are soft. Nina says, "I can't hear you." I find the comment interesting, as I realize that, as five-year-olds, the students may regard this statement only as a statement of fact, not implicitly understanding this to be a hint that they should raise their voices. In fact, three more students state their lines with volume equal to those preceding them. Nina shouts, "I can't hear you!" Finally, the next student says his line at a volume that resonates throughout the room. Nina interrupts once again: "Give him a hand for being so loud!" All the students clap, but most important, all students recite their lines at an audible volume level equal or better from here on out. Inferred lesson learned! The play ends, and Nina asks the children to give themselves a hand. Then she asks for a silent pause for them to become attentive to their next task, "Get yourself focused, please!" They do the play again, from memory; this time at a strong, confident volume level.

Upon completion of "Living Things around the World," Nina asks the children to recite three poems: "Dreams," "Giggles," and "Rudolph Is Tired of the City." All three poems are kinesthetic; they have specific gestures the students have choreographed. All the poems are expressive; students give most important words stress, change in tone, and change in length. All the poems are rhythmic. At times, it seems that one can take the musical tones that are the children's voices and record them as written notes on a musical staff.

NINA: In December excitement is high because we will finally perform our drama production and recite and sing the poems and songs we have rehearsed for the last few months. Final touches are made as we create a program for our families and our school audiences. We also practice another form of writing when we send out personally made invitations.

ERIC: On the day of the performance, I arrive early. Nina is working with students through their regular morning routine. Following school announcements, Nina conducts music time with a soft song and the lights off. During the song, Nina guides the students: "Keep yourselves focused. We need to stay under control."

Nina puts the lights on to find that Virginia has taken another student's pen. Denise has walked to Virginia's desk to pick up the pen and place it on Aubrey's desk. Nina, seeing all of this, walks to Virginia, kneels down to look at her at an equal head level and asks, "Are you in control of yourself?" Virginia nods. Nina smiles and says, "Good, because we really need you today."

Suddenly, there is a knock at the door, and Gloria Barnes, the principal, walks in. The children do "Dreams," by Langston Hughes, for her. They're very proud of themselves. The children continue listening to Nina's instructions. Meanwhile, Gloria comes up to me and says, "Nina really understands that for many of these children, school needs to be the best six hours of each day."

While Miss Barnes and I speak, we can hear Nina engaged in the following conversations.

Andre, who had been fighting other students for books, didn't fight today.

Nina: "Andre, give me a hug. You didn't fight over that book!" (Looking at Virginia.) Virginia, what nice new braids you have! Who helped you? Your father? Your sister? Your babysitter?
Virginia: You!
Nina: I did not! (Smiling.)

At approximately 9:00, there is a knock at the door. Marc's and Andre's mothers are there, asking where the play is going to be presented. Nina asks me to accompany the mothers to the library, get them some coffee, and wait for someone to come and get us in about a half hour to take us to the performance.

  I walk the two women to the library and get them some coffee. I sit down and ask how they feel their children are doing. Both women are clearly proud of their children. They mention how their boys enjoy school so much. Marc's mother is Haitian but speaks good English, noting how important this play is to Marc and to her. She points out that she wore her special yellow Sunday dress for the occasion and that she dressed Marc in his Sunday best, including a black bow tie. I am happy to see Andre's mother there. She expresses her thanks to Nina for calling her to tell her how Andre was doing. She was proud of Andre, saying, "Oh, Andre does like to write. I'm going to buy that boy a computer. He needs a computer."

At 9:30, a child walks into the library and motions for us to follow her. We walk together in silence to the cafeteria. As we enter the cafeteria, a child hands us a program. The room is filled to capacity, maybe even as many as a hundred people are there to see the kindergartners perform. Some family members are standing against the wall. Miss Barnes is there too. There is a low din of conversation, but then all hush as Nina walks to the stage to welcome the parents and introduce the children.

NINA: Here's how our program looks:

Winter Poetry/Drama Recital
Kindergarten Class
of
Dr. Zaragoza and Ms. Person
Little River Elementary School
December 9, 1999

Hello Song
Invitation by Shel Silverstein

Drama Production: Living Things

Dreams by Langston Hughes
Hope by Langston Hughes
The Giggles by Martin Gardner
My Little Sister by William Wise
Two Friends by Nikki Giovanni
My People by Langston Hughes
Merry-Go-Round by Langston Hughes
Winter Snow by Langston Hughes
Mother to Son by Langston Hughes
What a Wonderful World
Goodbye Song

Many times for our first performance we forego using the large auditorium and perform the play in our classroom. This smaller venue enables the softer-voiced children to be successful. Also since this first performance is focused on the language arts aspect of the production and there is much less energy put into scenery and costumes, the intimate setting serves us well. We usually set the room up with the audience sitting in a circle or semicircle, with the actors performing in the middle. This is quite powerful because the audience is so close and actually seems part of the piece. This year, though, we performed the piece on stage and it went well. But you don't just need to hear it from me. Here is what Larry wrote to his pen pal about the play:

December 9, 1999

Dear Joshua,
When I had my play in the cafeteria on December 9, 1999. You should have seen my play. It went very well. All of the kids did it loud. You should [have] come and see my play. You should [have] see my father taking pictures of the whole class. Write back soon. Merry Christmas to your whole family.
Love, Larry

And here's Darrius:

Dear Andrew,
Some of our poems are "My Little Sister" by William Wise, "The Giggles" by Martin Gardner and "Mother to Son" by Langston Hughes. We did the play and then we got off stage nicely. We had fun at the party after the play. We did all the poems in the party. Write back soon. Merry Christmas.
Love, Darrius.

And finally this is Roderick's letter:

Dear Daniela,
Yes, I'm getting good grades. How are you? You missed our play. It was fantastic. I'm sorry you didn't come. Thank you for the pink paper. Merry Christmas. Write back soon.
Love, Roderick

As Darrius noted in his letter, after the performance the children and I host a cast party with their families as our guests. It is such a perfect time because you can almost touch the sense of pride in the room. The children are pleased with their performance and during the party even offer to recite some of the poetry again. The families are beaming at their children's success and can hardly contain their pleasure, and I feel exactly the same! And can you guess what the children begin to talk about right away? Yes! They start planning their next performance:

Roderick: So what should our next play be?
Nina: Well, what do you think?
Roderick: Maybe about superheroes?
Nina: That's an idea. I guess we can start thinking about it. Let's talk about it after the party.

And that's exactly what we do. I actually would like to take a rest, but the children insist! Why do you think the children are so excited about working on a new piece immediately? I think that the play, because of the total absence of competition, and the inclusion of poetry and music, is an enjoyable, rewarding experience. Have you ever been in a play? I have and I will never forget the feeling—or my lines!

By December the children have internalized the idea that learning is a process and that we are never really finished with anything. Just as in writing, when we finish with one story we begin another one, and then another one, and another one; so it is in play writing. And now that we know so many poems it is time to learn some new ones, which we will most probably include in our next drama production. We continue to learn, because learning is a process and my children don't want to take a break from such a purposeful, productive use of their time.

And so we get right back to work after the party. Did you notice that the children write to their pen pals on the day of the play? Doesn't it seem like the natural thing to do? After they share their work with the present community they share it with a community they stay in touch with through writing. I see it as just perfect for my students, and for me. We are writers and we want to express ourselves and share our experiences through writing.

Before going on to contextualized lessons, let me share another beginning-of-the-year play that a first-grade special education class wrote with me:

City or Country?

Deb: I like the stores in the city.
Lia: What kind of stores do you like?
Deb: I like holiday stores. What kind of stores do you like?
Lia: I like costume stores.
Andy: In the city you can go to lots of parks.

Tommy:	What do you do at the park?
Albert:	I play on the swing.
Ken:	I like the country. I like the cows because they make milk.
Matt:	What kind of milk do you like?
Ken:	Chocolate milk.
Alex:	I like the city because there are tall buildings.
Cathy:	I like the tall buildings too and I like all the cars.
Roy:	My favorite car is a Corvette.
Candy:	I like the city because there are lots of community helpers like police officers and firefighters.
Donny:	I like the country because I like cows and chickens.
Albert:	Cows make milk and they say, "Moo."
Donny:	Chickens say, "Buhk, buhk, buhk."
All:	We love the city and country! Let's sing some country and city songs. (All sing "Did You Feed My Cow?" by Ella Jenkins, and recite "Rudolph Is Tired of the City," by Gwendolyn Brooks.)

And here is our end-of-the-year play. Enjoy!

Title: *Save the Rainforest*

Characters

Anaconda	Albert
Sun Bear	Giselle
Toucan	Lia
Leaf Frog	Tommy
Spider Monkey	Donny
Chameleon	Andy
Lizard	Gilbert
Jaguar	Matt
Butterfly	Cathy
Tiger	Candy
Vampire Bat	Alex
Boa Constrictor	Roy
Crocodile	Alan
Parrot	Sam

Setting: Rainforest

Problems
People cut down trees and there is not enough places to live or food for animals to eat in the rainforest. Also, there is less medicine and oxygen to breathe and the water is dirty from people's pollution.

Solutions
People need to stop cutting down so many trees and they need to keep our air and water clean.

Anaconda:	I want to walk in our forest. Let's go!
Sun Bear:	Okay, Anaconda, let's go play Hide and Seek.
Toucan:	Hi Sun Bear! I want to play with you too, but the people cut down the trees and I can't fly like a toucan should.
Parrot:	I know! And now there are not enough trees to make our nests! I'm sad and don't feel like talking even though I'm a parrot.
Leaf Frog:	Oh, I'm sad too, because I don't have so many leaves and I'm a leaf frog.
Spider Monkey:	And I'm a monkey and I like to climb trees. (Monkey starts to cry.)
Chameleon:	Don't cry, Spider Monkey. There are still some trees left. I know because I'm a chameleon and I change to the color of whatever tree I'm on.
Lizard:	I'm a lizard and I'm chameleon's friend and we want to stay alive. I hope people take care of our rainforest.
Jaguar:	Jaguars like to climb trees too, and we need trees. Oh look, here comes a beautiful morpho butterfly.
Butterfly:	I want some food and I need to get my food from the trees and flowers. People need to get medicine from trees and plants too.
Tiger:	How sad people cut down all the trees. Don't they know how it hurts all of us?
Vampire Bat:	Yes, Tiger, I know. I hope the people stop destroying the rainforest so I have a place to live. Look, here comes a crocodile.
Crocodile:	People are also dirtying my water and I need clean water to live in. Oh, there's Boa Constrictor.
Boa Constrictor:	Hi! The forest is my home too. The forest is sad without the trees and clean air and water. Please help save the rainforest.

All: We hope people learn to take care of the rainforest. We need
                   our trees and we all need clean air and water and enough
                   medicine. Please help save the rainforest.

ERIC: If we compare the kindergartners' "Living Things around the World"
with the special education second graders' "City or Country?" we see the following things:

	Lines	Words	Number of Students	Average Line Length (words)	Lines with 10+ Words	Longest Line
"Living Things around the World"	72	464	23	6.4	15 of 72 or 21%	16 words
"City or Country?"	47	462	14	9.8	15 of 47 or 32%	24 words

Hence, there are probably fewer lines since there are fewer students to ac-
commodate. However, the second graders (not surprisingly) have longer lines
to learn, at just over three words per line longer. Additionally, for second graders a third of the lines are more than ten words long, rather than the one fifth
found with the kindergartners. As a result, we can see how well kindergartners
do, but note how they relate in terms of reasonable expectations when compared to the second graders.

Contextualized Lessons

NINA: There are so many lessons going on all the time in my room that by
December it becomes very difficult to separate by categories. So while we are
officially doing drama when we work on our play, we are also working in various other areas. Actually, you can see the expansion and deepening of skills as
you examine the scripts written over time. Notice that in this last script we
are working on the elements of a story: title, characters, setting, problem, and
solution. The children focus on this all year, and when it is time for our final
production, the script emerges easily as we use these elements to guide the
discussion and its writing.

ERIC: Can you also see how our question formation guides the process? By
looking at title, characters, setting, problem, and solution, we ask the broad
range of questions. For title, characters, and setting, we can ask *what*, *who*,
where, and *when* (the latter for setting) questions. Then for problems and so-

lutions, we can ask how and why. Note that the solution ultimately becomes a selection from an abundance of possibilities. Nina asks students, even this young, to defend their selections and solutions.

Mathematics

Math manifests itself in many ways in Nina's class. Often it is a natural outgrowth of the daily announcements. At Little River, the announcements often include a word problem. Regardless of the age of the student the problem is geared toward, Nina asks children to do their best to work with it. Sometimes Nina will ask a quick math problem during roll call. Today, she does a quick math lesson while collecting homework:

> Quick: What's 10 take away 1?
> 3 plus 3?
> 3 take away 3?
> 10 take away 10?
> A billion take away a billion?

However, some of the deepest moments for math come during language arts and writing process.

NINA: Believe it or not, we do talk about dialogue during math. My children are writing addition and subtraction number stories by December and we actually talk about writing concepts like problem and solution, dialogue, and detail. Here are a few examples:

> Once there were four ladies. They were dancing. One fell. There were three left dancing. $4 - 1 = 3$ Alexander

> One day there were two kids playing hide and seek. Then they saw three bunny rabbits. They said, "Hello bunny rabbits. Do you want to come and play with us?" They said, "Yes." Now there were five. $2 + 3 = 5$ Roderick

> There were five cats and one went away because his paw was broken and he had to go to the hospital. There were only four cats left. $5 - 1 = 4$ Darrin

> One day there were three little children and two other little children saw them playing. They came over and said, "Can we play?" They

said, "Yes, you can." So there were five children playing together. 3 + 2 = 5 Shaquilla

One day there was a big brother. He had the music blasting. The police came to say cut it down. The brother did not cut it down. They put him in a crazy house. So there is no big brother. 1 − 1 = 0 Cal

Interesting word problems, don't you think? My students love writing these, and I love editing them because they are like compact short stories. Don't you want to know more about the big brother Cal writes about? And I wonder if that poor lady who fell while she was dancing is okay. It definitely makes math much more interesting for me. I think for the children, too. Word problems become more alive as children take control of the concepts through creation.

Reading Aloud

NINA: By December the children's identity as authors is strong, so they approach almost everything they do as writers. This is very evident as we talk about the piece we are reading aloud together. By now the children have internalized the language of an author, so I can easily use this vocabulary to guide and deepen the literacy concepts we speak about. Do you remember when we talked about the word *suddenly* last month because Dahl uses it so much? Well, since then we have been talking about transition words in our writing like *finally, then, suddenly,* and *all of a sudden.* Because they experience this concept concretely through *James and the Giant Peach,* the students more readily use it in their own writing. Also, when children see something in another piece of literature that they have already used, the concept is validated and confirmed:

Nina: (Reading from the book.) ". . . the really marvelous thing is to have no legs at all and to be able to walk just the same." Oh who do you think I'm thinking about now? (No response.) Who used the word "marvelous" in their writing? Remember?

Cindy: Me! In my diary.

Nina: Yes, I'm thinking about your diary entry the other day. Would you read it to us again?

Cindy: Okay. (Finds her diary and reads.) "Today I look marvelous because I have a new dress."

Nina: So Roald Dahl used the same word as you did. How does that make you feel?

Cindy:	Good.
Nina:	What other words do authors use?
Darrius:	"Suddenly."
Nina:	Yes, I think that's one of Roald Dahl's favorite words!
Denise:	Mine too!
Nina:	I know. What other words?
Andre	"Said."
Nina:	When do authors use that word, Andre?
Andre:	When they have talking in their story.
Nina:	Yes, when they use dialogue. What other words can we use to show that there is dialogue?
Danielle:	"Screamed."
Marc:	"Yelled."
Roderick:	"Cried."
Nina:	All those words could tell us that someone is talking. Let's continue reading and see what words Roald Dahl uses. "'You call that walking!' cried the Centipede." Oh, he just used the word that you said, Roderick, "cried." Let's read on: "'You are a slimy beast,' answered the Centipede. 'I am not a slimy beast,' the Earthworm said." Oh, so here the author used "answered" and "said." Most of us use "said" a lot, I think. What other words are you going to use to show that someone is talking in your story?
Shaquilla:	I'm going to use "screamed."
Nina:	Why do you think you'll use "screamed"?
Shaquilla:	'Cause there's going to be a monster in my story and the boy will scream "Aaaah!"
Nina:	Wow, you already have a plan for your story. Do you know what's going to happen at the end?
Shaquilla:	Not yet.
Nina:	That's okay. A lot of authors don't think of an ending until they start writing.

So you see how I connect to a book and continue connecting to the children's writing and back again to the shared piece of reading and then back to their own writing again? Isn't it cool?

ERIC: Nina also embeds reviews of such important concepts the day following these discussions. The day after Nina had this discussion, she built the concepts into her roll call. (She had forgotten to take roll earlier, and Danielle reminded her that she needed to take attendance.) Nina gathered the class together as a group:

Nina: Oh, thank you, Danielle! You're right! Everyone, when I call your name, please tell us where you had the peach go next, and get on line for lunch.

Silent Reading and Reading Discussion Groups

NINA: Now watch how I do this during silent reading and reading discussion groups. After about fifteen to twenty minutes of silent reading:

Nina: Excuse me, everyone. As we finish up with silent reading I'd like you to look for some of the words your author uses to show that there is or will be dialogue. Let's take about three minutes to do that. (After about three minutes or so.) Okay, let's see what some of you found. Aubrey?

Aubrey: "Called."

Nina: Read the dialogue that shows us what the character said.

Aubrey: "The dragon called, 'Where are you, cat?'"

Nina: Oh! Yes, I remember that book. Thank you, Aubrey. Let's have one more person share before we go into reading discussion groups. Aaron, what's a word that your author used to show dialogue?

Aaron: "Said."

Nina: Read the part that shows us who was talking and what they were saying.

Aaron: "Mom said, 'What a mess.'"

Nina: Okay. Who was she talking to?

Aaron: Andrew.

Nina: How was he making a mess?

Aaron: He had dirt all over him and brought it in the house.

Nina: What would your mom say if you did that?

Aaron: "Stop!"

Nina: Would she say it or would she scream it?

Aaron: "Scream."

Nina: So if you wrote a story about it would you say, "Mom screamed" or "Mom said"?

Aaron: "Mom said."

Nina: I think I would too. Thanks for sharing some of your book with us. Now when you get into reading discussion groups what do you think I want you to talk about?

KeAndre: Dialogue.

Nina: Why do you think that?

D'Andre: Because we talked about it now.

Nina: Okay, does anybody else have an idea about what we will talk about in groups?

Shaquilla: We'll ask questions.

Nina: What kind of questions?

Shaquilla: Like what's your favorite part, your favorite character, like that.

Nina: Yes, all the questions we usually ask. Let's read them together. (Children read chorally the questions written on a chart; for example: 1. Do you like your book? Why or why not? 2. Who is your favorite character? Why? 3. What's your favorite part of the book and why? 4. Why did you choose this book? 5. Why do you think the author wrote this book? See October for complete list.) Now when you go into your discussion groups you need to talk about the dialogue your authors use and what words they use to tell you that it is dialogue. When you're finished with that you can ask your friends questions about the books they are reading. Let's get into groups.

Here I continue contextualizing the concept we started talking about with *James and the Giant Peach* and continue the discussion through silent reading. Do you notice, though, that I don't start directing what the children should look for during silent reading until the very end? Why do you think I wait until then? What would happen if I told them what they needed to look for at the beginning of the silent reading session? My direction would definitely change how the children read, don't you think? If I asked about question marks at the beginning they would most probably look only for question marks. If I asked about adjectives they would most likely skip around the book looking for adjectives. For my students the purpose of silent reading is to read for enjoyment; I don't want to interfere with this enjoyment, so I wait until the very end of the session to focus in on a skill.

ERIC: Do you remember last month when we talked about *why* questions? Do you remember that the children, though, didn't ask these types of questions? Well, you see here how Nina has tried to take care of this. She gives specific examples of critical thinking questions students can offer one another. I could hear how she does this with her voice. Even though she comes to the end of a question, she pauses for only a second—not really a length of time suitable for someone to interrupt—and she adds a *why* or *why not* question. In other words, *why* should be viewed as a natural extension to most questions. As you try to answer these questions, note how the dynamics change when you add a *why*.

Now, we then wondered if children were using such language with one another. Our assumption was that they would need practice and a bit of direction in order to start asking why questions. Here's what Nina found.

NINA: When the children are in discussion I monitor them by entering into the groups to listen to and facilitate some of the conversation:

Roderick:	Virginia what book are you reading?
Virginia:	Cat.
Roderick:	*The Cat in the Hat*?
Virginia:	Yeah.
Nina:	So you're looking at Virginia's book. Good.
Roderick:	Yeah, I see the word "said."
Nina:	Show it to Virginia, Roderick.
Roderick:	Look at the word "said," Virginia.
Nina:	Point to the word "said," Virginia. (Virginia points.) So Dr. Seuss uses the word "said." Say "said," Virginia.
Virginia:	Said.
Nina:	Okay, Roderick. Show Virginia some of the dialogue and words your author uses.

(Another group.)

Danielle:	Here's my book *Where the Wild Things Are*. (Begins reading.) And the monsters cried, "Do not go. We love you so."
Larry:	Oh yeah, I read that book. Max was the king.
Andre:	What's your dialogue, Larry?
Larry:	"You can't catch me I'm the gingerbread man."
Danielle:	So does the author say "said" or something else?
Larry:	"Said."
Nina:	I hear some great conversation here. Whose turn is it now?
Andre:	Mine. My author uses "asked." "'Are you my mother?' asked the little bird."
Nina:	Do you see that authors use different words to show that there will be dialogue? You usually use "said," right, Andre?
Andre:	Mmmm.
Nina:	So what other words do you think you will use in your next stories?
Andre:	Maybe "cried" or "asked."
Nina:	Okay! Keep talking and when you're finished with dialogue go on to our other questions.

I facilitate the groups according to their needs. Because Roderick needs help with facilitating Virginia's language, I give much more guidance in this group than in the one with Andre, Larry, and Danielle. I make sure I visit each group at least once, and most of the time I visit them twice. In this way they receive the support they need throughout the session. I don't see myself as the children's sole source of support, though. Do you notice that I teach my students to support each other? Do you see how Roderick got a quick lesson on how to support Virginia? We'll talk more about this when we discuss interdependence and expectations.

Some teachers ask me how I know that children are talking about what they are directed to talk about. I also get this question in relation to silent reading: "How do you know the children are reading, Nina?" Actually, it's really not that difficult. You ask them. What are you talking about now? Are you talking about dialogue? If they're not, the question will immediately help them to refocus. I know that children read during silent reading because they answer questions and are fully involved in full-class and small-group discussions about their books. Remember, too, my students can choose the books they want to read. They learn to choose books that are interesting because they know they will have to read and talk about them! Also, the questions we ask encourage personal and interesting discussions. Why wouldn't my children want to share their thoughts? My class is safe and noncompetitive, so there is no fear about sharing and answering questions. So how do I know that children read and discuss their books? I know because I ask and I am an engaged member of the community.

ERIC: Our notes indicate that actual discussion occurs. We see such evidence in two different areas: during the actual reading discussion time, and during free learning time.

During actual reading discussion time, children look at books together. On this December afternoon, Damine and Latisha are laughing as they point to parts of their book. Nina doesn't stop children from expressing their enjoyment of books. It's also common to find pairs of children who enjoy reading to one another, especially from a book they agree is one of their favorites. On this day, it's Christian and Jamal each taking a page of a book they know very well. Nina does have to review the rules, but it doesn't take long for her to start the reading discussion time by saying, "I'm not going to tell anyone what to do" followed by "I love how cheerfully you go into discussion." Marc and Denel then ask each other questions about the book, and the questions they choose seem to resemble the *T* from Nina's TAG system.

Marc:	What do you like about the book?
Denel:	I like this picture.
Marc:	Why?
Denel:	Because it's funny. He has a long tail.

In a different group, Shaquilla, Jarrell, and Tommesha are discussing a book:

| Jarrell: | We had some corn? |
| Tommesha: | There's some corn here? |

Later in the day, during free learning time, Shaquilla holds a book about Kwanzaa. She walks around the room holding the book until she finds someone who wants to discuss it. In one group, Denise reads as Aubrey, Tommesha, and KeAndre look over her shoulder and point to various parts of the pictures. Shaquilla doesn't find a partner, so she returns to her desk to read the Kwanzaa book herself. When she finishes, she picks up a yellow primer book for first graders and tries reading. On this day, Nina starts the free learning time with instructions:

| Nina: | You may read poetry or books, write, do flash cards, edit, publish, do math papers, or practice numbers. You may not hang around or do free drawing. Please think in your head what you need to practice. Please think in your head about what you enjoy. If you want me to test you, bring me your yellow book. You'd better make certain you're learning something today. Jamal and Marc look like they're learning something. |

Following Nina's introduction to free learning time, I wandered about the room to take notes on students' conversation. Here's one between Darrius and Jamal:

Darrius:	I write my name.
Jamal:	I write neat.
Darrius:	When I go home, I'm gonna get my own paper. (Darrius lifts up his work and shows it to Andre, who is seated to the side. He then sets it down and starts a think-aloud process as he writes.) It's a Christmas book. And I write this. And these! You wanna trace it? I'm gonna make this a Christmas book.
Jamal:	You gonna write about a Christmas tree?
Darrius:	I'm going to make this a Christmas story.

Students are working on varying projects but all are busy. Marc works on math papers, Darius works with paper coins. Aaron and Jarrell are working on their penmanship, and today they're practicing writing numbers. Denise works to identify numbers by calling out their names and then pointing to them, clearly an indication of her use of a flash-card–type learning strategy. Darrin continues working on the story he began to compose earlier during writing process. Danielle, Larry, and Virginia are listening to stories on cassettes.

It is important to note that during silent reading and reading discussion, students are now choosing each other's publications from the bookshelf on the side of the room. As a result, it is perhaps not surprising that children are mixing the conversations about the books they're reading with talk about the works they're creating. Notably, during the TAG phase of writing process, Nina has amended the *G*, which was once "Give suggestions" to "Give suggestions and connections." With the fluidity of conversations observable during free learning time, we may indeed be seeing some of these connections coming to fruition.

Poetry

Nina: The Langston Hughes poem "Mother to Son" (1995) is a fantastic poem to discuss dialogue. This poem lends itself perfectly to a conversation about dialogue, trying one's best, life for blacks in America in the forties and fifties, and so on. And of course, the type of conversation surrounding the poem would depend on the age and background of the students. Listen to how my children and I connect to "Mother to Son":

Nina:	So who is talking in this poem? (No response.) Let's say the title again.
All:	"Mother to Son."
Nina:	Who's a son in this class? Andre, are you a son?
Andre:	Yes.
Nina:	Marc, are you a son?
Marc:	Yep.
Nina:	Shaquilla, are you a son?
Shaquilla:	No.
Nina:	What are you to your mother? Are you her son or her daughter?
Shaquilla:	Her daughter.
Nina:	Yes, you're her daughter. What about you, Aubrey? Are you a son or a daughter?
Aubrey:	A daughter.
Nina:	And what about me? Am I a son or daughter?
Larry:	A daughter.

Nina:	Yes, but what else am I? (No response.) I have three sons. So what else am I? What do my sons call me?
Denise:	Mommy.
Nina:	What else can they call me?
Virginia:	Ma.
Nina:	Yes, and they can call me Mother because I'm their mother. So let's look at the poem again. What's the title?
All:	"Mother to Son."
Nina:	Who are the characters in this poem?
Roderick:	A mother and son.
Nina:	Yes, that's why it's called mother to son. Who's talking in the poem?
Danielle:	The mother.
Nina:	How do you know that?
Danielle:	Because she's saying, "Well son I'll tell you."
Nina:	Yes, let's all say that line.
All:	"Well son I'll tell you."
Nina:	So she is telling her son something. KeAndre, what does your mother tell you?
KeAndre:	"Hurry up."
Nina:	What does your mother tell you, Roderick?
Roderick:	She says, "Read your book, Roderick."
Nina:	Oh, I'm glad she's telling you to read! What is this mother telling her son? (No response.) Does she tell her son to keep going?
Darrien:	Yeah.
Nina:	What does keep going mean?
Shaquilla:	To keep trying.
Nina:	Yes, to keep trying and to not give up. Raise your hand if you try hard. Everyone in our class tries hard. Is this mother's life easy? (No response.) Larry, remember the time you got that splinter?
Larry:	Yeah.
Nina:	Did it hurt?
Larry:	Yes.
Nina:	So Langston Hughes used the word "splinter." Do you think the mother's life was easy or hard?
Aubrey:	Hard.
Nina:	Yes, this mother's life was hard, but did she give up?
Andre:	No.
Nina:	What does she say to tell you that?
Andre:	"I'se still climbin'."
Nina:	Yes, or "I'se still goin'." So who's talking in this poem?

Danielle: The mother.
Nina: Who is she talking to?
Aaron: Her son.
Nina: Yes, and even though Langston Hughes doesn't say "she said" we know that she's talking because of the title and we hear her telling her son about her life. Let's read the mother's words again. (Everyone repeats each line after I recite them, one by one.)

We have many, many conversations around this poem as the year progresses and we make many connections to it throughout the year. For example, when we read *Cinderella* we connect the glass slipper to the crystal stair. We also connect this poem often to the Hughes poem "Dreams" because they both touch on the same theme of standing firm, and holding fast to dreams and life no matter what the circumstances. A nice vocabulary discussion would connect the words "barren" and "bare" from these same two poems. I know you can think of many other discussions that you could facilitate using this poem as a foundation. Can you think of all the civil rights themes you could develop? When I teach this poem to older children many are so touched they write their own poems as a response. One young girl entitled her poem "Mother to Daughter" and it spoke of her own mother's resilience in the face of difficult circumstances.

ERIC: What? You ask how kindergartners can have a conversation about literature? Well, in addition to Nina's examples here, we see that doing so actually helps us with curriculum—not only in terms of what we're teaching today, but also in terms of what we're preparing our students for. Let's look at some standards in curriculum where work with a poem like "Mother to Son" is clearly beneficial. Linguistically, the poem helps us look at the following items: rhythm in language, categorization of poetic language, contextualization of unknown words, cultural standards and variations of sight vocabulary, contractions, introduction of text as story, meaning, and imagery, eliciting of comparative information, recall of information in a song or poem, fostering of discussion of sequence of events, including the main idea of the poem, and probably even more.

So, how does "Mother to Son" stack up in light of our job mandates? One can choose any state's standards for early education, but it's fun to match Nina's concepts with the standards that are delineated in the manner Ohio has done. Ohio has stipulated (as have most other states) specific competencies educators feel children should have, particularly those of an academic nature, and particularly those dealing specifically with literacy. If you'd like, you could take a look at these competencies as outlined by the Ohio Department of Education and see what Nina and her children are doing achieve and surpass these standards (chart based on Ohio Department of Education 2000).

Phonemic understanding
- Read own first and last name.
- Identify and complete rhyming words and patterns.
- Distinguish the number of syllables in words by using rhythmic clapping, snapping, or counting.
- Distinguish and name upper- and lowercase letters.
- Recognize, say, and write the common sounds of letters.
- Distinguish letters from words by recognizing that words are separated by spaces.
- Hear and say the separate phonemes in words, such as identifying the initial consonant sound in a word, and blend phonemes to say words.
- Read one-syllable and often-heard words by sight.
- Reread stories independently or as a group, modeling patterns of changes in timing, voice, and expression.

Contextual understanding
- Understand new words from the context of conversations or from the use of pictures within a text.

Conceptual understanding
- Recognize and understand words, signs, and symbols seen in everyday life. Identify words in common categories such as color words, number words, and directional words.

Tools and resources
- Determine the meaning of unknown words, with assistance.

Concepts of print
- Demonstrate an understanding that print has meaning by explaining that text provides information or tells a story.
- Hold books right side up, know that people read pages from front to back and read words from left to right.
- Know the differences between illustrations and print.

Comprehension strategies
- Visualize the information in texts, and demonstrate this by drawing pictures, discussing images in texts, or dictating simple descriptions.
- Predict what will happen next, using pictures and content as a guide.
- Compare information (e.g., recognize similarities) in texts using prior knowledge and experience.
- Recall information from a story by sequencing pictures and events.

- Answer literal questions to demonstrate comprehension of orally read grade-appropriate texts.

Self-monitoring
- Monitor comprehension of orally read texts by asking and answering questions.

Independent reading
- Identify favorite books and stories and participate in shared oral reading.
- Use pictures and illustrations to aid comprehension.
- Identify and discuss the sequence of events in informational text.
- Tell the main idea of a selection that has been read aloud.
- Identify and discuss simple maps, charts, and graphs.
- Follow simple directions.
- Identify favorite books and stories.
- Identify the characters and setting in a story.
- Retell or reenact a story that has been heard.
- Distinguish between fantasy and reality.
- Recongize predicatable patterns in stories.

Prewriting
- Generate writing ideas through discussions with others.
- Choose a topic for writing.
- Determine audience.

Drafting, revising, and editing
- Organize and group related ideas.
- Write from left to right and top to bottom.
- Use correct sentence structures when expressing thoughts and ideas.
- Reread own writing.
- Use resources (e.g., a word wall) to enhance vocabulary.

Publishing
- Rewrite and illustrate writing samples for display and for sharing with others.
- Dictate or write simple stories, using letters, words, or pictures.

There are more standards that Ohio has established, but many repeat these fundamental competencies. As you can see, we're only in December, and our children can already perform the majority of these tasks. The goals named in this list suggest that children have quite a bit of proficiency with these tasks by the end of the year. We're just approaching the halfway mark in the school year, and we've already made tremendous progress, even completion in some cases, toward many of these goals. However, for Nina and me, to be at this stage is our goal. If we're aiming for high expectations, then to only achieve the goal at the end of the year would be to potentially leave some students catching up next year.

Speaking of standards, you may be asking how we dare use literature that doesn't demonstrate standard American English. I mean, how dare Nina and Eric teach from the very beginning material including nonstandard forms such as "I'se" and "Ain't been no"? I can still hear the mantra of my peers when I was in third grade. I quoted my grandmother with such confidence and disdain regarding the word *ain't*. I would protest, and the other children would mock, "Ain't ain't a word and you ain't suppose to say it." In other words, they knew the rule and they didn't care. Even as I type this sentence on Microsoft Word, implementing the self-correcting dictionary, the word processing program puts a red squiggle underscore under "ain't" as if to point out that it isn't a word.

Norbert Schmitt (2000) and other linguists (see, for example, Nation 2001; Lewis 2000) might look at this word a bit differently. Schmitt points out that native speakers of languages know a great deal of information about almost any single lexical item, and that knowledge isn't limited to the meaning of a word. As a result, what differences can we point out between the use of *ain't* and *isn't*?

	Ain't	Isn't
Meaning	negative "to be"	negative "to be"
Gender	not applicable	not applicable
Number	not applicable	not applicable
Grammar	verb (negative)	verb (negative)
Subject agreement	any subject	he/she/it
Formality	informal	formal
Rhetorical use	Can be used in the company of other users of the word; may be addressed as a word not to be used with people sticking exclusively to formal language	Can be used in both formal and informal settings.
Identity of speaker	May relate to regional dialect and/or educational level..	Traditional use, occurring in formal and informal settings, not related to specific dialects.
Dictionary use	In a few dictionaries; found in slang dictionaries.	In all dictionaries except slang dictionaries.

Hence, you see how we can know a lot of information about any word other than how to use it in a sentence. Furthermore, millions of people use the word *ain't* on a regular basis, with its having the same meaning almost all the time. Hence, communities agree upon its use. Perhaps more important, even people who don't use the word regularly understand its meaning fully. Finally, to suggest that it's not worth using because it's not in the dictionary would also suggest that we shouldn't use people's names, especially those spelled in unusual ways. After all, *McDonald's* isn't in the dictionary, yet it is certainly one of the first lexical items children from the United States learn to read.

In sum, to use the word *ain't* is only to add another word to one's lexicon, with no more implications for doing so than learning any other words. Is it more confusing? Is it more confusing for you to use the words *soda, pop, soda pop, Coke, tonic, fizzy drink, carbonated beverage,* or *soft drink*? If you were able to learn many of these words that all represent the same thing, as well as learn the situations in which they are appropriately used, why would it be unrealistic to learn the word *ain't*? Clearly, we can add one more category to our previous list of informational items:

	Ain't	Isn't
Social acceptability	Occasionally (though not always) controversial.	Almost universally acceptable.

One final point: a number of the children in this class arrived with the word *ain't* as part of their regular language. They've spent five years coming to know that word as normal and regular. Any native English speaker understands the word, and any native-speaking *ain't* user is most likely able to understand the word *isn't*. Hence, what good reason would there be to tell children they've been wrong for their entire life, that their families who taught them have always been wrong, and that they now have to do it my way? What ramifications would that have?

And here's the best part! To suggest that *ain't* is less than appropriate would be to deny that the poetry of Langston Hughes and other artists offer us nothing because their language standard somehow doesn't match someone else's. To accept *ain't* as viable communication is to incorporate the warmth and beauty of his masterpieces into all lives.

Writing Process

NINA: By this time my children know as well as I do what we will be talking about during our writing session. Yes: dialogue and the words we use to denote this dialogue. I'm sure you can guess how the conversation will proceed:

Nina:	I see everyone is excited about writing. You all got out your writing process notebooks so quickly. Let's talk a little before you continue. What do you think we're going to talk about?
Andre:	Dialogue.
Nina:	Okay, Denise, I saw your hand. What were you thinking?
Denise:	Dialogue too.
Nina:	Yes, today we're going to talk more about dialogue. Since we already spoke about it with our new poem, when we were reading *James and the Giant Peach*, and during silent reading and reading discussion, let's talk a little about it in your own writing. Why do you use dialogue in your stories, Shaquilla?
Shaquilla:	'Cause I like when things talk.
Nina:	Why do you think readers like to have dialogue in stories?
Felicity:	It's funny.
Nina:	Yes, sometimes if the character says something funny it makes the story funny. Thank you, Felicity. Someone else?
Danielle:	It makes it interesting.
Nina:	Yes, I like stories with dialogue because it makes it more interesting for me to read and write. Why else do writers use dialogue?
Cal:	So we know what happens.
Nina:	Yes, sometimes the characters who talk are telling us the story, like the mother in our poem "Mother to Son." Raise your hand and tell me if you're using dialogue in your story. Oh, I see a lot of you are! Darrin read me your dialogue.
Darrin:	"Ahhh!"
Nina:	Oh, who said that?
Darrin:	Me.
Nina:	So did you write "I said"?
Darrin:	No, "I screamed."
Nina:	That's great, because you didn't just say it but you screamed it. Would someone else like to read the dialogue in their story? Andre?
Andre:	"Let's get out of here!"
Nina:	What character is saying that?
Andre:	Roderick.
Nina:	So what do you write, "said, cried, screamed"?
Andre:	"Roderick screamed."
Nina:	Wow! You all have a lot of screaming in your stories! Why was Roderick screaming?
Andre:	Because we saw a shark.
Nina:	Oh! Did you get away?

Andre:	Yep.
Nina:	And what did you say?
Andre:	(Reads.) "Thank God we got out of the water because the shark was going to eat us!"
Nina:	Well, I'm glad it didn't eat you! So raise your hand again if you have dialogue in your story. Okay, people who want to try dialogue you can ask these friends to help you if you need to. Thanks for listening. Let's continue writing.

As you can probably tell, dialogue is not as difficult a concept for kindergartners as some might think. As a matter of fact, it's pretty easy because it is very concrete. Don't you think? All children of this age know what talking is, right? So, it's just a matter of helping them with getting what they already know on paper. As we read, write, and edit together we note the words authors use to describe how the dialogue is spoken: said, screamed, whispered, cried, yelled, laughed. In this way, children begin to include a variety of such words in their own writing. Of course, the play is such a perfect vehicle to talk about dialogue since it is pure dialogue. It's at about this time, after the performance of our first play, when children sometimes try to write their own plays and continue to deepen these skills.

What begins to emerge at this time is coauthoring. Why do you think this might be happening? Do you notice that I am encouraging children to seek help from each other during draft writing? They are used to seeking help during editing but now I am encouraging them to work together as they draft—and they do!

Expectations, Friends, Families, and Guests

By December my students are so verbal and know how to interact successfully around academic work, so I push them even more. Now they begin interviewing each other with the use of questions we develop together:

Nina:	Now we're going to talk about getting to know someone. How do we start getting to know someone? (No response.) What kind of questions do we ask when we meet someone? (No response.) What do you want to know about the new person? What's the first thing you can ask?
Danielle:	Like what's your name.
Nina:	Yes, that could be one of the first questions we can ask. What are some other ones?
Virginia:	Do you have a cat?

Nina:	Yes, Virginia, and I know you would ask that because you like cats, right?
Virginia:	Yep.
Nina:	What other questions can we ask?
Larry:	Do you have a dog?
Andre:	Do you have a bird?
Nina:	Okay, we can ask questions about pets. What else?
Christian:	About food?
Nina:	Yes, food, like "What's your favorite food?" We know everybody's favorite food in this room, don't we?
All:	Yeah!
Nina:	So let's think of other favorite questions: "Like what's your favorite . . . ?"
Aubrey:	"What's your favorite color?"
Nina:	Okay! What is your favorite color, Aubrey?
Aubrey:	Red.
Nina:	Oh, that's one of mine, too. Let's get some more questions.
Denel:	"What's your favorite car?"
Larry:	"What's your favorite toy?"
Roderick:	"What's your favorite TV show?"
Anthony:	"What's your favorite movie?"
Shaquilla:	"What's your favorite book?"
Nina:	We definitely have a lot of questions about favorite things. Let's think of some family questions. If you want to know about someone's family, what could you ask?
Darrin:	"Do you have a mother?"
Darrius:	"Do you have a father?"
Aaron:	"Do you have a sister?"
Cal:	"Do you have a brother?"
Nina:	Great! Now what about some questions about school?
Virginia:	"Do you like school?"
Nina:	Okay! Do you like school, Virginia?
Virginia:	Yep.
Nina:	I'm so glad you do! Other school questions?
Danielle:	"What's your favorite thing in school?"
Felicity:	"Who's your favorite teacher?"
Nina:	And now if we are interviewing an adult and they're not in school we can ask about work. Can you think of any about work?
Alexander:	"Do you like work?"
Denise:	"Where do you work?"
Justin:	"What do you do?"

So you see, as usual, I get them into the process not just by labeling what we're doing (I only say the word "interviewing" once) but by getting them involved with the foundation (questioning) of the process immediately. Within this process you see my students are developing their thinking, questioning, and speaking skills. I am especially proud of Virginia, who is just beginning to volunteer full-sentence responses. I build on these responses as I connect more fully to them as compared to others because she has made such progress!

As part of interviewing we make microphones for each child and practice with each other. We also invite guests into the classroom to practice and develop our interviewing skills. Some guests include: the principal, custodian, other teachers, cafeteria staff, and family members. As we get to know these people we also expand our questions to include categories like personal information and childhood questions; for example, "Where were you born?" "Where do you live?" "What do you like to do?" "What are your dreams?" "What did you do when you were little?" "What things did you like?" I love this interviewing and so do the children because we get to really know other people and it's fun. Just think, too, of how questioning skills deepen with consistent interviewing practice. And after each guest is interviewed we, of course, write thank you notes.

The expectations for letter writing have also increased as we expect children to ask questions of their fourth-grade pen pals and so build on some of the same skills we are developing in interviewing:

Dec. 9, 1999
Dear Sergio,
Roderick is my good friend. What do you watch on TV? I watch cartoons. Write back soon.
Love, Darrin

Dec. 9, 1999
Dear Melanie,
I eat french fries. What do you eat? My favorite book is Barney. I like writing process. I wrote a book called *The Doggie*. Write soon.
Love, Virginia

Dec. 9, 1999
Dear Elizabeth,
My favorite TV show is the Bascry Boy. What's your favorite TV show?

I behave good. Do you listen to your teacher? Do you have free learning time? Do you go outside and play? What do you want for Christmas? I want a video game. Write back soon.
Love, Andre

Dec. 9, 1999
Dear Michael,
What is your mother's name? Do you have a cat? Do you have a
pool?

What do you do after school? Do you play with your toys? Do you
color in your coloring book? Would you like to come to our school
and read books? We did a good job on our play today. My nana is doing a videotape and she lives upstairs. You can see the tape.
Love, Christian

And Christian's nana does tape the recital and she sends us party
things, too. She also washes Brownie:

12/5/99
Me and Brownie watched TV and then colored. Brownie went to the
laundry and Brownie was washed. Thank you for letting me take him
home. . . .
Love, Christian

Sometimes she even sends us new things for our science center. Her
name is Ms. Thomas and she is a fourth-grade teacher in our school,
but more than that she's our nana too! And when we see her in the hall
the children say, "Hi, Nana! Thank you, Nana!"

January

Just realized I haven't written plans for a few weeks. I better get writing! We've done so much—talking about characters, setting, exclamation points, question marks. I can hardly keep up with them!

(One of Nina's January diary entries)

NINA: I can't believe it's already January! Yes, this is usually what I say when we get back from the December break. Even though we've only been away for ten days, it seems like the children have really grown since December. Their excitement level (and mine!) is high as we begin to get into our regular schedule. Why do you think we can all get into it without much struggle or anxiety? Well, I think, for a number of reasons:

- We've created the structure ourselves, so it's within us.
- We are active participants within the structure and, in a sense, there can be no structure without us.
- Our structure is important and meaningful and so we get right back to what we need to accomplish.

ERIC: It's a new year, and for me the excitement lies in the yet-to-come. I have tremendous anticipation for the details that are about to be unearthed in the next five months. The children have come so far, and yet I can't wait to see how far they can go.

In spite of these eager feelings, there was no way I was prepared for the results I was about to observe. Perhaps Nina with her experience was ready, and I actually did believe something good was about to happen, but I wasn't really prepared for what that would be exactly.

Families

NINA: I'm so excited about beginning again with the students that I immediately include the families:

January 3, 2000

Dear Families,
   We are already off to a great start this new year! Thank you so much for helping your children with the yellow books I sent home! Most children have read these books beautifully and are already working on three new ones! You are going to be amazed at how quickly your children will be learning in the next few months! This is the time of year when everything comes together. Please continue to work with them consistently with their books and word lists. It really does make a difference!
   We will begin working on a new set of poetry this week, and this set includes: "Harriett Tubman," by Eloise Greenfield, "Sister for Sale," by Shel Silverstein, "Boa Constrictor," by Shel Silverstein, "Dream Variation," by Langston Hughes, "From African Poems," by Don Lee, "The Negro Speaks of Rivers," by Langston Hughes, "Hot Dog," by Shel Silverstein, "What a Day," by Shel Silverstein, and "Lift Every Voice." I will send home the words soon so you can enjoy the poems too!
   In Math your children will continue practicing addition and subtraction. This month we will also focus on counting money and telling time. You can help with this by allowing your children to practice counting by fives and tens with you. This will help them with counting nickels and dimes.
   A new project we will begin is quilting. This will help us with counting and measuring and also be lots of fun. Please send in patches of square material measuring 2 inches on each side with your child. Thanks! I'd love you to come help us sew them together, too!
   In Science and Social Studies we are talking and reading about the planets in our solar system: Jupiter, Saturn, Neptune, Uranus, Earth, Mars, Venus, Mercury, and Pluto. We are also working on our next drama production, which will focus on traveling through space. We finished *James and the Giant Peach* and have already started a new book called *Stuart Little*. They already love it!
   As always, please make sure your child is in school every day and on time (8:15).
   *Also, make sure your child comes with a book bag, pencil, and homework folder (with pockets) every day.
   Congratulations! I know you are proud of your children's work! I am!

   Sincerely,
   Dr. Zaragoza

As I think I've mentioned before, these letters to the families are very important for the families, the students, and me. When I sit down and write these letters they help me reflect on various aspects of my curriculum. I need to look back at what we have accomplished, look at what we are doing in the present, and make projections about the future. When I compose these letters, I am actually forced to share plans in the most succinct form possible and it really helps me to sharpen my thinking. And as you read in the above diary entry, though, I realized I hadn't written official plans; you can see with this letter how the plans are all in my head!

I also think these letters are a powerful way to connect with the families. Do you agree? I really depend on the families for their help and I know they appreciate that I treat them in a respectful and professional manner as I share some of the details of our community. I know that my consistent and deep connections to my families are a big part of our children's success. Because I am specific about our work and what kind of support we need, they really become invested in this kind of help.

I do believe, too, that the families become colearners with us, and their children's success is also their success. It is so heartwarming to hear adults and siblings recite the poetry at the recital along with our kindergarten performers. They also know their children's lines in our drama production. It is our poetry, our productions, our reading-aloud selections, our personal publications, and, of course, Brownie that form the thread that unites our families with our classroom community. And as you can see, this thread is very strong by January. Isn't it interesting that the major way I connect to the families is through the curriculum? I think it's unfortunate that many families only hear from their children's teachers when there is a behavioral or academic problem. I think when we treat families as collaborators it is much more productive for all concerned.

How do you think children feel when their parents or grandparents run into class, waving Brownie when he is accidentally left at home? What message are the students getting when a family member delivers forgotten homework? I think they feel valued and supported knowing they are not striving alone but have support from their families, their teacher, and their friends.

ERIC: In a bit, we'll discuss the expectations of the children the Brownie experience leads us to, but first, I want to concentrate on this collaborative relationship in shaping the Brownie reports. In January, we see the following kind of data emerging from Brownie missives:

A number of key phenomena are immediately visible, particularly when compared to the Brownie data of October. Again, just as we observed in October, students and families continue to write timelines of what they did sequentially. The children often took Brownie to a friend or relative's house and they played or watched TV. Families continue to give Brownie baths and report doing so. Additionally, games, TV, food and cooking, and sleep are regular subjects. These issues may not be so surprising, but what stands out to me is

Name	Number of Sentences	Sentence Breadth	Topics	Decorations
Jamal	3	7, 21, 11	Coming to my place	2 Brownies, circles, 5s, 6s; own name: *a* with long side line; other letters looking good
Christian	6	5, 2, 8, 8, 10, 5	Sequence: washing Brownie, my turn, love the teacher	Letters: *BMOPMONQISIqnM9nr EplDD19noDmnMAA9EN OnMqMPbLrBM91qcMq MqMqqqEmqBrqoMqp13L qLqNAsD6rMaNaslqMqLq LoDDOM51209341*
Adell	9	6, 9, 5, 9, 5, 9, 7, 10, 6	Sequence: eating, nap, playing, church, why pray, movies	
Danielle	4	12, 5, 13, 8	Family members, playing, bed; great having Brownie at home	Cursive writing
Shaquilla	7	6, 4, 5, 4, 4, 19, 7	Back flip, food, TV, bath, Mom, thanking the teacher	Brownie with underwear
Aaron	3	8, 6, 5	Sequence: football, TV, Elmo	Brownie, football, portrait of Aaron
Aubrey	3	17, 8, 5	Went to friend's house, pizza	Brownie
Marc	5	10, 4, 6, 17, 14	Sequence of things done last night: playing outside, ice cream, paint, bath, looking at the moon	
Denise	5	44, 27, 9, 8, 22	Sequence: Grandmother's house, bicycle, playing ball, cooking, bath, bedtime, picnic, park, store	Brownie and Denise
KeAndre	1	17	Watching TV, playing together, going to sleep	
D'Andre	1	9	Came home from school	2 Brownies
Alexander	5	17, 12, 9, 13, 20	Aunt's house, doing his mom's hair, TV show, cooking, PlayStation, sleep	
Unable to read name	2	25, 9	Eating snacks, playing on the porch, praying, bed	Brownie

that as the month progresses, the sentences get longer and longer. An analysis of the sentences shows that the principal reason for the longer sentences is that the families are now including simple clauses continually linked by the words "and" and "then." It is indeed curious that these data are more involved than those from October, in spite of their near tendency to be a reported sequence of events. We must wonder if a number of things are happening here:

- a sense of sophistication among children and families exists with respect to a belief that a longer missive is a more sophisticated missive;
- the children are gaining confidence in reporting the details of what is occurring in their lives; hence, to add details is much easier for them, meaning that as a new idea enters their head, they just add the next detail by using the words "and" or "then"; or
- families are editing more and more, thereby increasing their own adeptness at writing longer missives.

This adeptness is also demonstrated in family members who are learning English as a new language. Note this example from the Brownie entries. This one from a family member writing on behalf of the student:

> Me and Bowien went to my Grandmother House And we play With my Sisster And we Rid the bike And play Ball and my Mom call us And the House to wash are Hand and Ate Some Good Food that my mom cooking Good She told us to Going And wacth T'V And We Went And take a Good Bath and Had Some Snack to eat Befo we Go to Bedtime on Satday we Went to the park And play We Had pinknet outther to the park. On Sunday my mom take me And Bowien went with my mom To The Store And buy food us to eat?

I know this example is not an easy read for native English speakers, but it is ultimately understandable. It's important to note that this missive is one of the longest of the month from any family member. Furthermore, it represents a full report of what happened with this child and Brownie through the day. The grammar is there. The spelling is fairly close—at least close enough to make out words and ultimately sentences. Most likely this family member isn't spending concentrated time improving English at a detailed level, but is very willing to spend time helping their child. This family member is most likely, through the deep investment in the child's progress, practicing English at a level this person may not have experienced yet. As a result, the English of this person is indirectly improving.

Now in the Brownie journal the children are not practicing letter formation but are solely illustrating. Students are still practicing letters regularly in their writing process and daily journals, but there now is seemingly an unspoken agreement that this type of practice is not to happen in the Brownie diary that is passed from person to person.

Curriculum

NINA: We have five copies of *James and the Giant Peach*, and two copies of *Stuart Little* that we have just begun to read. They are eating up math and already are beginning to understand the concept of counting by fives (nickels) and tens (dimes). We are already counting our books in piles of five. And so it goes! We have begun a new play and a quilt—they won't let me forget! (A January diary entry)

The children definitely do not let me forget what we need to do. Isn't it interesting that while I sometimes forget to write down plans on the standard plan sheet there is definitely always a plan? I think that the plan is actually there within the structure. Here again we can discuss the natural connection between curriculum and structure in our room. There are certain foundational curriculum columns that keep us anchored. What do you think they are? I think we could come up with varying correct answers: poetry, writing, silent reading, reading discussion, reading aloud, and, of course, drama. In fact, it's incredible how these children have connected to drama. Even in January some are still talking with their pen pals about the last performance and at the same time looking forward to the next one:

Dear Jazmine,
The play we did on living things was great. Our parents, teachers, and other students came to see us. Everything went perfect. After the play we had a party. Now we are working on a play about planets. Please write soon.
Love, Aaron

As I type Aaron's letter here I realize what an edifying experience the drama production, both process and product, was for him. I can feel that he doesn't want to let go of that feeling of pride and confidence. I can actually see him basking in his success and the success of his classmates. But he doesn't sit on our laurels; he desires to forge on toward the next production! And as Andre notes below, we begin working on it every day. Notice, too, how he wants to share his new vocabulary word with Elizabeth:

Dear Elizabeth,
I like the Wheel of Fortune. Tell your teacher thank you for the paper. Do you go outside? We are doing good at take away. We do our new play every day. It's about going to the solar system because solar means sun. Write back soon.
I love you, Andre

The children also share the titles of their latest publications with their pen pals:

January 19, 2000

Dear Yanet,
I like the books we read. I wrote a book about an ice cream truck. We are doing new poems. I love "Harriett Tubman." I am going to school every day. It's fun. I love school.
Write soon please!!
Jarrell

January 19, 2000

Dear Melissa,
Yes, I like writing stories. The last story was *The Heart and the Balloon*. I like our new poems. The ones I like the best is "Sister for Sale." Write soon.
Love, Latisha

January 19, 2000

Dear Patricia,
I've published a new book called *The ABC Store*. My favorite color is pink. Our play is about planets. Our new poem is "Harriett Tubman" and another poem is "Hot Dog." What are your poems?
Love, Danielle

January 19, 2000

Dear Andy, I have four sisters and I have three cousins. I don't have any brothers. I don't have Pokemon cards. Thank you for the paper. We take homework books. Tomorrow my teacher said I can read *The Carrot Seed*. I write. I finished a book called *West Palm Beach*.
Write soon,
Love, Denise

Can you hear their confidence in these letters? Look how Denise states so clearly, "I write." In just these two words I hear her confidence, her pride. I see her standing tall with her head held high, holding her book about West Palm

Beach. She's an author. She works at her craft, and she wants to make sure that her pen pal remembers!

The children definitely realize how much work they do, and Shaquilla is indignant when her pen pal seems to suggest that there is sleeping going on in kindergarten:

January 19, 2000

Dear Nicole:
I don't sleep in kindergarten because we do a lot of work in kindergarten!! We do poems. One poem is Harriett Tubman. The play is about the solar system. In the play we're traveling to all the planets. We're doing a quilt. My teacher is crazy because she forgets to do all the things we have to do.
Love, Shaquilla

ERIC: Let's look at these letters even more in depth. Below is a chart of fifteen of these letters.

Name	Number of Sentences	Sentence Breadth	Topics	Decorations
Marc	2	5, 7	Gives thanks for the calendar	Letter format; picture of himself with an opened calendar showing an alligator; a circle; a building (maybe his school)
Tommesha	4	7, 7, 3, 8	Sequence: she got a dolly for Christmas, about learning to count by fives and tens in class, doing everything in class, and what her favorite poem is	Letter format; bands of colors, a colorful Christmas tree and dolly in a big purple circle on the back side
Jarrell	8	6, 8, 5, 4, 6, 2, 3, 3	Sequence: likes books he reads, wrote a book about an ice cream truck, new poems in class, loves "Harriet Tubman," loves school every day, asks person to write soon	Letter format; a purple turtle inside big bands of colors; fills back of page with a lot of different colors
Darrin	6	5, 5, 3, 3, 8, 2	Sequence: favorite Pokemon, working on something new, likes poem on Boa Constrictor, finds it funny	Letter format; bands of colors to the side and across page midpage, a colorful house on back of page with a big red heart in the middle of it, trees, lollipops, hearts, and squares on each side of house

Table continued on next page.

Name	Number of Sentences	Sentence Breadth	Topics	Decorations
Marc	6	5, 9, 5, 13, 9, 4	Sequence: her sister Julie and her age, birthday, her class learns new poems and is practicing for a new play about the nine planets, asks person to write back soon	Letter format; colorful borders surrounding letter, back of page filled with diagonal bands of colors
Latisha	5	5, 9, 5, 10, 2	Sequence: likes writing stories, wrote about "The Heart and the Balloon," likes the new poems, likes the poem "Sister for Sale," write soon	Letter format; orange and purple border, the word "love" on the bottom, different intriguing shapes, a little boat, letter *k*s or chairs near her name at the end of the letter, a big red-filled square with a sun in the middle of the back of the paper and some blue circles
Damine	5	5, 7, 10, 7, 3	Sequence: asks two questions to addressee (does she like Pokemon cards? what is she doing now in her class?), class learning the solar system, learning new poems, write back	Letter format; a brown Pokemon figure, blue box with a blue star in the middle, green box with a brown star in the middle; back of page has a brown abstract image
Danielle	6	9, 5, 5, 7, 6, 4	Sequence: published a book called *The ABC Store*; favorite color is pink, solar system play, poem on Harriet Tubman, remembers another poem called "Hot Dog," asks about other person's poems	Letter format; orange balloon, a four-color flower, big and small yellow suns, a heart-shaped pool, a bird, tree, little opened and closed books scattered around; on back of page: two orange ponds with two brown hearts in the middle, clouds, trees, orange birds, a yellow sun in a blue square, a blue/green/black car
Aaron	6	9, 10, 3, 7, 9, 3	Sequence: did a play on living things, parents, teachers, and students went to the play; everything was perfect; after the play they had a party; they are working on a new play on the planets; write back soon	Letter format; nothing on front; on back of page: a green ghost, a yellow sun, other abstract figures
Alex	6	6, 6, 8, 5, 6, 4	Sequence: loves to color and draw, likes to take tests, play on planets, her favorite planet is Mars, thinks Mars is pretty, write back	Letter format; nothing on front; on back of page: girl with a big blue face and black hair with a blue bow

Table continued on next page.

Name	Number of Sentences	Sentence Breadth	Topics	Decorations
Larry	4	15, 9, 8, 4	Sequence: favorite poem is Harriet Tubman, favorite book is *What Color*, class doing a play on outer space, class also making a quilt; write back	Letter format; letters in a square: *ooyssWreMdoJ/ DrrWHRDBmbp/rEFr rLBAv/SNVellss*; nothing on front; on back of page: abstract shapes in different colors
Denise	11	4, 4, 5, 5, 5, 5, 4, 10, 2, 8, 2	Sequence: has four sisters, three cousins, no brothers, doesn't have Pokemon cards, gives thanks for paper, takes homework books, teacher will let her read *Carrot Seed*, she writes, finished a book called "West Palm Beach," write back	Letter format; pink and red borders, balloons with strings and two yellow heart shapes; on back of page: red and brown abstract shapes
D'Andre	6	6, 6, 8, 8, 14, 3	Sequence: watches wrestling, favorite TV show is *Martin*, loves to read and do poems; favorite poem: "My Little Sister," play on planets, write back	Letter format; brown, red, and blue wrestling ring with people on the top and a big yellow cross in the middle; on back of page: a red person, many colors criss-crossed, and a red and green comb-shaped figure
Andre	8	5, 8, 4, 7, 7, 11, 3, 3	Sequence: likes *Wheel of Fortune*, tells addressee to say thank you for the paper, asks if she goes outside, says they are doing good at "take away," class doing a new play on solar system, says "solar means sun," write back, I love you	Letter format in a red square; "We Knew MaMa's Song" in a box; The Dog Shot hiDSc; a glass, a basketball; on back of page: hills or rocky mountain with a tree and a red heart balloon on top of it; two stars (purple with a green circle in the middle and a red star with a green circle in the middle); blue dots in the sky representing stars; yellow sun in top left corner of page
Jamal	6	4, 6, 11, 4, 3, 3	Sequence: his friend is Anthony, does not have a PlayStation, likes Boa Constrictor poem, write back, I love you	Letter format; colors splashed around on page

Let's have a quick look at these pen pal letters and some of the data they display. Of the 15 letters examined, the average number of sentences per letter is 5.93, ranging from no fewer than 2 to no more than 11 among the examples. Furthermore, of all the letters, 7 are 6 letters long. Of the 89 sentences from the sample, the average sentence length is 6.00 words, with sentences ranging from 2 to 15 words per sentence. In addition, 9 of the letters contained a sentence of 10 words or longer, but no single letter had more than one of these sentences.

Finally, a summary of the topics examined in these letters is listed in the following table:

Topic	Number of instances
Poetry	9
Science	7
Practicing for a new play	6
What I wrote about or what I'm writing about	6
Reading	4
Thanks for correspondence	3
Hobbies, other than TV or Pokemon	3
Family	3
Pokemon	2
TV	2
Presents	1
Friends	1
Favorite color	1
Math	1
Quilt	1
Tests	1

Finally, it is worth noting that Nina and paraprofessionals assisted the children with the body of each letter. However, both the dates and the signatures of the children were accomplished by the children themselves.

After I analyzed these data, I spoke with my fellow teacher-education colleague Mark about the results; however, I didn't tell him who the subjects were. First, I asked him to listen to this list of topics of pen pal letters. He said, "Okay!" Then I said, "Who do you think wrote these letters?" And Mark said, "I'll guess that they were written by the students in your on-line master's education course." I then told him that the students were five years old, and his jaw broke when it hit the floor.

NINA: I actually do go a little crazy sometimes trying to keep up with everything! Luckily, I have my students and the structure of our curriculum to keep me sane and organized and as long as I don't forget the major things—play, poetry, *Stuart Little*, Brownie, and the all-important quilt—we're all fine!

Reading Aloud

Do you notice that Denise mentions reading aloud to her pen pal? At this point I am not the only one reading aloud to the whole class—the children are doing this as well. Doesn't this seem like a natural progression in our classroom? They have read their own pieces since the first day of school and by January many children are ready to read works written by other authors. They sign up to read aloud and usually we make time for one or two students to read right after lunch. A child may also choose to share another author's book during writing process sharing. The only requirement is that the child has practiced it enough so that it is read fluently:

Nina: So, Denise, I see you've signed up to share *The Carrot Seed*. So you're ready?

Denise: Yep.

Nina: So how do you know you're ready?

Denise: Because I practiced it with my mother and sister for homework and read it about five times to them.

Nina: Great! I can't wait to hear you read!

Most children practice their book for homework. Sometimes I will give individual children more support and listen to the reading before they read it in full community:

Nina: Virginia! I see you're going to share a book! Wow! What book are you going to read?

Virginia: *Toys*.

Nina: Oh, that's the red book you're working on. Can you read it like you're talking?

Virginia: Yeah.

Nina: Good! Get me the book so you can practice with me.

Of course, children have a choice of which book they want to share. Some children—Andre, Shaquilla, Danielle, Larry—are now able to read full-length primary books so I might ask them to choose a favorite part to read if we're running out of time. More times than not, though, they and the rest of the class beg for the whole book and I surrender!

At the end of the reading the audience responds with TAG. Let's listen to Denise's TAG session after she reads *The Carrot Seed*:

Denise:	T: Tell what you like.
Virginia:	The carrot.
Denise:	Why? (No response.) Why do you like carrots?
Virginia:	They're good.
Denise:	Another T?
Latisha:	I like when the carrot got big because it was funny.
Denise:	A: Ask questions.
Andre:	Why did you pick that book?
Denise:	Because I can read all the words.
Andre:	Very good.
Nina:	Andre, that was so friendly of you to say "very good" to Denise! I have a question for everyone. Why do you think the carrot grew so big?
Felicity:	Because the boy put water.
Nina:	Okay, and why did it grow with water?
Damine:	Plants need water.
Nina:	Yes, anyone else?
Latisha:	The boy puts water every day.
Nina:	That's true. He never gives up. He knows that all living things need water. What other things need water to grow?
Aaron:	Flowers.
Christian:	Trees.
D'Andre:	Fish.
Nina:	Ha! I never thought of that. Fish would die without water. What else would die without water? (No response.) Who else is living?
Andre:	Animals like dogs.
Nina:	Raise your hand if you have a dog. Oh, that's right, Larry, you wrote a story about your dog, Sugar. So when do you give Sugar water?
Larry:	In the mornings.
Nina:	Yes, dogs need water and so do other animals. Do we need water?
Shaquilla:	Yes, because my mom makes me drink water every day.
Nina:	I try to drink water every day too, because we need water to stay alive. So the carrot grows because the boy keeps watering it. Thank you, Denise. Go on to G.
Denise:	G: Give ideas.
Felicity:	Next time you can read that Dr. Seuss book that you always take for homework.
Denise:	Okay, thank you for that idea.

There I go again, contextualizing a science lesson using literature. By now I guess you expect it, right? The above is an example of how I cover other curriculum areas within our literacy program. To extend this activity I might ask them to draw or write about living things, nonliving things, and so on. I also could connect this to the poem "Dreams," by Langston Hughes, because the boy doesn't give up even though everyone in his family says that the carrot won't grow. Of course, we can always write a play about it. Ha! Ha! I'm only kidding—for now! In March you'll get to read our play about the solar system and hear how we learn and reinforce science concepts. But as long as we're talking about writing, let me share a morning song usually composed around January so that we start with a new song for the new year:

Hello!!

Hello, my friends!
How are you?
I hope you're fine and great!
I hope you're awesome and terrific!
I hope you're wonderful and marvelous!
I hope you're absolutely perfect!
I hope you know you're gorgeous, too!
I hope you will be helpful and kind!
We'll read and write and have some fun!
Hello, my friends!
We all are special!

When I read *Stuart Little* aloud, we also touch on science and math concepts. For example, because Stuart is a mouse born into a human family the discussion of mothers and babies emerge as I ask questions such as:

- Can a mother dog have a baby kitten?
- Can a mother cat have a baby dog?
- What kind of baby did your mother have, Darrin and Darrius?
- Is your baby sister a human baby or a mouse, Larry?

Then we talk about how *Stuart Little* is fiction because a human mother can't really have a mouse baby.

We also study measurement when we read about Stuart because it is mentioned that Stuart is two inches tall. So we all get rulers and measure our fingers, our feet, and anything else we want to! Measurement is further reinforced when we read about a young girl who helps her grandmother finish a quilt and we begin our own.

Poetry

As some of the children mention in their letters, the newest poem is "Harriett Tubman," by Eloise Greenfield. It is a very long, rhythmic poem that the children love because it presents such a clear picture of how the underground railroad worked. They also love the strong lines that celebrate freedom. As the children become familiar with the social studies concepts in this poem I add the Langston Hughes poem "A Negro Speaks of Rivers," which further deepens these concepts. It is a wonder to see and hear such young children recite these poems and truly understand the meaning behind every word they say.

While many of our poems are serious and deal with social issues, I do include poems that are just pure fun! "Hot Dog," "Sister for Sale," "Boa Constrictor," and "What a Day," all by Shel Silverstein, are some of the children's favorites. They are very silly, fun to recite, and generate great conversations:

Nina: Why do you think this person wants to sell his sister?
Aubrey: Because she bothers him.
Nina: Okay. So you think the person saying this is a brother? Why do you think that?
Aubrey: I saw the picture in the book.
Nina: Oh! That's right, there was a picture for this poem. So what's another reason a brother would want to sell his sister?
Denel: 'Cause she touches his stuff.
Andre: 'Cause she gets him in trouble.
Larry: 'Cause she cries a lot.
Nina: I guess those are all reasons! If you had a sister how much would you sell your sister for?
Virginia: A dollar.
Denise: A million dollars.
Nina: Oh, Denise, you have four sisters, don't you?
Denise: Yeah.
Nina: Would you really want to sell any of them?
Denise: No.
Nina: Why not?
Denise: I love them!
Nina: I know you do! So what can a person really sell? (No response.) What do people sell in stores?

Do you see how I can go right into money concepts now? Shel Silverstein includes a dollar, a quarter, a dime, a nickel, a penny in this poem—just what we're studying!

ERIC: So you see how the poem lends itself to a quick math lesson, right? Certainly with our December look at contextualization, such orientation should not be such a surprise. But do you think the children are thinking, "Oh how clever. Dr. Zaragoza just combined a poem into a math lesson"? Probably not. But also look back at our data set on the January 19 pen pal letters. Look at Danielle, who wrote about the solar system play—a collaboratively authored science lesson—and ultimately (following her own recognition of a poem she loves) what her pen pal's favorite poems are. Note that she doesn't ask whether or not her pen pal loves poems; there is just an assumption that she would. To me this indicates that some of the children in Nina's class are connecting the reflection of the world demonstrated in the artistic work of poetry, story writing, and drama to the world around them.

Writing Process

NINA: We've already spoken about the children's profound identification as authors. A part of normal conversation for our young authors includes what they are reading and writing. Let's look at some of their written pieces:

My Father by Alexander
One sunny day there was a man. He was walking and he said, "Can I have one of your ice creams?" I said, "Sure." The man was my father.

The Cookie Store by Denise
Yesterday me and my mom went to the cookie store. We got cookies and chocolate milk. A monster came in and said, "What are you buying?" I said, "I'm buying cookies. Do you want some?" He said, "Yes." I bought the cookies.

The Jail Boy by Denel
Once there was a boy driving. Another boy was following him because he wanted money. He caught him and took him out of the car and beat him up. Then the police came and that boy went to jail.

The Flying Burger by Aaron
One day me and my brother went to Burger King. He dropped the burger and it started to fly. He ran to catch it. He caught it and ate it.

The Giant Man by Demeatric
When I went to the beach there was a big giant man who came out of
the water. He ate my boat and then he ate me. A crowd came and they
cut his stomach and got me out.

The Friendly Shark by Jamal
One day I was walking and I went to the beach. Then I went in the
water. A shark came. It let me ride on him. It said, "Do you want to
go for another ride?" I said, "Yes." Then I went home. I went to see
him every day.

The Hungry Dog Dad by Darrius
My Daddy keeps eating dog biscuits. I wanted to stop my Dad from
eating dog biscuits. I said, "Stop eating dog biscuits. You are not a
dog. You are a human." Then he stopped.

Silent Reading and Reading Discussion

NINA: Our reading program continues as usual. Children continue to choose
their books and are encouraged to choose books that they love and books that
are new and a bit challenging. As you read in the family letter, the children
are also working on "yellow books." These books (also "red books") are part
of a leveled, mechanistic reading program that we are required to implement.
They are usually very sparse and uninteresting. ("Sally makes a cake. It is
good. Mom says 'Yum.'") I can hardly stand them! Why do you think my children are okay with them, and I am okay with allowing them to use them? By
this time my children are very confident as readers and with choosing from a
variety of materials, so for them these stilted little books are additions to a very
large library. I see it the same way. These things can't really harm my children
now because they know and partake in real writing and reading. These flimsy
little books will not deter them from seeking more meaningful material. They
also serve as a springboard for a discussion on making writing interesting:

Nina:	How can we make this story about Sally more interesting? (No response.) What could you add?
Shaquilla:	Like more characters.
Nina:	Yes, if I were the writer I would add more characters. What else?
Danielle:	I would add more dialogue.
Nina:	Okay. Why would you add more dialogue?
Danielle:	'Cause it makes it more interesting and I like talking.

Nina:	Thank you. What else? (No response.) What is missing from this story? I actually wouldn't even call it a story because it's missing something. (No response.) Remember? What do all the stories we write have? Characters, setting . . .
Andre:	Problem.
Nina:	Yes, problem and what?
Alex:	Solution.
Nina:	Yes! Interesting stories have problems and solutions. They also have settings, too. This story doesn't even talk about a setting. What are some of the settings you used in your stories?
Aubrey:	The store.
Alex:	The street.
Denel:	Jail.
Nina:	Okay, all the stories you all write are interesting because they have settings, problems, solutions, dialogues, and characters.

ERIC: Up to now, you may have been thinking to yourselves, "Eric and Nina, there you sit in your ivory tower, giving us permission to do what we want. Don't you understand that we have an established curriculum to follow that our bosses give us? And if we don't follow the curriculum to the letter, we could lose our jobs? How could you possibly think that we could be this open?" We do understand this, and actually Nina has a set curriculum to follow at this school.

The point we make is not to promote one's own independence in what gets taught. We actually believe in good guided curricula. If implemented appropriately, a step-by-step approach in a curriculum that leads to student success is most probably the most efficient guideline a school supervisor can give a teacher. Furthermore, administrators, teachers, supervisors, superintendents, and families scurry at conferences, workshops, and publisher displays in hopes of finding the newest, greatest textbook series that will apply one hundred percent to their curriculum. However, I have to say that in this day and age, I wholeheartedly doubt that, unless teachers have the time and resources to write their own books for their own classes (resources that would stay only in the confines of their classroom), such materials even exist. Why would I paint such a pessimistic picture here? It's no one's fault. It's just good business. Textbook companies need to appeal to as broad a spectrum of their audience as possible in order to sell as many books as possible. As a result, they are willing to accept that their materials will touch most people of the world. For example, it is not uncommon for a textbook to have lessons on how to use a subway. For a large number of students in the world, perhaps even a majority of students, the subway is an integral part of daily life. And if such a textbook series is adopted by a famous urban school district, other districts looking to the famous district as a model may select the same text, even if their location is out in a cornfield in the heartland.

This is where you come in as a teacher. Often we don't have the power to say, "This book is ridiculous." Or even though we say it, the book remains as the basic text. I say that if we're really the good teachers that we are, we can take the flimsy red book and make it (a) interesting and (b) applicable to our students lives, while (c) learning about a different perspective that perhaps doesn't fit our lives so well.

NINA: The personal connections that are encouraged and enabled in the classroom community give whatever curriculum mandated its relevancy. Let's listen to some connections we make to the books we read in our classroom:

Nina: Why do you all cheer when we start reading *Stuart Little*?
D'Andre: It's funny.
Felicity: It's about a cute animal.
Shaquilla: It's in a city and I like cities.
Denise: It's exciting.
Nina: What part is exciting to you?
Denise: When he is in the window shade and everyone thinks the cat got him.
Nina: Oh, that is an exciting part because it's a problem and we want to see how it will be solved.

The little yellow or red books that my children are reading and practicing are not a danger to my reading community (though I do believe they are deadly if they are a major element of a program) and I easily integrate them into our reading program. The children like them because they are easy and they breeze through them quickly so as to move on to the next book. The families like them too, because they are short and sweet and are an easy way to mark progress.

While generally I do not believe in drilling children on isolated words within a word list, I allow my families to help with these lists as part of homework. I don't think they hinder my children, because these lists are such a small part of an incredibly vibrant literacy environment. These lists, though, if used alone and as a major piece of a program, would, I believe, be quite harmful because they promote an isolated, uninteresting curriculum that encourages isolated word calling and denies the dynamic nature of genuine reading. What do you think?

Structure

Yes, I do write down weekly plans, and each day I write down my daily plans and share them with my students. Remember I talked about how each morning we list "Things to Do Today"? Well, that's my daily plan. Here's an example:

Things to Do Today
1. Diary writing
2. Poetry ("Harriet Tubman")
3. Writers' workshop
4. Silent reading
5. Reading discussion groups
6. Lunch
7. *Stuart Little*
8. Quilt
9. Drama
10. Goodbye Song

Now let me show you the plan sheet that helps me plan for the entire week:

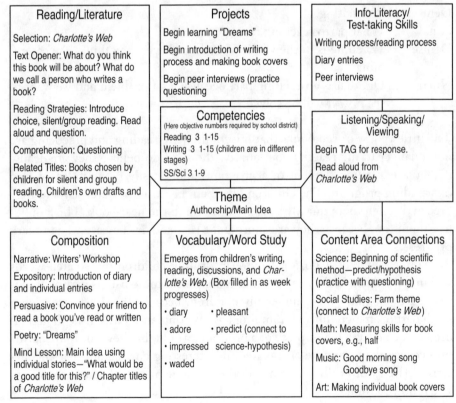

Reading/Literature

Selection: *Charlotte's Web*

Text Opener: What do you think this book will be about? What do we call a person who writes a book?

Reading Strategies: Introduce choice, silent/group reading. Read aloud and question.

Comprehension: Questioning

Related Titles: Books chosen by children for silent and group reading. Children's own drafts and books.

Projects

Begin learning "Dreams"

Begin introduction of writing process and making book covers

Begin peer interviews (practice questioning

Info-Literacy/ Test-taking Skills

Writing process/reading process

Diary entries

Peer interviews

Competencies
(Here objective numbers required by school district)
Reading 3 1-15
Writing 3 1-15 (children are in different stages)
SS/Sci 3 1-9

Listening/Speaking/ Viewing

Begin TAG for response.

Read aloud from *Charlotte's Web*

Theme
Authorship/Main Idea

Composition

Narrative: Writers' Workshop

Expository: Introduction of diary and individual entries

Persuasive: Convince your friend to read a book you've read or written

Poetry: "Dreams"

Mind Lesson: Main idea using individual stories—"What would be a good title for this?" / Chapter titles of *Charlotte's Web*

Vocabulary/Word Study

Emerges from children's writing, reading, discussions, and *Charlotte's Web*. (Box filled in as week progresses)

• diary   • pleasant

• adore   • predict (connect to

• impressed   science-hypothesis)

• waded

Content Area Connections

Science: Beginning of scientific method—predict/hypothesis (practice with questioning)

Social Studies: Farm theme (connect to *Charlotte's Web*)

Math: Measuring skills for book covers, e.g., half

Music: Good morning song
            Goodbye song

Art: Making individual book covers

As you know, many of the elements on the weekly plan sheet are carried over to future weeks because so much of our work is ongoing. Actually, I guess you could say that my whole program—not just the writing—is a process program. Everything is done over time and when final products are created or completed the process begins again. As you have already seen, a structure founded within a process orientation is actually quite stable and predictable, so planning is not too difficult. We know we will always read aloud, so planning is only a matter of choosing the next book. We know we will always do poetry, so it's only a matter of which poems to read and when to read them. We know we will always be doing a drama production, so it's just a matter of writing and performing it. We know we will always be writing and reading, so it's just a matter of deciding what to write and read. In this kind of classroom, too, deciding what skills to talk about is not difficult. All writers and readers need to talk about certain aspects of literacy, and these aspects are always emerging in whatever literary pieces we are focusing on at the time. Here are some common concepts discussed within all literacy communities:

- dialogue
- setting
- beginning, middle, end
- problems and solutions
- main idea
- character traits
- character development
- character change
- character relationships
- audience
- style
- theme
- genre
- voice
- suspense

Can you think of any others? There are also the many skills related to form and mechanics that are discussed during editing and final publication, such as spelling, punctuation, and illustrations. Definitely lots to talk about, so I am never at a loss when it comes to planning. There is always so much to do and so little time!

Expectations and Interdependence

The higher I raise the expectations the more the children learn! I am even amazed. We talk about going to college and making our dreams come true. Andre raises his hand and says, "My mother goes to school and she's learning not to live on the street and come back and live with me." (A January diary entry)

> It is amazing to me how much these children really work, and it confirms my belief that kindergartners can do so much more than many of us expect. And so expectations remain high in January and vary according to each child's need. The children are comfortable with being pushed; they push themselves, and actually push me to remember what I'm supposed to remember. But they're easy on me and very forgiving if I forget or can't fit something into our schedule on a particular day. Just as long as it doesn't become a habit!
>
> In January, too, I find that the families are very comfortable with supporting their children and graciously help with whatever our classroom community needs. For example, the amount of material sent in for our quilt is enough to make many quilts! I think they are so happy with their children's progress and their children's desire to be in school that they themselves are inspired. Isn't that powerful, children inspiring their families? I know that Andre's mother is working hard to succeed herself. She is determined to give Andre all he needs for school, evident in his new sneakers, pencils, backpack, and books. When she visits our class her eyes reflect the light of Andre's progress and this inspires her to continue to strive.

The Brownie entries also illustrate the families' willingness to support the high expectations placed upon their children. They place Brownie right in the middle of family activities and push their children to fully describe events. Notice the amount of details written:

1/21/00
Me and Brownie went to my grandmother's house and we played with my sister and we rode the bike and played ball and my mom called us in the house to wash our hands and we ate some good food that my mom cooked. She told us to go watch TV and we went and then took a good bath and had some snack to eat before we go to bedtime. On Saturday we went to the park and played. We had a picnic out there in the park. On Sunday my Mom took me and Brownie to the store and bought food for us to eat.
By Denise

1-9-00
Brownie was lying in the bed with my nephew while I was playing Monopoly with my sister and brother. I was playing with Brownie

throwing him in the air. I made a mistake and hit my brother in the face with Brownie's nose. Jamal

You can tell, too, that families are not only pushing their children to verbalize more but are also connecting to current events and the curriculum:

January 20, 2000
Brownie and me played outside. We played football and we ate ice cream. Then we made a beautiful painting and Brownie made a big sun and a moon to look at. At night we took a bath and when it was night we read a book that was about the moon.
Love, Marc

1/17/00
Brownie and I went to Blockbuster and got a good movie for kids. And we had a fun, fun time watching it with my family. Brownie, it was nice having you over. See you next time. Bye, Bye Brownie.
Happy Birthday Martin L. King.

Our families take their partnership with me quite seriously, and their involvement has surely enabled me to heighten my academic and social expectations for their children, my students. The children continue to push each other along no matter what present levels they might be working at. So while Andre is reading at a first-grade level and continues to be challenged, Virginia is also challenged as she begins to learn how to write her name. Here's another one of my January diary entries:

> Virginia is learning to write her name with the help of her class and can now write "V," "I," "R," "G" by herself. She is reading words, too, and beginning to talk in full sentences.

And the whole class does help Virginia with her name:

Nina: Oh listen, everyone. Thank you, Latisha, you looked at me right away. Thank you, Denel, you are ready to listen. Thank you for letting you interrupt you. Let's look at this word that Denise just wrote: "Vacuum." Raise your hand if you help vacuum your house. Oh, I see a lot of you do. Raise your hand if you help sweep your house. Why do we vacuum or sweep?
Aubrey: To clean.

Nina:	Okay, thank you. Someone else?
Aaron:	To pick up things.
Nina:	Okay. What do we clean or pick up when we sweep or vacuum?
Felicity:	Like garbage or dirt.
Nina:	Okay. What else?
Darrin:	When you spill something.
Nina:	Okay, maybe when you spill out little things from your backpack. I also have to vacuum up dog hair because I have two dogs. Raise your hand if you have a dog. Raise your hand if you have a cat. Okay, so you all know what I mean. Now whose name in this class starts with the same beginning sound as "vacuum"? Let's all say the word "vacuum." (Children say "vacuum.") So whose name begins with this same beginning sound?
Alex:	Virginia.
Nina:	Yes, Virginia. Virginia, say your name.
Virginia:	Virginia.
Nina:	Okay, now say "vacuum" and "Virginia." "Vacuum Virginia."
Virginia:	"Vacuum, Virginia."
Nina:	Now, everyone say "Vacuum Virginia."
All:	"Vacuum Virginia."
Nina:	Let's all write the first letter in the air with our fingers. Now let's all write the rest of Virginia's name with our fingers in the air and let's say the letters when we write them. You can look at her name on the class list to help you.

Can you just see Virginia glowing as everyone recites her name and then writes it altogether with her? It is so beautiful to see and hear the community help in such a tangible, cohesive way. Some might wonder why all the children have to spend their time on concepts they probably know (the letters and beginning sound of Virginia's name) when they can be involved in more useful work. They need to do this because we are all a community and we help each other succeed. If you notice, too, Virginia isn't the only one connecting. We use a word from Denise's story and we all connect to it in a meaningful way through conversation. So everyone wins here while we help Virginia write her name.

February
Dr. Zargoza, I'm tired of talking!

NINA: By February I am pushing my children even harder as first grade comes into closer view. Every minute is precious and so I insist on attendance and punctuality. When you review my schedule you will agree that even if children are five minutes late they have missed some learning time. Remember? When my students first walk in they choose silent-reading books, sharpen pencils, write an entry in their diary, and even recite a poem. All of this happens before the schoolwide announcements. Actually, we might do some learning as we walk together to the classroom. We might talk about *Stuart Little*, yesterday's homework, or a word they saw on the television program *Wheel of Fortune*. The rhythm of our community begins immediately, and a child who is late misses the first important beats.

ERIC: It's the first day of February, and Nina is taking the opportunity to use the new month as a teachable moment. Here are some of her quotes:

- When you call out, you don't let other people think.
- What does it have to be?
- Why can it not be February 23rd?
- So what would the number be for today if February just started?
- Give me any answer.
- Would it be zero-day of February?
- What comes before two?
- What day comes . . . ?
- It starts with an /f/.
- Where's the chalk for the math?

- What day is it? Is it Sunday, Monday, or Tuesday?
- You can know the date from the sign-up sheet.
- Why is the January calendar different from the February calendar?
- We don't have to write numbers for our January calendar, so what can we do with our new calendar?
- Do you have to do everything the same way as everyone else or can you be different?
- Name on top.
- If you don't have a pencil, please figure out what you need to do.
- I'm watching how small you're doing your letters.
- Remember to space your name. Write ____. Then put your finger and then write ____.
- Look how nice that looks when it's not so big.
- What do you need to do?
- You never put loose paper in your desk.
- Latisha, I'm giving your name to Miss Barnes to call your family. I'm not calling anymore.
- What story has that thing that you cut down a tree with?
- Yesterday, Denise _____ so fast that no one could catch her. It starts with an /r/.
- What thing with paint in it rhymes with ran?
- When you grow up, Denel, you're going to be a . . .
- Congratulations! Is this beautiful or what? Everyone brought their homework.
- Denel, you're going to have a beautiful week.
- You just wasted a minute of our time.
- Starting tomorrow, I'm going to make a paper with adding and subtracting mixed up.
- Shaquilla, you're looking at the word on the board since I don't have letters on my face.
- (Interruption with a knock at the door.) I'm not getting that when I'm in the middle of a sentence.
- Keep your eyes closed because your opinion counts, not your friend's.

Diaries

ERIC: We haven't much discussed what children put in their diaries every day to this point. We only have two rules for diary writing: write the date for each entry written and write an entry every day, and so, for the most part, children mark the page in whatever way they want. Let's look at some of the diaries we have in February.

Diary descriptions:

- Numbers: 12, 3, 9 – 6 = 3, some pencil abstracts; on the back: letters: tAMePOD /Dr2
- Letters: Tet? 2 t MY / me; Numbers: 9–17, 0000000; on the back: Te 2 t me2 rNM
- Numbers: 94; pencils marks all over the page; on the back: a girl and a boy smiling, boy wears a crown; a worm and the numbers: 180000000000 and 12000000
- Many pencil marks all over page; some flowers; letters: F B n e (randomly around); numbers: 3; on the back: letters: MOA; numbers: 10 – 7 = 3; pencil marks all over page
- Numbers: 9 6 3; 3/9632; letters: te?r; pencil marks all over page; on the back: pencil marks all over page; numbers: 6; letters: ? o T M e 2 y / M N
- Letters: tleRCOWM; numbers: 15, 100, 75; three crossed circles; on the back: pencil marks all over page; eight smiley faces
- Letters: WmeA; a house done in pencil; on the back: numbers: 1445 — =7, 24 – = 18; letters: Ve2; a house
- A sun and a house with windows on roof; on the back: a house with one window on roof
- Letters: Vne2MeSH / Fe; on the back: numbers: 2000, 189
- Letters: VeiWM; on the back: Feb282000; letters: Wme2VA
- Pencil marks all over page and a house in the middle; on the back: a car; numbers: 800000000; letters: ANDY (?)
- Pencil marks all over page and a house in the middle; on the back: letters Feb29; numbers: 2000 – 25 = 1975; 24, 25
- A house; letters: haao; on the back: numbers: 6 2 3 = 11; 6 2 + 3 = 11; 623 = 11; a penciled house

Letters, numbers, and shapes seem to be the most salient features, particularly those that relate to our daily lessons. There are a few attempts at pictures, as well. However, just as often, we just see zigzagged pencil marks across the page. Furthermore, even though there are slightly more numbers and letters in the diaries than we'd found in October, the diaries are for the most part the same throughout the year. Why might this be? I'm not sure with the information we have that we can draw any certain conclusions, but I do have one hunch. I'm wondering if the children are merely warming up each day, much as a symphony does with scales or athletes do with stretches. Could it be that children are loosening their muscles and slowly getting into the flow of the day by going through some rhythmic exercises that help them focus, and the effort of connecting a pencil to a piece of paper then helps them gear up for the task at hand? I hope so, but without conducting a separate study, I'm not really sure if we can make that conclusion or not.

However, there is a further reason I speculate that this is a warm-up. We often observe that children choose the same story over and over. Families often have to read the same story again and again, and children ask for the same story day after day and night after night. Well, one Friday night, Nina and I were having dinner when we brought up this question. And we discussed these issues, pretty much as I've just listed for you here. After dinner, Nina went to her Greek class held downtown, and we agreed to meet the next morning for coffee.

When we met Nina said, "Eric, Eric, I've been dying to tell you what happened last night. You won't believe it." I'll let Nina tell the rest of the story here.

NINA: Yes, I do remember what I realized so clearly after my Greek lesson—I always chose to first read a piece of text that I could read fluently before attempting new material. I guess I was warming up and easing slowly into the more challenging task ahead. I also remember doing this when I began to learn Russian. Even now as a almost fluent speaker of Russian I usually read a familiar poem or two before attacking a never-before-seen piece of literature.

Curriculum

ERIC: Just after the starting bell one early February morning, the school announcements for the day begin. Miss Barnes, the principal, issues the daily math problem. Most children have already begun their diary. Some of the children try Miss Barnes's math problem. Others, however, continue writing in their diaries.

Darrin draws a Christmas tree. Denise tries to put letters together, especially Darrin's name, copying one letter at a time. Darrin erases some of the wrong letters. Darrin, himself, is writing in a new notebook. Denise writes from the side to form her letters. Shaquilla concentrates alone, copying small letters. She has trouble placing the letters on the lines, but Nina helps her with a starting place. Danielle and Christian argue over an eraser. Larry is in the bathroom, and we can hear him singing the ABC song.

Nina sees that no one has signed up for sharing stories. Cal volunteers to practice reading in front of the class. As I write my notes on all these events, Latisha, who is sitting next to me, looks at my notebook and comments, "You need to skip lines."

Writing Process

During writing process, Tommesha is coloring a folder. Marc and Darrius have started their own makeshift writing process with Marc as an editor and Darrius as a storyteller. Jarrell and Denise are working together, as are Latisha and Felicity. Damine looks at two books on his desk, one with a picture of a cheeseburger and the other with a picture of a pit bull. Then he tells Danielle a story about a dog eating a cheeseburger.

NINA: The children are working hard on their writing pieces, and their stories are becoming more developed. All my young authors understand that fictional pieces have a problem and solution and most of them easily create these. Children who need to be supported in this area are conferred with during revision of a draft they want to publish. Let's listen:

Nina: Hi Chris, I see you signed up for editing. Are you ready?

Chris: Yep.

Nina: So this is the story you want to publish?

Chris: Yeah, it's about church.

Nina: Oh. Do you go to church?

Chris: Yes, with my grandma.

Nina: Oh, I go to church with my son. So is your grandmother a character in your story?

Chris: No, a cat.

Nina: Wow, a cat in church! I can't wait to hear it. Read it to me.

Chris: "One day I went to church and we sang 'Lift Every Voice.' Then a cat came in."

Nina: You're finished?

Chris: Yep.

Nina: Well, can we think of a problem? (No response.) What is the cat going to do in church?

Chris: I don't know.

Nina: Well, just think about it. You're the author, so you can make the cat do anything you want it to do. Raise your hand when you think of something and I'll come back and help with editing. Remember, think about a problem and then a solution to the problem.
(Three minutes later.)

Chris: I got the problem.

Nina: What?

Chris: The people are going to scream.

Nina: Really? Then what?

Chris: The cat's going to start singing and the people will laugh.
Nina: That's funny!! So the people aren't afraid anymore?
Chris: No, because the cat sang.
Nina: So, you have a problem—the people are afraid—and a solution—the cat sang and they weren't afraid anymore. Great! Now read it to me so I can edit it.
Chris: "One sunny day . . ."
Nina: Wow! I like how you added the word "sunny" so we know what kind of day it is! Go on—
Chris: "One sunny day I went to the church and we sang 'Lift Every Voice.' Then a cat came in the church and people screamed, 'Ahhh, it's a cat!'"
Nina: So, should I put an exclamation mark here?
Chris: Yeah.
Nina: Why?
Chris: Because the people are screaming.
Nina: Okay, go on.
Chris: "The cat started to sing 'Lift Every Voice.' Yes, it's a cat. It can sing too. Everybody laughed."
Nina: Ha! Ha! I would laugh too if I heard a cat sing. So what's the title of your story?
Chris: "The Church Cat."
Nina: Oh! I like that you have the setting and your main character in the title. Did you sign up to share?
Chris: Yeah!
Nina: I bet your friends are going to love it! Go get publishing paper!

Isn't that the cutest story? I think I say that about all their stories! Do you see how I just needed to push Chris a bit to include a problem and solution? She had it in her head but just needed to be nudged a little. Because the children are so immersed in literacy work it usually takes only a question or two to help them connect to the elements needed in a particular piece. Remember, we are talking about literacy all day, so my students have an amazing amount of input to work with. Let's hear the TAG session for "The Church Cat" and then we'll talk more about some of the literary skills deepened in February.

Chris: T: Tell what you like.
Shaquilla: I like when the cat sang "Lift Every Voice" because that's my favorite song.
Nina: Thank you for telling us why you liked it, Shaquilla. You didn't make Chris have to ask you, "Why?" Go ahead, Chris.

Chris:	Another T: Tell what you like.
Virginia:	I like the cat.
Chris:	Why?
Virginia:	They're nice.
Chris:	Okay, A: Ask questions.
Danielle:	Why did the cat go in the church?
Chris:	Because he heard the people singing. Another A: Ask questions.
Nina:	Let me ask the class something. Is this story fiction or nonfiction?
Andre:	Fiction.
Nina:	Why?
Andre:	Because cats really can't sing a song.
Nina:	And why does that make this story fiction?
Andre:	Because fiction means fake.
Nina:	Yes, fiction means fake. What else does fiction mean?
Denise:	Not real.
Nina:	Yes, not real. Anything else?
Latisha:	Like pretend.
Nina:	Okay! That word reminds me of a poem we know. Can anyone guess what poem I'm thinking about? (No response.) Let me hum it for you. (Nina hums.)
Aaron:	"Invitation"?
Nina:	Yes, I was thinking about when Shel Silverstein wrote, "If you're a pretender come sit by my fire for we have some flax golden tales to spin." Oh! I just did G, give ideas, suggestions, and connections. I connected to a poem. As long as we're talking about it let's all stand up and recite it together. (All recite "Invitation" by Shel Silverstein.) Great! Isn't it cool how we can do poetry and writing process together? Chris, why don't you do one more G?
Chris:	G: Give ideas, suggestions, and connections.
Shaquilla:	I connect to nonfiction.
Nina:	Why?
Shaquilla:	Because it's the opposite of fiction.
Nina:	Do you like to write nonfiction?
Shaquilla:	Sometimes—like about the planets.
Nina:	Oh, yeah, most of the books we took out of the library were nonfiction because they were about real things, not fake—the planets. Raise your hand if you like nonfiction books. Raise your hand if you like fiction books. Raise your hand if you like both. Okay, we definitely all like books! Let's give Chris a hand. Who's next?

The children continue to work on the major skill areas all authors work on. Do you notice how many elements I touch on even in my short conversation with Chris? Let's look at it again. Well, we definitely focused on problem and solution, but we also touched on other areas like adjectives, use of exclamation mark, main character, and setting. Do you see how these authors really begin to understand and use what they need? While my children might not yet know the formal word "adjective" they definitely know how to use the concept.

In the larger conversation the concept of fiction is developed as the children are pushed to come up with synonyms. I like how I jump off from Latisha's word "pretend" into the poem. I love when I do that kind of stuff. It is fun, and keeps the conversation vibrant and fast-paced. These links also help intensify the learning experience because of the physical movement and plain excitement of it all! Do you see how Shaquilla took my lead as she connected to nonfiction? Notice, too, that I help everyone become involved with the concepts of fiction and nonfiction as they raise their hands to show their preferences. With a little here and there all the children will soon be striving to make their own connections.

Let me share some of the pieces written in February. I am sure you will notice how developed the children's stories have become. Enjoy!

The Big Giant Hotdog by Tindale
One day I saw a big giant hotdog. When I took it home I ate a little piece. Then the hotdog came alive. He said, "You can't eat another piece. No more pieces." My mama wanted to see it. She said, "Let me get a bite." Then the hotdog said, "No, no, no!"

I'm Sorry by Felicity
Once upon a time my sister was playing with me. Then I hit her mouth and her tongue started bleeding. My mama put a paper towel in her mouth. I said, "I'm sorry."

The Dead Lion by Alexander
Once there was a lion. He was trying to scare me. Then he chased me and he ate me up. Then I got a knife and cut him open. I got out and the lion died.

The Birthday Party by Denise
One day it was my sister's birthday. She was nine. She ate all the cake. Then she was dancing and she fell. Everybody laughed. She laughed too.

The Dead Cat by Denise
One night I went outside and saw a dead cat. I called Christian, "Come here. Go call my mom because I see a dead cat." She called my mom and my mom took the cat to the hospital. They checked it and it was really alive. Me and Mom took it home. We named it Missy.

A Rainy Day by Denel
One night there was a boy. He went home and it was dark and raining. He had a hole in his roof and water was falling in his house. A lot of water flooded the house. He opened the door and the water went out.

School by Virginia
I like reading and playing in school. School is fun.

My Friend by Virginia
One day Christian came to my house. We played with toys. It was fun.

The Cat by Virginia
One day the cat died. A man got a gun and he shot the cat. Poor cat!

The Party by Virginia
One night Christian had a party. It was fun. We got wet in the pool. We got something to eat. Dr. Zaragoza came to the party. We were happy. We went home.

The Chasing Guinea Pig by Jarrell
One day Christian went to the store to buy stuff for a party. The party was for Dr. Zaragoza. It was a nice party. Suddenly, my guinea pig started talking. He said, "You all better get out of my house." The guinea pig started chasing them. They ran out of the house. Then they came back and gave him candy and he was friendly.

Skateboarding by Darrius
I was home and I was practicing skateboarding so I could be good at it. I had to practice with my helmet because if you fall you'll bust your head. You might need knee pads too because you might scrape your knees. I scraped my knee but I still love skateboarding.

The Monster by Darrius

The monster was by my window and I got out of my bed and got a piece of wood. Then I banged the window with the wood and the monster fell. Then he was dead and I went back to sleep.

Super Glue by Aaron

One day me and my brother went to school. In school he spilled super glue on the floor and the teacher stepped in it. She screamed and fell. They said, "Are you okay?" She took off her shoes and she walked. She cut the shoes off the floor. My brother was sorry and he never did it again.

The Hungry Dinosaur by Demeatric

We were in a dinosaur place. We hit a dinosaur with a piece of pot. He woke up and he ate us. Then I took a stick and opened his mouth. Then me and Darrius got out and never went to that place again.

The Friendly Fish by Danielle

One day me and Denise went fishing. We saw a fish in the water. We caught it. It jumped on my face. Then Denise started laughing and I started laughing. The fish started laughing. The fish became our friend and he played a fishing game with us. Then he went back into the water. Then we went in the water and we swam with him. Every Saturday we went to swim and play with him.

The Rainy Night by Jamal

One night I was walking down the street and it started to rain. It was lightning, too. I got really wet and I was scared, too. So I ran home as fast as I could. The next time I go out at night I'm going to take my umbrella with me.

The Scared Dinosaur by Jamal

One day Ms. Trunchbull was looking behind the school. She saw a dinosaur. She said, "What is this dinosaur doing behind this school?" Then he ran away because she yelled so loud.

So what do you notice about some of these stories? What similarities or differences do you see? Can you see some of the concepts we've been working on illustrated in some of the stories? One of the first things that jump out at me are the titles. Almost every title is three words long, contains a main character and a word that describes that main character. Can you just hear me scaffold these titles? Listen as I finish with editing and ask the author about the title:

Nina: So, Jamal, what's the title of your story? (No response.) What's your story about?

Jamal: A dinosaur.

Nina: Yes, good. So can you think of a title?

Jamal: The dinosaur.

Nina: Can you add another word to tell more about the dinosaur? (No response.) How does the dinosaur feel in this story?

Jamal: Scared.

Nina: So what word could you add to your title?

Jamal: "Scared." "The Scared Dinosaur."

Nina: Yes, "scared" describes your dinosaur to us. I understand why he's scared! Would you be scared of Miss Trunchbull?

Jamal: Yeah! She's so mean!

Nina: Do you think your dinosaur would be scared of Miss Honey?

Jamal: No.

Nina: Why not?

Jamal: Because she's nice.

Nina: Yes, she is. Let's ask the class about Miss Trunchbull and Miss Honey. Everyone, let's come together for a minute. Thank you, Christian, you look ready to listen. Thank you, Jarrell. Jamal and I are talking about Miss Trunchbull because the dinosaur in his story is scared of her. Why do you think the dinosaur is scared of her?

Virginia: She's mean.

Nina: What makes her mean? What does she do that is mean?

Denise: She screams.

Shaquilla: She throws children out the window!

Roderick: She calls children bad names.

Nina: Yes, she does a lot of things that are mean! What about Honey? What kind of person is Miss Honey? Remember we talked about this before—about how authors describe their characters.

Latisha: Miss Honey is nice.

Nina: Okay, she's nice. Let's think of other words to describe her.

D'Andre: "Good."

Christian: "Pretty."

Nina: Yes, those are other words that describe Miss Honey. Why do you think Roald Dahl named her Miss Honey? (No response.) Think

	about it. Raise your hand if you have ever tasted honey? When did you taste honey, Alex?
Alex:	When I was sick my mother put it in my tea.
Nina:	Yes, some people put honey in their tea. How did the honey make the tea taste?
Alex:	Like sweet.
Nina:	Yes, honey makes things taste sweet. We can also call a person sweet when they are nice. Whose mother calls them honey? Yes, Darrin, I always hear your mother call you and your brother "honey." And what does your Nana call you, Christian?
Christian:	Sometimes she calls me "sugar."
Nina:	Oh, because sugar is sweet! Larry, is your dog Sugar a sweet dog?
Larry:	Yeah, she always licks me.
Nina:	And you're a sweet person, right, Christian? Just like Miss Honey? So I guess Roald Dahl could have called Miss Honey Miss Sugar! What else could he have called her?
Roderick:	Miss Sweet.
Nina:	Ha! That's true. Does your mother ever call you "sweetheart," Roderick?
Roderick:	Sometimes.
Nina:	And what nice words do I use for my students?
Danielle:	"Honey."
Nina:	That's true. I use the word "honey" all the time. Don't I sometimes call the girls "missy"?
Denise:	Yes! You always call me that! And Aubrey, too.

I love this kind of lesson because it's just so filled with connections. I love going from a child's story, to a piece of literature, to the children's own experiences, and then back to the examination of the piece of literature in a different way. These kinds of conversations really enable children to internalize the concepts under discussion because the concepts are looked at from many different angles. Because they are also linked to the children's own life (which is already internalized) they are brought into the children's own worldview more easily. I guess some might call this connecting the new information to something already familiar. I think it's more complex than that, though, and doesn't happen hierarchically. It really isn't just a matter of naming and practicing the skill. Notice that I don't label what we are doing as "character traits" but just dive into the conversation. This depth of learning happens in a literate community whose members are totally immersed and engaged in purposeful, personal reading and writing.

Most of the children's stories contain a problem and solution, but naturally the story elements included depend on the individual child. Look at Virginia's stories now. Remember, Virginia in September needed to work on verbal skills and we worked with her by scaffolding one-word answers through a step-by-step process of repetition and positive recognition. Inclusion in all activities of the classroom also gives Virginia equal access to all information and concepts shared, and this enormous amount of input moves her along. Now, as you can see from her stories, she speaks in full sentences, tells a simple story, and shows evidence of a beginning understanding of problem— "Poor cat!"

What is most powerful to me, though, is the happy tone of most of Virginia's stories. She includes herself in a party, has a best friend, eats magic bread, and even her monster is a good monster. She feels secure, safe, and is happy to be part of our community. That is a blessing.

Looking back at the children's pieces, do you notice that they are a mixture of fiction, nonfiction, and both? I think that children using characters from other stories (if you haven't guessed, Miss Trunchbull is a character in Roald Dahl's *Matilda*) exemplifies how alive our literacy program is! Larry later also uses Miss Trunchbull as a character in one of his stories. We also talk about Matilda as if she is a student in our classroom—well she is, really. Isn't she? She's with us every day as we read about her and live what she lives through. My adult students think I'm crazy when I talk about a character we are studying as if he or she is real. We were reading *The Catcher in the Rye* when one student felt he had to remind me: "Nina, remember, Holden Caulfield is not real! He is a fictional character!" I guess the questions I pose about the characters in our books (What would Matilda say if she were here right now? Would Miss Trunchbull let a child do that? So, what would Holden say about that?) keep them alive and keep the program alive. And what's wrong with that?

TAG

By February the children can really run our TAG sharing sessions on their own. To reinforce this independence and interdependence on each other I sometimes do not interrupt at all. I also recognize their growing ability with comments like:

- Wow, I can see you don't need me at all, do you? You know how to do this all by yourself!
- I bet if a substitute teacher came in here she wouldn't have to do a thing. You all know exactly what you need to do.
- You don't need my help. You all know what to do next. I'll wait until you remember. Help each other!

What's interesting is that the few times I've been absent the substitutes have commented that the children were the most well behaved during writing process. Why do you think this might be? I think that the structure of the program has really enabled them to be independent and confident about knowing what to do and when. I think, also, that the work is so meaningful for them that there is absolutely no reason for them to misbehave. I jokingly tell a substitute when the children begin to get out of hand just do writing process. They'll love it.

ERIC: You can see how the approaches toward story writing are incorporated into math. Remember Nina shared some of the math problems the children wrote in December? Let's look at some of the story problems the children have come up with this month:

There were nine children playing ball and three went away. There were six left. Demeatric

There were four happy faces and one went away because it was sad. So there were only three happy faces left. Jarrell

There were two children and one died. Now there is only one left. Virginia

One day there were four flowers. Then one day one other flower grew. Now there are five flowers. Marc

There were five heart balloons. Then five more came. Now there are ten. Latisha

There were three clouds and one floated away. Now there are two left. D'Andre

There were four cats and one was alone and he went with four cats. Now there are five cats. Justin

There were seven stars, but three were covered by clouds so there were only four showing. Larry

There were four kitty cats and one more came. Now there were five all together. They were happy. Jamal

If we examine the word problems written by the children this year we see a number of interesting phenomena. Let's have a look at the following chart of these math story problems:

Name	Number of Sentencs	Number of Words per Sentence	Topic of the Math Problem	Included Illustrations	Included Math Problem?
Alexander	4	5, 3, 2, 5	Dancing ladies	Dancing ladies	Yes
Demeatric	2	10, 4	Children playing ball		No
Danielle	3	8, 8, 5	Kittens, baby crying	Kittens	Yes
Roderick	6	10, 6, 5, 9, 3, 4	Kids playing Hide and Seek, bunnies adding kids and bunnies together;	Bunnies, friends	Yes
Darrius	2	12, 5	Two people eaten by alligator	People; then no people	Yes
Jarrell	2	13, 8	Happy faces; one becomes sad	Happy faces and a sad face	Yes
Tommesha	3	8, 7, 5	Heart; two get broken	Hearts (two with zigzags)	Yes
Virginia	2	7, 6	Two girls; one dies	Two girls, one circled	Yes
Marc	3	6, 7, 5	Flowers; one grows		No
Denise	2	13, 6	Children; mom calls one home		No
Andre	2	8, 5	Hearts	Hearts	Yes
Justin	2	14, 5	Cats; one is lonely and joins others	Cats; joining cat marked with an arrow	Yes
D'Andre	2	8, 5	Clouds; one floats away	Clouds (one with an X in it)	Yes
Latisha	3	5, 4, 4	Balloons; others come	Balloons	Yes
Cal	6	7, 5, 8, 7, 7, 6	Big brother, sequence: blasts music, police come, doesn't cut it down, police take brother to a crazy house	Person, circled with an arrow going out.	Yes

Table continued on next page.

Name	Number of Sentencs	Number of Words per Sentence	Topic of the Math Problem	Included Illustrations	Included Math Problem?
Jamal	3	9, 6, 3	Kitty cats, one comes		Yes
Christian	2	8, 6	Cats, some go away		No
Shaquilla	4	15, 8, 5, 7	Children playing, others join the game	Children	Yes
Larry	1	16	Stars; covered by clouds	Stars; three circled with arrow out	Yes
Typical	**3.33**	**6.67**			

The common baseline math structure seems to be: There are number (nouns) and number (verb). Now there are -----s. *Here's an example. There are 4 crows and 2 fly away. Now there are two crows.* Some of the common verbs used within the problems include *come, cover, take, float (away), call, eat, grow, die, hide,* and *jump (on).* Clearly these verbs lean us toward a subtraction problem, while others take us to an addition problem.

Silent Reading

NINA: Now the children can easily read silently for thirty minutes or so. Often, though, because of time restraints, silent reading is cut shorter. When this happens I hear groans and comments like, "Oh, five more minutes, please!" I understand totally because I want five more minutes, too! I think that part of the reason for our great success with silent reading is that I am as passionate about it as they are. I always have my own personal reading material every day and relish the opportunity to read. By February silent reading takes place right after lunch. I think this time slot has also contributed to its success. By the time we are finished with lunch we are very ready to relax. The lunchroom is usually very loud and very hectic, so to enter the classroom and be allowed to relax and not talk is a real luxury. Actually, when you think about it, not talking in my classroom is a real treat. I'm sure you've noticed how interactive we all are! Once I was sitting with my children during lunch and I asked Denise, "Why aren't you talking to your friend next to you?" She answered, "Dr. Zaragoza, I'm tired of talking!"

Talk! Talk! Talk! If we're not talking about what we're writing and reading, we're talking about the planets. And if we're not talking about that, we're talking about a poem or reciting it. And if we're not talking about poetry or reciting it, we're rehearsing our drama production or singing. And if we're not doing all that, we're helping someone do it all! Exhilarating but exhausting, and silent reading comes at the perfect time!

ERIC: Up to now, we've emphasized stories and books as our means of reading or understanding that reading leads us to entertainment. However, there are many other kinds of reading (and writing) that we may wish to start including in our library. Now, I can imagine you're saying, "Well, apart from the library, where am I going to get those materials? I don't have much money and books don't grow on trees, Eric!" Fortunately, the list I'm going to share with you contains things that are essentially free. Imagine bringing any of the following items and placing them in your reading library, as recommended by Pat Killian (personal communication 1999) and H. Douglas Brown (1994), and placing them in your reading library:

Advertisements	Cinquaines	Headlines	Paragraphs
Anecdotes	Comic strips	Horoscopes	Phrases
Anthems	Complaints	How-to-do-its	Plays
Apologies	Conversations	Instructions	Poems
Articles	Data sheets	Interviews	Policies
Autobiographies	Definitions	Introductions	Polls
Awards	Descriptions	Invitations	Postcards
Ballads	Diagrams	Itineraries	Predictions
Beauty tips	Dialogues	Jokes	Problems
Bedtime stories	Diaries	Jump rope rhymes	Questionnaires
Billboards	Dictations	Labels	Questions
Biographies	Diets	Legends	Receipts
Bio-poems	Directions	Letters	Recipes
Blurbs	Dramas	Lists	Reports
Book jackets	Exclamations	Love notes	Rules
Booklets	Explanations	Lyrics	Schedules
Books	Fables	Magazines	Sentences
Bulletins	Fairy tales	Manuals	Signs
Bumper stickers	Fantasies	Math problems	Songs
Calendar quips	Forms	Memories	Summaries
Cartoons	Fortunes	Menus	Thank you notes
Cereal boxes	Free writes	Nursery rhymes	Timelines
Certificates	Game rules	Observations	Travelogues
Chain stories	Graffiti	Odes	Verses
Character sketches	Greeting cards	Opinions	Weather report
Charts	Grocery lists	Pamphlets	

Can you see how this list relates to reading as real life? Often we look at reading only in terms of being able to negotiate a novel or news. But isn't it equally as important to be able to read, or at least recognize, these snippets of language? And if they're so short and sweet, why wouldn't we want to include them in our reading library? And by the way, this list isn't complete. Are there any other elements you'd like to add to what we've got here?

Finally, at this point, we've been placing the burden of gathering reading library materials on you. But is there any rule that states that you have to be your only resource? In fact, to suggest such would violate the philosophy of constructivist philosophy with respect to teaching. Who is the most valuable resource in a socioconstructivist view? The children are. What kinds of materials could the children bring? And what kinds of materials could the children's families bring?

Reading Discussion Groups

NINA: I think you have a good idea of how our discussion groups happen. Remember the guiding questions we use? Remember the contexualized lessons I shared with you a few months ago? Well, this is all still happening in February, but with much less intervention from me. The children do not need to be prompted as much to help each other form groups or to begin conversations. I, of course, circulate and facilitate discussions, but there are times when I let them go along on their own. This really can happen, too, because the children have such a grasp of what is expected of them and what needs to be discussed. Doesn't this make sense, though? They've had months and months of contextualized lessons and understand that whatever we talk about in writing process or reading aloud is usually touched upon again during reading discussion:

Nina: So when you get into discussion groups what will you talk about?
Shaquilla: Like what are the characters like.
Nina: Okay, tell me more.
Shaquilla: If they're sweet or mean or scared.
Nina: Yes, what kind of personality the characters have. Someone tell me about a character in a book they're reading.
Jarrell: One character is Brother Bear.
Nina: Oh, you're reading a Berenstain Bear book. So what kind of bear is Brother Bear?
Jarrell: He likes to learn.
Nina: What is he learning?
Jarrell: To ride a bike.
Nina: Oh! So what would you call a person who likes to learn? (No response.) What would you call a person who likes to read?
Larry: A reader.
Nina: And a person who writes?
Felicity: A writer.
Nina: So, Jarrell what would you call a bear that likes to learn?
Jarrell: A learner.

Nina:	And does Brother Bear try hard?
Jarrell:	Yeah, he keeps trying.
Nina:	A person who keeps trying can be called what?
D'Andre:	A tryer.
Nina:	Okay, another word for that is "persistent." Everyone say "persistent."
All:	Persistent.
Nina:	Who else do we know who is persistent? (No response.) Who tries and tries until they get something?
Darrin:	Andre.
Nina:	What do you mean?
Darrin:	He keeps trying to read until he can read.
Nina:	Okay, Andre is very persistent when he reads. How is Matilda persistent? (No response.) What does she keep doing until she gets it right?
Aubrey:	Using her magic.
Nina:	Yes, remember how persistent she was? She kept practicing until she could make the things move with her mind. So when you go into your discussion groups talk about someone in your story and what kind of character they are.

Families and Field Trips

The children have many more books to talk about in February because our class now makes monthly field trips to the local public library. These trips are such a pleasure and we all look forward to them. They are not complicated, they are free, and we get to walk there together. It is so much fun to walk through the neighborhood, see some family members walking on the street, and see where everyone lives: "Look, Dr. Zaragoza, that's where my grandma lives!" "Look, there's my church! Larry comes to that church with me too!" "That's where my auntie works!"

This monthly event also gives our schedule variety, becomes part of our schedule, and enriches our literacy program. The librarian usually reads two or three books aloud—with great expression and theatrics! I think it is just so powerful for the children to see others as passionate about literacy as we are. It also helps them to see that literacy can happen anywhere and everywhere—not just in the classroom. The librarian loves it too, and because we visit every month she gets to know the children and encourages them to visit after school and on Saturdays, too.

After the librarian reads, the children get to borrow books with their own library cards. Can you guess some of the books they pick? Well, many run for copies of *Charlotte's Web*, *James and the Giant Peach*, *Stuart Little*, and *Matilda*. They love having a copy of one of these books for themselves. Last month I encouraged each child to get a nonfiction book about space. These books supported our field trip to the planetarium, and the books and planetarium together enabled us to write our play about the solar system. Cool!!! You'll see how all these connections come together when you read the play next month.

There are always a few family members that join us on our field trips. For some reason the families really enjoy the library trips—maybe for the same reasons I do: they're not complicated, only take about an hour, they're free, and they're easy! I love when my families can join us because it's just another opportunity to strengthen our partnership. Speaking of which, here's the monthly letter:

February 7, 2000

Dear Families,

Just a short note to let you know how everything is going. As usual, we are doing lots of learning! Almost all children know their lines from the play and we are planning the performance for the middle of March.

We had a wonderful time at the planetarium and the library last month. Please make sure that you read the library books that your child has chosen. I know you will be pleased at how your child is reading. Please continue helping them read their new word list every night.

You probably noticed that I have been sending home the same math homework for the last week or so. I will continue to do this until the children can add and subtract without using their fingers. Help them memorize the answers of these examples.

It is imperative that your child comes to school every day and on time. I am working very hard to get each child ready for first grade. If they are absent or late it will be difficult for them to be successful.

Reminders:

Please make sure that your child:
• is on the morning line by 8:15 each morning;
• completes all homework every night; and
• comes to school with two sharpened pencils every day.

**Your child also needs to bring in a hard-covered composition notebook. This notebook will be kept in school and used for writing every day.

Please be assured that I am working very hard to make sure that your child is ready both academically and socially for first grade. A strong foundation in kindergarten will influence your child's success in school. Thank you for your continued help and trust.

Sincerely,
Dr. Nina Zaragoza

I'm sure you now can understand why I am so adamant about children being in school every day and on time. They would miss so much talking!

March

That's why we call it the solar system
because solar means sun.
Oh! I remember we read that in one
of our books!

NINA: So it's the beginning of March and we have a full month ahead of us. Usually March is a long month with not many days off. It is also a time of year when in many parts of the country the same kind of weather is dragging on and people are ready for a change. In March, too, many teachers and children are feeling tired and perhaps a bit bored with the now very familiar schedule. This is the time when I think it is especially important to keep our classrooms vibrant and alive. What better time, then, to do another drama production? Remember how the excitement of the last production carried over even to the next month? So right in the middle of the month we will perform our play. That will keep us going, don't you think? What also keeps us excited is receiving letters from our pen pals. And another new element in our classroom is a bear called Venus! Here's the family letter to give you an idea of our March plans, and then we'll get into the details:

March 6, 2000

Dear Families,

Hello! I hope you are all well. As usual, we are working hard in school and are learning new things every day. We are almost ready to perform our play for you and have scheduled the performance for *March 17 at 9:00 a.m. in the cafeteria.* We hope that every family will be able to come. We also invite you to our cast party after the play.

Thank you for helping your children take care of the public library books. As you know we went to the library again this month and got new books. Please help them read these books and pick out familiar words. Most children are also taking home red or yellow reading books. Please read these every night so that they can progress rapidly to the next level. Also, please continue helping them read their word list every night.

We will continue to work on addition and subtraction until all children know the basic facts without using their fingers. We are also reviewing telling time ("o'clock" and "thirty"); which number is bigger/smaller; and the value of a penny, nickel, dime, and quarter. Please help your children with these concepts during your regular activities; i.e., counting change, telling time, etc.

We have finished reading *Stuart Little* and are well into *Matilda*. Ask your children about Matilda and her family. They will have lots to tell you! Ask them, too, about the stories they have written! They are all excellent authors! We've learned some new poems, too! (Ask them to recite "A Negro Speaks of Rivers.")

Reminders:
Please make sure that your child:
• is on the morning line by 8:15 each morning;
• completes all homework every night; and
• comes to school with two sharpened pencils every day.

May you have a peaceful and productive month!
Nina Zaragoza

I realize as I share this letter with you that I guess I'm a bit of a nag! I am always reminding my families of things. I think they mostly appreciate it, though. I think that these monthly letters help my families feel safe because they are predictable, clear, and concrete. They know what's happening in our community and they are given clear direction on how they can help their children each month. I wish I would have gotten letters like these from my own children's teachers—especially in middle school. There were times when I had no idea what was happening within my children's classrooms. It would have been nice!

Anyway, when I happen to forget the monthly letter for my families one or more of the families remind me as they drop off or pick up their children. Actually, even the children remind me. Did I mention that when I have these letters ready the children and I read them together before they are sent home? Why not? They're part of the family too, right? Shouldn't they know what is being written about them and their community? Sometimes, too, I ask what they want me to share in these letters. Remember, they are becoming expert letter writers since they write at least once a month to their pen pals.

Which reminds me, I forgot to share some of the letters from last month with you. As I read them over I see the relationship between the fourth graders and kindergartners developing around academic and social issues. These younger and older children connect easily academically because they are involved in the same kind of community. The fourth graders' teacher, Debbie Feria, was one of my undergraduate students and she also did her student teaching in my classroom, so the philosophical foundations and curricula of our classrooms are similar. The children recite many of the same poems ("In my class I'm doing a poem called 'Mother to Son'") and sing some of the same songs ("Yeah, I like 2 Pac even though he is dead.") They also write and perform drama productions ("We aren't doing a play on the planets. We are going to do a play and I hope it's called 'Haunted Millenium'.") They are involved daily in writing process including TAG, silent reading and reading discussion groups, and reading-aloud activities ("In my class we are reading a book called *Roll of Thunder, Hear My Cry*. Mildred S. Taylor wrote the book.") and the majority of their letters to each other now focus on what they are reading and writing:

Dear Melanie,
I wrote a book called *The Monster*. It was blue. Do you write books? What books do you like? Write back soon, love, Virginia (Name written by herself with a little teacher guidance.)

Dear Elizabeth,
I do know Jarrell. He's in my class. I think your favorite pokemon is Picachu. I read *Rosie's Walk* yesterday. I wrote a book called *Math Homework*. I know a lot of poems. I know all of them by heart. Please write back soon, love, Andre

March 17, 2000
Dear Roderick
How are you? I'm glad that you are getting good grades. I have heard that the books *Stuart Little* and *Matilda* are good books. I'm sure you will like the book *Matilda*. In school we are doing many projects. We are studying the Great Depression. Are you studying anything in particular? Yes, I do like sports. My favorites are tennis and basketball. Please write back soon.
Your pen pal,
Daniela

March 20, 2000
Dear Larry,
First of all, what is the story *Rainbow Fish* like? The books I like are mystery like code master. It teaches you codes of all kinds. One is the *The Popsicle Stick Code*. But my favorite is *The Shadow Code*. Be careful! One letter might have the message on the bottom!
Sincerely, Joshua

March 22, 2000
Dear Melissa,
My name is Demeatric. I am new to this class. We went to the library
yesterday. I liked the new books I got. Write soon, Demeatric
*Damine went to a new school

Dear Michael,
Do you do silent reading and reading discussion groups? Do you go
to the library? I went to the library and we got library books that we
wanted. We hope you write back soon.
Love, Christian

Once in a while the fourth graders remember that their pen pals are only in
kindergarten so they give them some encouragement, advice, and a look into
fourth grade and the future. Here are some examples found in the March pen
pal letters:

- I'm very proud of you on how you are writing. You are writing your
  name better.
- Your writing is coming out perfect and your handwriting and your draw-
  ing great!
- Your handwriting is improving a lot!
- I hope you are getting good grades.
- I don't like taking tests. Here in the fourth grade things are a little hard.
- We are practicing a big test called the F-CAT!
- When I grow up I want to be a paleontologist. That's a person who stud-
  ies old things left by ancient people.

Can you believe there is also a letter in our play? I'm sure you can:

Our Solar System
Scene 1: Classroom
Danielle: We haven't been on a field trip for a while.
Alexander: Where should we go?
Roderick: Let's go travel through space!
Aaron: Yeah! Let's go!
Darrin: We'll travel around the sun so we can see the planets of our solar
                    system.
Darrius: That's why we call it the solar system, because solar means sun.
Aubrey: Oh! I remember! We read that in one of our books.
Jarrell: How are we gonna get there?

Tommesha: Well, just like the astronauts, we need a spaceship.

Darryl: We should write a letter to the space center and ask if we can use one.

Virginia: They call that place NASA.

Marc: Let's go write the letter!

Scene 2: Classroom

Denel: Here's the letter.

Denise: Let's read it together to make sure it makes sense.

All: "Dear NASA,
"May we please use a spaceship so that we can travel to the planets of our solar system? Thank you, Kindergarten class at Little River Elementary School, Miami, Florida."

Andre: Let's hurry and mail our letter!

Scene 3: Classroom

Damine: Oh, we got our answer from NASA.

D'Andre: It says we can go to the space center and use their spaceship and suits.

Latisha: Wow! That's great! Let's get going!

Cal: I guess we should write a thank you note before we go! (Children laugh.)

Scene 4: The Moon

Jamal: Wow! Look at our moon!

Christian: Let's land there first before we travel to the planets.

Shaquilla: Okay, but let's remember to keep our helmets on because there is no air.

Larry: Wow! It's so dark!

Adell: That's because there's no air so the stars don't twinkle.

Alexander: And the sky stays black!

Danielle: But it's fun! Look how high we can jump because there's no gravity.

Roderick: Be careful. Don't fall in that crater!

Aaron: It's a little scary! Let's get going.

Scene 5: Venus

Darrin: Look, there's Venus!

Darrius: We better stay in our spaceship because it is really hot!

Aubrey: Yeah, it's so hot we would be fried!

Jarrell: It rains most of the time on Venus and the rain is poison!

Tommesha: It's getting really hot!
Virginia: It's because we're near the sun.
Darryl: The next planet is even closer to the sun.

Scene 6: Mercury
Marc: Look, there's Mercury!
Denel: Wow, it's so orange.
Denise: We definitely can't land there.
Andre: No way! We'd be roasted alive!
Damine: Yeah, like a piece of toast!
D'Andre: Or a turkey in the oven.
Latisha: Let's get out of here!

Scene 7: Sun
Cal: Look we're passing the sun!
Jamal: No! We can't look! Close your eyes!
Christian: The light of the sun can blind you!
Shaquilla: We better get going to the outer planets.

Scene 8: Mars
Larry: There's Mars.
Adell: It looks hot!
Alexander: But it's not. It's really freezing cold.
Danielle: That's good! I still feel hot from being so close to the sun.
Roderick: Let's land.
Aaron: So this is Mars.
All: Achoo!
Darrin: It's so dusty!
Darrius: Maybe we should cover our noses.
Aubrey: There's no plants or animals.
All: Achoo!
Jarrell: My asthma is killing me! Let's go back on the spaceship.

Scene 9: Jupiter
Tommesha: Here we are on Jupiter.
Virginia: It's pretty far from the sun.
Darryl: I know. Look, the sun looks so small from here.
Marc: I can hardly see it. There's so many clouds.
Denel: But look at Jupiter's moons.
Denise: Yeah, I see! Jupiter has sixteen moons. Let's count them.

All:	One, two, three, four, five, six, seven, eight, nine, ten, eleven, twelve, thirteen, fourteen, fifteen, sixteen.
Andre:	Oh, did you see that?
Damine:	It's lightning.

Scene 10: Saturn

D'Andre:	Look! My favorite planet, Saturn.
Latisha:	It's my favorite too, because I like the rings.
Cal:	Let's fly through them.
Jamal:	Oh, they're made of dust and rocks covered with ice.
All:	Wow!
Christian:	Let's hurry because the next planet is so far away.

Scene 11: Uranus

Shaquilla:	We're finally here on Uranus.
Larry:	Look, Uranus has rings too.
Adell:	Just like Saturn.
Alexander:	It's really dark!
Danielle:	Yeah, I feel like going home now.
Roderick:	Well, we only have to pass two more planets.
All:	Okay, let's go!

Scene 12: Neptune

Aaron:	Look at Neptune!
Darrin:	It's big.
Darrius:	I know but it's mostly gas and liquid so we can't land.
Aubrey:	Oh well! I want to go home anyway.
Jarrell:	Okay, okay, one more planet to go!

Scene 13: Pluto

Tommesha:	There's Pluto.
Virginia:	It's really small.
Darryl:	Yeah, it's the smallest planet in our solar system.
Marc:	It's made of all rock and it's farthest from the sun.
Denel:	Okay, we've seen all the planets and our moon and sun.
Denise:	Let's go back to our own planet now.
Andre:	Yeah, I'm hungry!
All:	Me too!

Scene 14: Earth

Damine:	Here we are! Our own planet!

D'Andre:	It's perfect because it's not too hot and not too cold.
Latisha:	And we don't have to wear spacesuits to breathe!
Cal:	And we can eat some real food!
All:	Home sweet home!

What a play! Do you see how long it is? Talk about high expectations for kindergartners! Remember the length of the last one? Do you see the growth? Look at the length of sentences and the concepts embedded in the piece:

- NASA
- solar system
- names of planets
- distance from sun, atmosphere, size, temperature, composition of each planet
- gravity
- craters
- poison rain
- inner versus outer planets
- life-supporting versus non–life-supporting planets

ERIC: Let's look at the data of this play and compare it with our first play.

	"Living Things around the World"	"Our Solar System"
Lines	72	111
Words	464	701
Number of students	23	25
Average line length (words)	6.4	6.3
Lines with 10+ words	15 of 72 or 21%	24 of 111 or 22%
Longest line	16 words	18 words

What developments do you see? First, it's longer. Each student is responsible for three or four individual lines plus eight lines they say as a group. The average line length is about the same, but the more sophisticated lines have become slightly longer. Perhaps most important, the number of words has increased by approximately 73 percent.

NINA: There are a few lines that the children always laugh at whenever and no matter how many times they are said. Can you guess which ones? The one about the thank you note makes them laugh because we are *always* writing thank you notes. The one about toast and then when D'Andre says "Or a turkey in the oven" always gets us howling. I guess it's the image! Also, when Jarrell says, "My asthma is killing me!" the children laugh and closely identify with him because many of them suffer from asthma and know how harmful dust can be.

This play is a clear illustration of our discussions of the planets. Indeed, the development of this drama production connects directly to our science curriculum. As a matter of fact, during the time of the script writing we visit the planetarium and the library and are virtually immersed in our solar system:

Nina: So everyone got at least one book about our solar system from the library. Raise your hand if you got two about the solar system. Three? Four? Wow, we are going to be reading a lot about the planets and space! Everyone hold up your favorite book about space so everyone can see. Denel what book is that?
Denel: *The Moon.*
Andre: Oh, I already read that book. It's a big book we have.
Nina: Oh yeah, I remember a few of you reading that during free learning time. Weren't you reading it too, Christian?
Christian: Yeah, it has a big picture of a crater.
Andre: It looks cool.
Nina: Tell the class something about a crater, Andre.
Andre: It's like a big hole in the ground.
Roderick: I saw one on *The Magic School Bus.*
Nina: So maybe we can put something about a crater on the moon in our play. What could we say about it? Any ideas? Oh, Denel, let's show the class a picture from your book while they're thinking.
Danielle: Maybe one of us could fall in it.
Nina: Okay, anyone else?
Darrius: And someone could throw a rope to get him out.
Nina: Okay, so you're connecting to Danielle's idea. Others?

Conversations like these happen throughout the day and I jot down the children's ideas for script development. Can you imagine how many books we have related to space? Let's use our math skills. If each child has at least two space books from the public library we have forty-eight! Many children, though, have at least three or four! That is definitely a lot of reading aloud. Much of our reading aloud during the month of script writing is from these books. In fact, the children all beg me to read their books. But you know me, I turn to the families and ask them, "Please help them read these books and pick out familiar words." Many children come in ready to read a few pages from their books themselves—so I don't have to do all the reading aloud!

While I try not to interrupt our silent reading time too much, when we have a need to find information for our play I will be more directive:

Nina:	I know we just usually read what we want during silent reading, but today could you please read your space books so we can finish up with our script? What other information do you think we need?
Shaquilla:	Like where all the planets are.
Nina:	Yes, do you have that book with the picture that shows the planets?
Shaquilla:	Yeah.
Nina:	How can you tell where each planet is?
Shaquilla:	By looking at the picture.
Nina:	I know, but can you see which planets are next to each other and which are next to the sun?
Shaquilla:	Yep.
Nina:	Okay, so that's what we need to know. Look that over and then in your reading discussion group you can talk about the order of the planets. Okay, I think we need more information on Mars. Who has a book about Mars?

So now we are using silent reading and reading discussion groups to gather the information we need to finish the script. While the children are in their smaller discussion groups I will circulate around and help them choose what we might need:

Nina:	So what are you talking about?
Aaron:	Saturn.
Aubrey:	I like Saturn because of the rings.
Nina:	Oh, maybe we can talk about our favorite planet in the play. What do you think? Virginia, what's your favorite planet?
Virginia:	Pluto.
Nina:	Why?
Virginia:	It's a dog.
Nina:	Oh! That's right, there's a dog named Pluto. But now we're talking about the planet named Pluto. Is the planet Pluto big or small? Look at the picture in your book.
Virginia:	Small.
Nina:	It's the smallest planet. Should we write that in our play?
Virginia:	Yeah.
Nina:	What else can we write about Saturn besides the rings? (No response.) Well, let's look and see what the rings are made of. Let's

see. Oh, here it is. Look, I'll point to the words, read with me. (All read and decide to use this information for our play.)
(The discussion group with Shaquilla.)

Nina: So are you looking at the picture of the solar system in Shaquilla's book?

Alex: Yeah.

Nina: So let's look and see which planet is closest to the sun.

Shaquilla: Mercury.

Nina: So how do you think it feels on Mercury? (No response.) Do you think it's hot or cold?

Shaquilla: Very, very hot!

Nina: So, why do you think it's so hot, Aaron?

Aaron: It's so close to the sun.

Nina: It is. I'm glad we're not that close to the sun! Darrius, which planet is farthest from the sun? Look at the picture.

Darrius: Pluto.

Nina: And do you think it's hot or cold on Pluto?

Darrius: Cold because it's far away.

Nina: So, Aaron, why do you think it's really dark on Pluto? (No response.) Does the sun make things light or dark?

Aaron: Light.

Nina: Yes, so do you think the sun's light reaches Pluto?

Aaron: No.

Nina: Why not?

Aaron: Because it's far.

Nina: Yes, it's very far. Would you like to live on Pluto, Darrius?

Darrius: Yes!

Nina: Why?

Darrius: Because it's a name of a dog and I like dogs!

Nina: Ha! You wouldn't be afraid because it's so dark and cold?

Darrius: Nope!

Nina: You're brave! So Shaquilla, could you please go get a paper and pencil and write the order of the planets so we can decide which ones we'll visit first and last. So make a list and start with Mercury and write them in order. Do you know what I mean?

Shaquilla: Yeah, like put number one Mercury, number two Venus.

Nina: Yes, thanks, have this group help you.

By March, all these information-gathering conversations are finished and the script is written, practiced, and almost ready for performance. As we read, reread, recite, and practice performing this play, the science concepts are being reinforced and deepened:

Nina:	So do you think we could ever have poison rain on Earth like on Venus? (No response.) Well, what do you think would make rain poison? What are some things we use that are poison? (No response.) Think about it. What are some things in your house that your family uses to clean?
D'Andre:	Ajax.
Nina:	What do we clean with that?
D'Andre:	The sink and bathtub.
Nina:	Yes, and you have to be careful that doesn't get in your eyes or mouth because it could be poison. What else?
Denise:	Bleach.
Nina:	Yes! That is very, very poisonous. Do you ever touch that, Denise?
Denise:	No! My mother puts it high so my little sister can't get it.
Nina:	That's good, and if you're mother forgets, make sure you don't touch it and remind her to put it up. So sometimes if poison gets in our dirt, water, or air it could evaporate into the atmosphere and become part of our rain. Raise your hand if you remember when we did that evaporation experiment. Demeatric wasn't here when we did that so let's tell him about it. Who wants to start? (No response.) What happens when a liquid evaporates? Well, first let's name some things that are liquids.
Alex:	Water.
Felicity:	Soda.
Darrius:	Milk.
Nina:	Demeatric, can you think of a liquid (No response.) What do you like to drink?
Demeatric:	Apple juice.
Nina:	Okay, apple juice is a liquid. So what happens when a liquid evaporates?
Darrin:	It disappears.
Nina:	Yes, we can't see it, but is it gone or does it just change?
Andre:	It changes from liquid to gas.
Nina:	Okay, so what does that mean?
Andre:	It goes into the sky—like in the clouds.
Nina:	And what happens when the clouds are full?
Danielle:	It rains.

Nina:	So when poison is in our water like the rivers and ocean and the water evaporates it could come down later in our rain. How could poison get in the rivers and ocean?
Aubrey:	Garbage?
Nina:	People do throw garbage in the water sometimes. Do you think that's good?
Aubrey:	No, it's dirty.
Nina:	Yes, that's called water pollution. Is that river by our school polluted? (No response.) Raise your hand if you know the river I'm talking about. Hey, I think that's why our school is called Little River! So is that river polluted? Dirty?
Jamal:	Yeah! Yuck. It smells.
Nina:	Also, some companies pollute the water with chemicals. Then what happens when the water evaporates with those chemicals?
Shaquilla:	It goes in the rain.
Nina:	So when this happens is the rain clean?
Andre:	No, it's like poison.
Nina:	So we need to take care of our water and air to keep it clean.

Wow, what a lot of science. And you thought I only taught writing and reading. You can see how much more we can do jumping off of this conversation—liquids, gases, solids, water cycle, environmental studies, and so on. We love it! And like everything we do, we will continue to connect and build on these concepts over time through a variety of mediums, including poetry and song. For example, a song we sing when we talk about pollution and our environment is Marvin Gaye's "What's Going On."

You might have noticed, though, that most of my poetry connects to social studies concepts and the drama productions either connect to science or social studies. When it comes to music I think most songs connect to being social (hello, goodbye, "What a Wonderful World") or social issues like pollution, or social studies—city, country, and so on). The math concepts are either included in the drama production (for example, "Let's count them") or through the use of number stories created by the children and children's literature (for example, *The Quilt*). But maybe it is really all too connected to even categorize!

This production we perform on the stage because the children are confident and loud! Included in this performance are our newly learned poems, which include:

- "Harriet Tubman," by Eloise Greenfield;
- "A Negro Speaks of Rivers," by Langston Hughes;

- "Mother to Son," by Langston Hughes;
- "Sister for Sale," by Shel Silverstein;
- "Boa Constrictor," by Shel Silverstein; and
- "The Giggles," by Martin Gardner.

While many teachers save their poems by African Americans for February because this month is designated as African American History Month, I do not like this separation. You can tell that my students learn a variety of poems from a variety of different-heritaged authors and we celebrate their work all year long!

Diaries

ERIC: Do you remember last month when I told you that diaries were warm-up exercises with pencil marks and occasional number and letter practice? Well, guess what! This month, we saw a dramatic change in the diaries. The pencil marks have started to disappear and the numbers and letters have begun to be the rule rather than the exception. Look at the descriptions of a few diary pieces from this month:

Decorations:
- Letters: March 102000; a bus-shaped object; on the back: a bus-shaped object with 3 smiley faces on it (maybe the kids on a field trip?)
- A bus-shaped object with 7 smiley faces on it (maybe the kids on a field trip?); on the back: numbers: 15 − 3, 00, 00, 47, 14 − 11 = 3; letters: March 72000
- A house in pencil; a bus-shaped object
- A triangle; on the back: a hand over some object
- Numbers: + 0, 400, 0; abstract figure in pencil
- Numbers: − 6, 10, 4, +, 3; a heart; on the back: a bus-shaped object
- Letters: Merz/Earvn; on the back: numbers: +, 10, 7, 3
- One person with no arms; abstract object; on the back: big letters: M M
- Letters: March1?; on the back: ve2r; numbers: 25, 17, 8
- Numbers: 3, 10, 36; on the back: WAtVNH; numbers: 8
- Numbers: 104; letters: teisVR; on the back: letters: WMeLH; March21200
- Letters: ve2AMW; on the back: letters: Ve2A; March212000; March 162000
- Letters: Dec; on the back: letters: WeHZS0R
- Numbers: 5 + 4 = 9; letters: We2NV; on the back: letters: Re?tH

Again, we can only speculate as to why this is occurring. However, it's interesting to note that we're starting to see text as the reason for doing diaries. Dates are more accurately written, and even a few correct math problems show up from time to time. You can see that a bus was a common theme for a while, so the drawings have begun to show some common purpose as well.

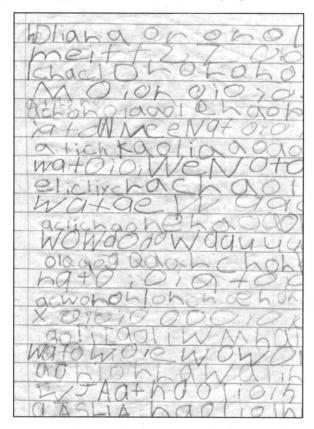

Writing Process

NINA: Even with all this immersion into science we never forget writing process. Well, there are times when, because of assemblies, special programs, or field trips, we can't do writing process. But even on these days—even when we are out for the whole day—I am scolded as we walk back into the classroom:

Danielle: Dr. Zaragoza, we didn't get to do writing process today!
Nina: Honey, I know, but we were at the planetarium all day.
Danielle: I know, but can we do it now?

Nina: But there's only about twenty minutes left. I think we need to work on our play.

Danielle: Okay, but we better do it tomorrow!

Nina: We'll do it right after our diaries and morning announcements.

Danielle: Promise?

Nina: Yes, if an emergency special program doesn't come up!

So, we continue with writing process as the children work through self-chosen topics. This might be a time when some teachers might require all students to write something about the planets, since that is a major focus in the classroom. For me, though, choice is sacred in writing process. And because children are reading more nonfiction books this kind of writing usually emerges naturally. My young authors are still choosing to create narrative pieces, and Larry (like Jamal last month) decides to include Miss Trunchbull in one of his pieces. Maybe writing process is a haven for the children—one place where they don't have to connect to the solar system—a place where they can decide to think about anything they want. Here's what Larry is writing:

> *One School Day* by Larry
> One day I went to Matilda's school and I saw Miss Trunchbull stomp-ing. I said, "Good morning, Miss Trunchbull." She said, "Get to your room, you little idiot!" I ran to my class. I told Miss Honey. She said to Miss Trunchbull, "Don't you ever do that to my kid." Miss Trunch-bull said, "You don't tell me what to do!" We ignored Miss Trunchbull and closed the door in her face.

> *My New Sister* by Larry
> One day I went to the hospital. My mother was in the bed and she was holding a new baby. The baby's name is Jeanette Shaw. She is my sister and she is home now. She cries like a cat, "Meow, meow." I love her.

> *The Lucky Boy* by Larry
> One day a boy was scared of bulls. I saw them chasing after him. I said, "I will help you." I had big muscles and pushed all the bulls away. He said, "Thank you."

Our New Bear: Venus

Remember I mentioned a new member entering our community? Well, her name is Venus, and she is a teddy bear that Alex brought in for us. The children are excited to be able to bring a new bear home and the families got right into it—after asking, "Where's Brownie?"

Me and Venus by Jamal
When I came home from school I showed my sister Venus and she said, "Where is Brownie?" So I said, "It's no more Brownie. It's Venus." And she said it looked like a girl. So me and Venus and my cousin played with Venus with my toys in the house. And then we had dinner together and then I went to take a bath and watch TV. I went to sleep so my mother woke me up to say my prayers and I gave my mother and Venus a good night kiss and we went to bed.

Me and Venus
Me and Venus had gone to aftercare. Then we went home and called my Auntie Bubbles but she wasn't home. Venus kept going to sleep. She didn't want to wake up. I said, "Venus, Venus wake up." When she woke up she wanted some milk. We wanted to go outside but it was raining so we watched TV until I had to take a shower. Then we went to bed. Christian

Me and Venus ate crab and squeezed some lime on it so it can taste good. Then we read *Goldilocks and the Three Bears* to my mother. My sister tried to eat Venus but I told her "No! No!" Alex

Me and Venus ate some cokes [cookies] and then we clod my bot [called my brother] and then we play and rid [read] are [our] red and blue books. Then we play some mor and then we rid goldilocks and the three Bears and rid a picture Bye Venus. I hope to see you again. [Last sentence written by mother.] Shaquilla (Written on her own.)

Many (including me!) didn't want Brownie to feel sad and jealous so we made sure that he was always taken home too:

Brownie Bear and I played at my daddy's job until it was time to go home. We didn't watch TV tonight because I had too much homework but Brownie kept me company while I was doing my work. After dinner I took a bath then Brownie and I went to bed. Mommy kissed us both good night. Jarrell

Before we talk a little more about Brownie and Venus I want to warn you about something. This teddy bear thing can really get out of hand! In one class

I taught, our first bear was Sasha and then a child decided to bring in another bear. We named this second bear Chrissy. And then another child decided to bring in a bear and we called that bear Princess, and so on and so on and so on. By January we had eleven bears and some of those bears had little baby bears attached to them with Velcro. Each bear also had a notebook for adventure writing. The children loved it because almost everyone got to take a bear home. But I was going a little crazy because all the children wanted to read aloud what they wrote in their bear's notebook and it took so much time. But the children loved it and they were reading and writing. I loved it too—once I figured out how to organize it all. We used the class list, and each bear with the notebook was placed in a plastic bag and once in a while all the bears rested in the classroom and did not go home. So, now that you're warned, let's get back to Brownie and Venus.

You can imagine the conversations that come from the adventures of Brownie and Venus. We talk about jealousy, brothers and sisters, bedtime, being stuck in a book bag all night, broken arms, and watching TV and videos ("Do you think it's good that Brownie watch that movie? Do you think that's a good movie for children to watch?"). We also learn what families do together and what they believe:

> My mom, me and my sisters went to church last night and I forgot Venus in my book bag. When I came home I took Venus out of my book bag and I told my mom I forgot Venus. My mom said to tell Venus that I was sorry for leaving him home by himself. This morning my sister was playing with Venus and broke Venus's arm. My mom tried to fix Venus the best way she could. My sister and I wrote a story about Venus but my mom didn't like what we wrote about Venus so she wrote it over and told the truth because she doesn't like when we aren't honest about my story about Venus. Thank you. Love always, Aubrey

Isn't it kind of funny that our community decided to name this new bear Venus? How appropriate! Venus—one of the planets in the solar system and now the name of our new bear! Why not? There's a dog named Pluto!

April

Would you like some tea?

NINA: After our spring break we are ready to "travel"! We will go to the Seaquarium in Miami, but we will also "visit" England and Japan. Hey, we've already gone around the solar system—anywhere else is a piece of cake! So as long as we're talking about cake, let's have a tea party:

Nina: Denise, you look so pretty today. Did you dress up for our tea party?

Denise: Yes, and I brought bread, too.

Nina: Oh! Everyone, let's say thank you to Denise for bringing bread.

All: Thank you!

Nina: Did anyone else bring anything?

Darrin: Me and my brother brought cookies.

Nina: Yummy. Let's all say thank you to Darrin and Darrius.

All: Thank you!

Nina: I brought bread and butter and jam and milk.

All: Thank you!

Nina: Why do you think I didn't bring tea?

Andre: 'Cause kids aren't allowed to drink tea.

Nina: Okay. Does anyone have any other ideas?

Justin: Maybe because tea is too hot.

Nina: Yes, I was thinking of both those things. Tea is usually hot and I don't want anyone to get burned. Also, many of our families don't think tea is good for children to drink. Everyone, since Justin is new to our class and didn't read *Matilda*, let's talk a little about her. Was Matilda allowed to drink tea?

Aaron: Yes.

Nina: Yes, she drank tea with her teacher, Miss Honey. In England chil-
         dren are allowed to drink tea. They're allowed to drink tea in Russia,
         too.

Crystal: My mother lets me drink coffee.

Nina: Oh! Café con leche?

Crystal: Yeah.

Nina: She puts a lot of milk, right?

Crystal: Yeah.

Nina: Everyone, *leche* means "milk" in Spanish. Let's all say "leche."

All: Leche.

Nina: Wow, very nice. You all have great Spanish accents. Now let's try
         and talk in a British accent like Matilda. Remember how some of the
         words she used in English sound a little different from our words?
         Who wants to tell Justin how Matilda says TV?

Aaron: Telly.

Nina: Yeah, raise your hand if you say "telly" sometimes now? I see a lot of
         you! Good! You know I was thinking, I wonder if in Japan children
         are allowed to drink tea. Let's remember to ask Eric when he comes.
         You know he lived in Japan and he speaks Japanese.

All: Wow!

Nina: Hey, maybe he could teach us some Japanese! Would you like
         that?

All: Yeah.

Nina: Okay, we'll ask him the next time he's here. So let's get ready for our
         tea party. Oh, I guess we can call it a milk party!

All: Ha! Ha!

Nina: (Attempting a British accent.) Now, don't forget, let's talk like Matil-
         da! Would you like some tea?

This was one of my favorite things this year because it came from one of my
most favorite books, *Matilda*, by Roald Dahl. One scene in the book has the
main character, Matilda, visiting her teacher Miss Honey and having tea. So
this is our "field trip" connection to this book. We traveled to England in our
minds and had the tea that Matilda and Miss Honey had: butter, bread, jam,
and milk. We set the tables with napkins and flowers, and had our own tea
party as we talked about the book.

Not only did we "visit" England, we also learned about Japan, and Eric
taught us how to count in Japanese. Listen as Virginia and her friends share
with their pen pals:

April 19, 2000
Dear Melanie,
My favorite ice cream is vanilla. My favorite movie is Rug Rats. My favorite book is Big Bird. I write books. I love to write books. I only speak one language and that's English but we're learning to count in Japanese. [Writes the numbers 1–5 in Japanese.]
Please write me back.
Love, Virginia

April 19, 2000
Dear Andy,
Hi Andy. I'm fine. And you? I don't go to P.E. yet but my sister does. She likes it a lot. I can't wait until I'm old enough to go to P.E. In my class we're learning to count in Japanese. Here are some of the numbers: [writes some numbers in Japanese]. Please write back. I love you, Denise

April 19, 2000
Dear Daniela,
I am getting some new shoes for Easter. We are having Easter dinner at my house. I do like *Matilda*. In school we are studying math, Japan, and we are readimg *The Littles*. What else are you learning in school? Write soon, Love, Rodcrick

April 19, 2000
Dear Jazmine,
For the summer I am going to come to school. I love school. I like to ride my bike with my twin brother, Anthony. Did you get a dog yet? I want a dog, too. Write soon!! We are learning Japanese. Love, Aaron

Dear Yanet,
I have lots of friends at my school. Their names are Larry, Tommesha, Virginia, Andre, and much more. I'm doing great in school also. In my class we're learning how to count in Japanese. Here's some of the numbers: [writes some numbers in Japanese]. Please write back. Love, Jarrell

I think it's a powerful thing to hear children as young as these talking about language, about how many they know, and the new language they're learning. A fourth grader agrees with me:

May 2, 2000

Dear Marc,

I'm so happy you're going to the Seaquarium. I can't believe you're learning Japanese. That's incredible. Well for my summer we're probably gonna go to the beach and pool. Then to Disney World for all the new theme parks and Typhoon Lagoon. It is so exciting. I can't wait. I'm in chorus. We're going to have a field trip to West Miami Middle School for the show. It is exciting. Write back soon!! Sincerely, Kimberly

Many make at least one connection to Japan and Japanese:

May 2, 2000

Dear Larry,

My class already knows Japanese stuff. Did you know that Leukemia is a type of disease caused by radiation? Also, the atom bomb that hit Japan was caused by WWII. Yes, I have been to field trips lately. I have gone to Colours Performing Group. Lucky you, you're going to Seaquarium. Tell me what you see in the Seaquarium when you write back, okay? Sincerely, Joshua

May 2, 2000

Dear Aaron,

Hi! How are you? I heard you are learning Japanese. Do you like to speak Japanese? I think Japanese is very different from English. Can you write me some words in Japanese and the meaning of them in English? No, I don't have a dog but my aunt has one and I love it like I would love a dog that I had to myself. Write back soon!! Love, Jazmine

May 2, 2000

Dear Jarrell,

I see that you're improving your writing a lot. Thank you for the Japanese numbers. They're great! How old are you? Well you're really doing good in school, right? Well I am too. Do you know Spanish? I do 'cause I was born in Cuba in Havana. I came here when I was little. Where were you born and how old are you because I'm in 4th grade and I'm 10 years old. I have 4 brothers and we are 6 sisters that makes 10 kids. Do you have brothers or sisters? Well, Bye! Love, Yanet

May 2, 2000

Dear Roderick,

How are you? I'm glad that you are getting new shoes. What kind of shoes are you getting? I got new shoes. They are Adidas. I like *Matilda* too. I've never heard about the book *The Littles*. What kind of math are you studying? Do you know any facts about Japan? In school we are studying about a Tesseract. Well, I have to go now. Bye. Your pen pal, Daniela

The children continue to talk about their academic and social affairs in April letters and the answers to the April letters. It is so interesting to me how the children's personalities become apparent in these letters. How wonderful that they feel comfortable and confident to use writing as a tool to express their thoughts, feelings, and individuality:

April 19, 2000

Dear Danielle,

My name is Justin. Aubrey left to another school so I'll be your pen pal. I like to read too. My favorite book is *Jack and the Beanstalk*. Happy birthday! Do you have any pets? I have a bunny rabbit. Write back. Love Justin

April 19, 2000

Dear Alex,

We are reading *The Littles* and reading is good. I do not have a pet. I like poetry like *The Giggles* and *The Negro Speaks of Rivers*. Do you have any pets? What do you play outside? Write back soon! Love, Jamal

Dear Michael,

I like when my class does reading discussion and my favorite cartoon is Pokemon. My favorite Pokemon is Pikacho. Have you read any good books lately? On Easter I'm going to my grandma's house to do an Easter egg hunt. Love, Christian

April 19, 2000

Dear Patricia,

I hope you got presents for your birthday. What did you get? I love to read and write. My new book I just wrote is called *The Magic House*. Do you like to write stories?

Write back soon, Love, Danielle

May 2, 2000
Hi Darrin.
How are you doing? I'm doing well in school. On my last report card
I got Principal's Honor Roll. In my class we are reading Harry Potter.
Has your class read that book? We are almost done with it. My class
is doing a play about the '50s, '60s and '70s. The play is going great.
Your friend, Sergio

May 2, 2000
Dear Cal,
Well, we took the SRI test. That is about all new we did here. In P.E.
we are playing baseball. I have batting gloves with me so that I can
swing hard. Do you have P.E.? I don't have pets.
Your friend, Daniel

These will be the last letters we exchange with our pen pals because the
end of the year is approaching. But that's okay, because guess what? We are
going to meet our pen pals in May. Yep! Debbie Feria will come from across
town with our pen pals and visit us at Little River. We are all very excited! Can
you guess what we are planning to do together? You'll see next month.

Family Connections and Expectations

You probably know that my expectations of the families and children don't
lessen. Even though we are into the final nine weeks of school we keep on going. Remember, this is a process-oriented room and things are always moving,
evolving, being published, and being read.

April 10, 2000

Dear Families,

Hello! I hope you all had a restful and peaceful break. I am excited to get
back to work with you and your children and I know we will get a lot accomplished in these last nine weeks.

I will really be pushing your child to read more and more. With your help
they will be reading at or above the first-grade level by the end of the year. Please
read with your child every single night. I want them to get through their red
books quickly so that they can move on to the first-grade books. The word lists
are very important because these are the words that are the foundation of the
first-grade reading program.

We will continue to work on addition and subtraction until all children know
the basic facts without using their fingers. Please work with your children on tell-

ing time; which number is bigger/smaller; and the value of a penny, nickel, dime, and quarter, and counting by fives and tens.

**All children need a spiral notebook for their math work. If you have not already done so, please send a dollar so we can purchase a notebook in the library.

We have finished reading *Matilda*. Did your children tell you about our little tea party? We will begin a new chapter book this week. Any suggestions?

Reminders:
Please make sure that your child:

- is on the morning line by 8:15 each morning
- completes all homework every night
- comes to school with *two sharpened pencils every day.*

Please send in the field trip form and money ($8) for the Seaquarium as soon as possible.

We're almost there! Congratulations on all your hard work!
Nina Zaragoza

Curriculum

The families are working hard with their children and this work is evident as the children continue to progress in all areas. We still have one more marking period to go and I am determined to get the children as close to first-grade level as possible or even above first-grade level. The stronger they leave kindergarten the stronger they'll be in first grade.

Reading Aloud

Families are working at home to get their children through those red and yellow books and each day some children are ready to read them aloud. By April these books dominate a lot of reading-aloud time. I get a little impatient because the books are a bit boring ("I like to read. I like to write. I like to cut. I like to paint. I like school.") The children don't seem to mind it at all. Even though they might have heard this great red book called *At School* at least fifteen times, they listen patiently while the sixteenth child proudly shows that she or he has also mastered it. They are so polite and very proud of themselves and their classmates, so how can I deny them this? I can't. So I know the red and yellow books by heart.

As you already read, the minute we finish *Matilda* we get into a new chapter book to read aloud. Why wait? This new book keeps the classroom exciting, and I would be nagged continuously if I didn't quickly start a new book. So, of course, I listen to my community and start reading. Luckily, I love to read aloud too.

Since this month we are going to the Seaquarium I encourage children to take out at least one nonfiction book about an animal that we'll see on our field trip. Do you think they take only one? Of course not! So, we have a lot of sea animal books to read and talk about—and there's our science for the rest of the year. Can't you just hear us connecting to pollution again?

Report Writing, Silent Reading, Reading Discussion, and Writing Process

Because we have done a good amount of nonfiction reading by the time we get to April, it is around this time that I help my children begin report writing. Their identity as writers is so ingrained that a new form of writing is like getting a new toy. I do not require everyone to write a report, but most of the time all children choose to—especially if the report can have something to do with animals. Here's a full-class discussion focusing on beginning report writing:

Nina:	Excuse me. I'd like to share an idea with you. Thank you, Justin, you're ready to listen; thank you, Aaron; thank you, Virginia. You know, since we've been reading so much about sea animals I thought maybe some of you would like to write about your favorite animal. Raise your hand if you might like to write about an animal. Oh, I see a lot of you do! What animal would you like to write about, Darrius?
Darrius:	A dolphin.
Nina:	Why a dolphin?
Darrius:	Because they're my favorite.
Nina:	Why?
Darrius:	'Cause they're pretty and smart.
Nina:	Okay, who else likes dolphins?
Danielle:	I do because they like to play.
Nina:	Do you know what dolphins eat?
Andre:	Other little fish.
Nina:	What else do you think they eat?
Shaquilla:	Maybe like shrimp.
Nina:	Okay, so one of the things you can write in your report about your animal is what they eat. What other animals can we write about?
Virginia:	A dog.
Nina:	Yes, someone can write about a dog. Is a dog a sea animal?
Andre:	It's like a pet animal.
Nina:	Okay, does anyone else have another answer?

Denel:	A house animal.
Nina:	And why do you think we call it a house animal?
Denel:	Because it can live in the house.
Nina:	And why do we call a dolphin a sea animal?
Alex:	Because it lives in the sea.
Nina:	Yes. So Virginia, do you want to write about a dog or a sea animal?
Virginia:	A dog.
Nina:	Why?
Virginia:	Because I want a dog.
Nina:	Oh! So maybe you can find a book that tells you how to take care of a dog. When we do report writing we talk about things that are true. What's another word for that? (No response.) Most of the time in writing process we write stories that are fiction, make-believe. What's the other word we use for things we write that are real, true? Non . . .
Denise:	Nonfiction.
Nina:	Yes, when we write information about things it is nonfiction because the things we write are real. So what kind of things do you think we should write about the animals we choose?
Shaquilla:	Like what they eat.
Nina:	Okay, so let's write them down, like questions to help us remember. (Reads as she writes each word on the board.) "What does the animal eat?" So what's another question we can ask about the animal? (No response.) What else would we want to know about an animal?
Latisha:	What color.
Nina:	Okay, so let's put that like a question. (Writes on the board and reads as she writes each word.) "What color is the animal?" Someone else give us another question.
Darrin:	About where it lives.
Nina:	Yes. (Writes on the board and reads as the question is written.) "Where does the animal live?" Thank you, Latisha and Darrin. Someone else? Let's get a few more questions. Are all animals born the same way? (No response.) How is a bird born?
Andre:	In an egg.
Nina:	Yes, the baby comes from an egg. Oh, that reminds me of a book we read a lot. Do you know which one I'm thinking of? Or can you make a connection to a book?
Danielle:	I'm thinking of *Charlotte's Web*.
Nina:	Why?

Danielle:	The part where the goslings came out.
Nina:	Oh, that's right! And remember when Templeton took that rotten egg?
All:	Yeah!
Nina:	The book I'm thinking of is *Are You My Mother?* Remember that one?
All:	Yeah!
Nina:	So that baby was born from an egg. How are other babies born? (No response.) Darrin and Darrius, do you remember when your baby brother was born?
Darrin and Darrius:	Yeah.
Nina:	Was he in an egg?
Both:	(Laugh.) No!
Nina:	Where was he?
Darrius:	In Mommy's stomach.
Nina:	Okay, the place where the baby is before it is born is the womb. So another question to help us with writing our report is (writes on board and reads as question is written): "How is the baby animal born?" Now do all animals move the same? (No response.) How do we move?
Felicity:	We walk.
Nina:	Yes, we walk. What other ways can we move?
Alex:	Skip.
Nina:	Yep, skip, walk, run. How does a fish move?
Virginia:	Swims.
Nina:	How does a spider move?
Andre:	Crawls.
Nina:	A bird?
Demeatric:	Flies.
Nina:	So another question can be (writes it on the board and reads as it is written) "How does the animal move?" So what do you think? Do you think we have enough questions here?
Danielle:	Maybe we need one more.
Nina:	Do you have an idea for one?
Danielle:	Mmm. Maybe like what kind it is.
Nina:	Oh, like if it is a bird or a fish?
Danielle:	Yeah.
Nina:	Okay, thank you. Let's write it. Everyone try and read it with me as I write it. Ready? Start looking. (Writes on the board and reads each word as it is written.) "What kind of animal is the animal?"

	Wow, we came up with some good questions! Let's read them all together. Ready, go.
All:	What does the animal eat?
	What color is the animal?
	Where does the animal live?
	How is the baby animal born?
	How does the animal move?
	What kind of animal is the animal?
Nina:	You know I'm thinking that instead of the color of the animal we can write other things that tell us how the animal looks. Like if it has fur. What else?
Felicity:	Like if it has wings.
Nina:	Okay. What else?
Alex:	How many legs.
Nina:	Yes, both those things tell us more about how the animal looks. So let's change the color question to "How does the animal look?" This way we can write more than just the color. So think about the animal you want to write a report on, and we'll talk about it more in reading discussion groups. Thank you for letting me interrupt you. Go back to writing.

This conversation is a bit long because I used it to introduce a new way of writing. I could have gone on even longer by introducing terms like *reptile*, *amphibian*, and *mammal*, but I think we did enough for one session. I will write the questions we created to guide our writing on a chart and hang this chart in a prominent place. We will practice reading these questions, and during this practice time I will extend the discussion and introduce the new concepts. These concepts will also naturally come up as we read and discuss books that focus on the chosen animals.

If children decide to report on animals that aren't sea animals I will make sure that I get the books they need for the animal they choose. Can you think of other subjects my students could report on? I could have also encouraged reports on England or Japan, don't you think? This would be another way to weave everything we do together. As usual, the books and subjects for our reports become part of our silent reading material and reading group discussions. Just as our play emerges from scaffolded small-group reading discussions, so does much of the material for the children's reports:

	(Last three minutes of silent reading.)
Nina:	Before we go into reading discussion groups take the last three or four minutes of silent reading to go over the questions we're using

to help us with our reports. Let's read the questions together. (Everyone reads the questions chorally.) Now before we go into discussion groups find some of the answers to the questions so you can share them with your friends.

(Reading discussion group with Denel, Larry, and Felicity.)

Nina: So are you talking about your animals in this discussion group?
Denel: Yes. I'm doing a bear.
Nina: Oh, not a sea animal?
Denel: Nope.
Nina: That's okay. So how does your animal look?
Denel: It's brown.
Nina: Okay, what else? Felicity, what else about his animal?
Felicity: It has fur.
Nina: Yes, it's furry. Larry, so did you help Denel find out what the bear ate?
Larry: No, but maybe honey.
Nina: Yes, that reminds me of Winnie the Pooh.
Felicity: And Miss Honey!
Nina: Ha! Ha! Great connection. So why don't you three look at Denel's book and find out what else bears eat. I'll come back in a few minutes to see what you find.

Little by little the children learn that they can get the information for their report out of their books. Just like when we studied the solar system, I will help them read and pick out the lines they want to include in their writing:

Nina: Did you find other things that bears eat?
Larry: Yes, see he's eating berries.
Nina: Good, you're using the picture to help. Let's find the sentence that tells us about the picture. Oh here it is. Let's read it together. I'll point to the words. (We read the line together.) Denel, do you want to write this in your report?
Denel: Yeah.
Nina: Okay. Go get a paper to write the sentence down. Larry and Felicity can help you if you want.

These reports will go through the same process as any other piece of writing. The author will work on a draft, have it revised and edited, and then will publish it. The author, too, will decide whether it will be shared during a TAG session:

Nina:	So did you finish the draft of your report, Latisha?
Latisha:	No, I'm still writing it.
Nina:	Would you read me what you have?
Latisha:	Okay. The fish is gold. He swims. He eats fish food.
Nina:	Oh, so this is about a goldfish?
Latisha:	Yeah.
Nina:	So do you have a goldfish at home?
Latisha:	It died.
Nina:	What happened?
Latisha:	I don't know. It was on top of the water.
Nina:	Oh, maybe they don't live that long. What else can you say about how a goldfish looks? (No response.) Do you know what those things are called that help the fish to swim? (No response.) Well, let's look in your book. Oh, see this picture? It has the names of the parts of the fish. See this word? Let's sound it out.
Latisha:	"Fin."
Nina:	Oh, you didn't need to sound it out. I bet you saw the word "in" right?
Latisha:	Yep, and I put the /f/ sound.
Nina:	You really are a reader. So you see that's called a fin. It helps the fish swim. Hey, that rhymes! Maybe you can write that in your report. Oh look, here's what helps the fish breathe. You can read it.
Latisha:	"Gills."
Nina:	Yes. There's some more information you can add to your report.
Latisha:	Okay.
Nina:	So let me know when you're ready for editing. Do you think you'll share this?
Latisha:	Yeah, I already signed up.
Nina:	For today?
Latisha:	Yep.
Nina:	Good! Maybe they can give you more ideas before you publish it.

(TAG session.)

Latisha:	T: Tell what you like.
Andre:	I like how you got the information out of your fish book.
Latisha:	Thank you. Another *T*?
D'Andre:	I like that you wrote about a goldfish because I have one.
Latisha:	Thank you. A: Ask questions.
Denise:	How many books did you use to get the words?
Latisha:	One. Another *A*.
Felicity:	Do you have a goldfish?

Latisha: It died. G: Give ideas, suggestions, connections.
Shaquilla: I connect to the Dr. Seuss book called *One Fish, Two Fish, Red Fish, Blue Fish*.
Latisha: Another one.
Danielle: Maybe you can add more about what else it could eat.
Latisha: Okay, thank you.

You see that, as usual, we follow the same process and structure whether we are writing narrative accounts or reports. Do you notice that in this TAG session I don't intervene at all? I could have interrupted with a bit of guidance—for example, "Latisha, maybe the class wants to know a little more about how your fish died." Or I could have built in another lesson connected to the Dr. Seuss book, but there are times when I think it's important to just leave the children alone to make their own connections. They hear my voice and guidance all the time and soon they won't hear it at all. They won't have me to scaffold them much longer, so I want them to get used to hearing their own voices in their heads. So especially now, as we near the end of the year, I push them toward even more independence.

The reports might be just four or five lines long, but they are reports and the children are proud of their final publication. Here's Latisha's:

The Goldfish by Latisha
The fish is gold. It swims. It has fins to swim. It has gills to breathe. It eats fish food. I like goldfish.

Poetry

Even though our formal performances are over, my children never give up their desire to recite poetry. In April they insist on practicing at least one or two poems a day. Oh, by the way, Danielle represented our class in a school district poetry recital and won first prize for her grade. She and I traveled to another school, where she recited "My People." When she returned she received a standing ovation from her classmates. They were proud of her and themselves, because when someone from our community wins, we all win. Let's listen a bit to how we worked with poetry in these last months:

Nina: So what poem should we do today? Let's go by the list so we all get a chance to pick. Alex, you're first on the list, so what poem should we recite?
Alex: "Hope," by Langston Hughes.
All: "Hope," by Langston Hughes. (We all recite the poem together.)

Nina:	Beautiful! Danielle, now what poem?
Danielle:	"Mother to Son," by Langston Hughes.
All:	"Mother to Son," by Langston Hughes. (We recite the whole poem together.)
Nina:	Okay let's go on to . . .
Andre:	No, one more please!
Nina:	One more?
Several children:	Yes, one more. No, two more.
Nina:	Okay! Two more and then we need to go on to something else. Roderick, you're next on the list. Which poem?
Roderick:	"Boa Constrictor," by Shel Silverstein.
All:	"Boa Constrictor," by Shel Silverstein. (We recite the whole poem together.)
Nina:	I can see you all love that poem! One more! Aaron, which one?
Aaron:	"A Negro Speaks of Rivers," by Langston Hughes.
All:	"A Negro Speaks of Rivers," by Langston Hughes. (We all recite the poem together.)
Nina:	Wow! You all sound amazing! Maybe later we can draw pictures for this poem. What pictures could we draw?
Larry:	Those pyramids. They're like triangles.
Nina:	Oh yes! Remember when we talked about them being in Egypt?
All:	Yeah.
Nina:	What else can we draw?
Darrin:	Rivers.
Nina:	Yes, Langston Hughes talks about a lot of rivers. Remember we put the rivers in alphabetical order? Let's name some of the rivers.
Shaquilla:	Euphrates.
Denise:	Congo.
Darrius:	Nile.
Latisha:	Mississippi.
Nina:	Do you remember which river is in our country?
Roderick:	Mississippi.
Nina:	Oh, I remember! You told us your grandmother lives in Mississippi, right?
Roderick:	Yeah, I visit her in the summer.
Nina:	Did you ever see the river?
Roderick:	I don't know.
Nina:	Maybe this summer you can. Why do you think Langston Hughes talks about so many rivers?
Andre:	He likes them.

Nina:	Maybe he did like rivers. Any other ideas? (No response.) Does the water in the rivers stay still or move?
Justin:	They move.
Nina:	Okay. So did Langston Hughes talk about one river or a lot of rivers?
All:	A lot.
Nina:	And who's talking in this poem? Remember? Look at the title.
Danielle:	A Negro.
Nina:	And what does that mean?
Andre:	Like an African American.
Nina:	Yes. A long time ago did African Americans live in America or in Africa?
Darrius:	Africa, but then they were slaves.
Nina:	Yes, when they first came to America they were brought here to be slaves.
Shaquilla:	Then they became free like in the poem "Harriett Tubman."
Nina:	Yes, and Langston Hughes is talking about slavery and freedom in this poem, too. The first rivers are in Africa and then the last river is in America. Like how the Africans traveled from Africa to America. How do you think they traveled?
Felicity:	Airplane.
Nina:	That's one way we travel now. What other ways do we travel?
Virginia:	Bus.
Nina:	Yes, you take the bus to school, right, Virginia?
Virginia:	Yeah.
Nina:	Thank you. What's another way we can travel?
Marc:	Train.
Nina:	Yes, train. Another way? (No response.) How do people travel on water?
D'Andre:	Boat.
Nina:	Africans were brought to America by boat. They were brought on slave ships. What do you think about this?
Shaquilla:	I think it was sad.
Nina:	Yes, do you think it was right or wrong?
Denise:	Wrong.
Nina:	Why?
Denise:	Because they weren't free.
Nina:	Is everyone free now?
All:	Yes.
Nina:	Let's say "A Negro Speaks of Rivers" one more time and then we'll go on to something else.

We continually talk about the poetry we recite, and over time we make many connections to the same poem. You can tell by the conversation above that we had already spoken about this poem before. My initial questions, therefore, were to help refresh their memory. After, we get to questions that enable them to more personally connect. Do you see how Shaquilla jumps to another poem? You know that this kind of discussion is prevalent in this community because we are connecting all the time! "Merry Go Round" and "Mother to Son" enable us to talk about the civil rights movement and the difficult time many black Americans had even though they were free. From here, too, we can create opportunities for report writing:

- author/poet study;
- a country in Africa; or
- the civil rights movement.

Do you have any other ideas?

Math

I'm sure you've noticed that over the past several months I have been urging families to help their children with the basic addition and subtraction facts so that they won't need to count on their fingers anymore. I do this when I am sure that all the children understand adding and subtracting conceptually. Usually by February or so, the children are comfortably creating addition and subtraction word problems and so are ready to memorize the basic facts. This type of memorization enables them to compute rapidly and concentrate on higher-level math concepts and paves the way for double-digit computation. Pretty advanced for kindergartners, many think. But all year, just as in writing and reading, I find that in a safe, structured, process-oriented classroom students progress and connect more deeply than traditionally expected.

Eric: The day I check in, the morning begins with announcements and a math problem, which ironically kind of ties into *The Littles*. It's a problem about Pinocchio's nose. Here's the problem:

One day, Pinocchio told a small fib, and his nose grew 2 inches longer. The next day, Pinocchio told a much bigger lie, and his nose grew 4 inches longer. How many inches longer did Pinocchio's nose get to be?

At this point, the voice stops and waits as classes work the problem together. Usually this delay is a minute or so. Nina rushes up to the blackboard, takes a piece of chalk, and writes the numbers 2 and 4, like this:

2   4

She says, "What goes in the middle?" A number of children raise their hand, and as Nina points to a number of them, each says, "A plus sign!" or "Plus!" Then she asks, "Why do we put a plus sign here?" One girl says, "When something gets bigger, we add." Nina then feels the pressure to solve the problem, encouraging the students to quickly figure out an answer: "Hurry before the man comes back on!" The children are indeed able to come to the answer "six" successfully.

When the announcements end, Nina notes that this problem relates to their reading *The Littles*. Larry goes to the front of the room to have his height measured. He's been there before. Nina suggests, "Let's measure Larry again." She pulls out the tape of the tape measure and shows the students. Nina asks, "Do we start in the middle of the tape measure or at the top?" Several students suggest starting at the top. There's a line on the wall where Larry was previously measured, but Larry has grown a tad. Larry smiles, takes his pencil and marks a small notched line just above the previous mark. Nina points out to the class: "Oh, look what he did to show the beginning and the end of the line. He put little itty bitty lines."

More Fun with Venus

NINA: The children are still taking home Brownie and Venus, and some, like Andre, write the entries all by themselves now:

April 23, 2000
Me and my yellow TeBear Venus was waching TV Playing to. Andre
(Written by himself.)

Others are very lucky and get to take home a bear for the weekend. Here's what Felicity, Venus, and her family did one weekend at the end of April:

4-28-00
Me and Venus came home from school and we went in my room and took a nap. When we woke up it was night and me and Venus took a bath, ate, and went back to sleep.

4-29-00

We got up, brushed our teeth and washed our face and then ate breakfast. Me and my sister played with Venus until we had our snacks and we played some more. Later we ate dinner and took a bath and we went to bed.

4-30-00

We did almost the same thing like yesterday. We had more fun today. Well, it's time to say good night. Venus and I will see you tomorrow in school. Oh yea, me and Venus and my sister had a little party and we danced. See you in school. Fun teddy!
Felicity

Fun class! Don't you think? See you in May!

May-June

Judy never saw the dog again.

NINA: Maybe the opening quote sounds a little depressing, but in a month school will be over for the summer. The end of school in this district is in the second week of June, and my children and I are not too happy about this ending. We all love school and we don't let the word "end" stop us from learning! Remember, there is no ending to a process!

Curriculum

We continue to work diligently as we write and read through our process program. We do really work through our schedule even on the last day of school before and after our final graduation ceremony and party.

Writing Process

ERIC: In the first week of the last month of the school year, students begin writing process without need of any teacher direction. Latisha and Roderick are reading their stories out loud with a partner. Latisha tells her partner that she thinks her story is too short because it doesn't take very long to read out loud. Shaquilla is practicing writing cursive script. A couple of students are working on the computer. A number of pairs are composing, scribing, and/or editing, including Darrius and Alex, Justin and Darrin, and Aaron and Shaquilla.

When students come together for TAG, no one has signed up. Nina then asks one of the children to describe the plot of the story he's working on. Nina writes two lines on the board:

Why _____?
Because _____.

For each plot item a student mentions in his or her discussion, Nina asks two or three "why" questions, expecting a "because" reply. At the end of the discussion, she notes, "Do you see how you can ask 'why' and answer 'because' and get more detail and more plot?"

Andre decides to read his story on skateboarding. His voice is a bit softer than we've come to expect, and Nina says, "Louder!" When Andre completes the story, Nina says, "T: Tell what you like." A number of hands go up. Andre puts his finger to his mouth, indicating that he's not sure who to call on. Nina says, "We acknowledge people who are behaving nicely." Andre calls on Darrin, but Darrin doesn't have anything to say. Nina scolds a bit, "Please have your comment ready before raising your hand." Andre calls on Jamal. "Why do you think the dinosaurs died?" Nina rejoices, "Great question! Why do you think they died?" A number of students indeed have suggestions, and a discussion ensues. Nina connects the conversation to issues of pollution and Marvin Gaye's "Mercy, Mercy Me (The Ecology)."

NINA: In the last month we work extra hard, especially in writing process because we are creating a class book for each child to take home as a gift from all of us. This book contains written pieces that the children choose to include. They choose stories written in September, but most also want to write newer pieces for this anthology. Much of the drafting is now done by the children, and they depend less on dictation to the editor. Let's look at some of the stories written in May and the beginning of June:

The Crazy Saturday by Shaquilla
One Saturday I was sick and I couldn't go out to play. I said to my mother, "May you do me a favor?"
    "Yes, my poor thing," she said.
"I want some juice with ice and it has to be cold, please." She went to get some juice in the kitchen and my Daddy said, "Where are you going?"
    She said, "I'm going to get Shaquilla something to drink."
    "While you're in there cook me something to eat." He said.
    My Mom said, "I can't do two things at one time!!!"
"Well you better do it and it better be good," said Dad.

When my mother came back to my bed she had an empty glass in one hand and a pot in the other hand. I said, "What is this? The glass is empty."

"I must have poured the juice in the food! Your Daddy's driving me crazy!"

The Burnt Chicken by Marc

One day me and mom had a birthday party for Dr. Zaragoza. We got cake and soda. Then we bought presents for Dr. Zaragoza. My sister asked Dr. Zaragoza, "What's your favorite thing to eat?" Then she kept asking because she kept forgetting. Then my sister was too tired and sent me to buy chicken. When my sister was serving Dr. Zaragoza she made a mistake and forgot the chicken in the oven. The chicken got burned. Dr. Zaragoza said, "That's okay. I'm a vegetarian."

As you can see the stories continue to develop in fluency and uniqueness. Many students, like Shaquilla and Marc, easily include dialogue in their stories to drive their pieces. Marc also writes successfully without using this technique:

My Best Friends by Marc

One day I went home and saw my best friend. He was in my house waiting for me to go outside and play football. We played football. When we threw the football the ball popped. I went to get it but I didn't see the ball. Another best friend took it. Then we all three played together.

My Funny Cat by Marc

One day I was sleeping and then my mom woke me up. She said, "Go eat breakfast and take a shower." I went to take a shower and my cat jumped in the water. I put him outside of the bath but he jumped on me. My mom took the cat out of the water. We both laughed.

Roderick writes about Pokemon cards, Superman, and his friends. He also seeks editing help from one of our many visitors in May and June and includes this editor, Derek, as a character in his final story:

The Scary Day by Roderick

One day there was a mean man walking down the street. He grabbed me and he pulled my arm off. He asked me, "Where do you live?" I said, "Raaaa," like a dinosaur and he ran away. I went home and put my arm back on.

The Super Gift by Roderick
One day when I was riding my bike I saw Superman flying in the sky. He flew down and gave me a gift. I told him thank you. The gift was two hundred and fifty Pokemon cards. I love Pokemon cards. Superman said he had to leave but he was going to visit me again.

The Beach by Roderick
One day Andre, Shaquilla, Derek and I went to the beach. We swam far out. We all jumped and splashed. We saw a fish and it said, "come with me." We got some money from the fish. We went back to the shore, and we got a coca cola and tortilla chips. We had a picnic with the fish because it jumped out of the water. We said, "Thank you." Then we ate and drank. (Edited by Derek Zaragoza, nine years old.)

These young authors have learned how their words can bring laughter, sadness, and other emotions to the audience:

The Scared Letters by Denise
Once upon a time my Mama took me to school. I opened my diary. The letters started to jump out and eat my name tag. I said, "Stop before I pow pow you." They ran out the door because I scared them.

The Homeless Lady by Cal
One day there was a lady. She walked everywhere I went. She asked me, "Can I wash your clothes in the washing machine?" She washed her clothes in the washing machine. Then I took her somewhere to eat. I gave her money and she took the bus and went away. She came back and said, "I got a new house with your money." I felt happy.

Judy's Dog by Shaquilla
There was this girl named Judy. She had a dog. She named it Mars. One day she kicked a tennis ball out of the house and the dog ran and got the ball. Then the pound came and got the ball and the dog. Judy never saw that dog again.

Here are some of the math word problems that the children include in the anthology:

There were two dogs in a cage and one was sad so he got out of the cage. There was one left. 2 – 1 = 1 Aaron

There were two people and an alligator came and ate them up. There were zero people left. 2 – 2 = 0 Darrius

Once upon a time there were six hearts. Four were broken and they went away. Then there were two left. 6 – 4 = 2 Tommesha

Here is a final story that we all wrote together to place as the first story in our end-of-the-year anthology:

The Surprise Party by Brownie, Venus, Nina Zaragoza and all the children of Dr. Zaragoza's class

One sunny, yellow day Brownie went to pick up his friend Venus in a bus. Venus said to Brownie, "How did you learn to drive?"

He said, "I took driving lessons."

"Where are we going?" Venus asked.

"Venus, we are going to the store to buy cookies, cake, spaghetti, ice cream, fruit, tofu, potato chips, and pizza."

"Then where are we going?" asked Venus.

Brownie said, "We have to pick up all of the children from Dr. Zaragoza's class."

"Why?"

"Because we are having a surprise party because she is our favorite teacher."

"Wow, we are going to have a nice party and Dr. Zaragoza is going to be so surprised," said Venus.

When Dr. Zaragoza opened the door she was so surprised. She said, "Wow! Thank you!" Brownie, Venus, and all the children were happy. Everyone ate a lot and then there was a parade with fireworks. It was a beautiful day.

ERIC: It's fun to look at the data from the last anthology and compare it to our benchmarks from the beginning of the year.

Name	Number of Submissions	Average Number of Sentences	Average Sentence Length (words)	Range (low)	Range (high)
Larry	4	4.75	9.26	2	16
Shaquilla	7	7.00	9.47	3	23
Christian	6	5.67	7.85	3	19
Jamal	4	5.75	8.35	3	15
Cal	4	5.75	7.83	3	14
Latisha	3	3.33	10.5	6	14
D'Andre	3	4.33	9.00	3	16
Justin	4	4.25	5.12	3	15
Andre	6	5.67	9.03	3	18
Denise	5	5.00	8.44	3	16
Denel	4	4.00	10.00	6	24
Marc	3	6.00	8.83	3	17
Virginia	6	3.83	5.34	2	11
Tommesha	5	4.80	9.50	3	23
Jarrell	3	4.33	9.61	3	15
Aubrey	2	5.50	6.91	5	9
Darrius	4	4.75	7.68	3	19
Darrin	4	5.40	9.00	4	19
Felicity	6	5.17	6.87	3	12
Aaron	3	5.67	7.12	3	15
Roderick	5	4.40	8.91	4	14
Danielle	4	6.25	8.24	3	14
Demeatric	4	3.75	9.00	3	13
Alexander	4	4.25	7.76	3	15
Typical	**4.29**	**4.98**	**7.57**	**3.08**	**14.46**

Note how each story is almost five sentences long, and a typical sentence is a little over seven words long. Finally, most stories range from about three to fourteen or fifteen words per sentence, but can get up to as many as twenty-four words in a story.

Do you remember when we looked at our data in November for the three-month period? Well, let's look to see how numbers work for this past three-month period, and see if there's any change.

Name	Number of Submissions, Sept.–Nov.	Number of Submissions, March–May	Average Number of Sentences, Sept.–Nov.	Average Number of Sentences, March–May	Average Sentence Length, Sept.–Nov.	Average Sentence Length, March–May
Larry	8	4	3.50	4.75	6.86	9.26
Shaquilla	6	7	4.00	7.00	4.79	9.47
Christian	7	6	3.43	5.67	8.46	7.85
Jamal	7	4	3.00	5.75	5.62	8.35
Cal	6	4	4.00	5.75	7.67	7.83
Latisha	5	3	4.67	3.33	5.79	10.50
D'Andre	6	3	3.33	4.33	8.30	9.00
Justin	n/a	4	n/a	4.25	n/a	5.12
Andre	9	6	3.67	5.67	6.09	9.03
Denise	12	5	4.17	5	5.50	8.44
Denel	n/a	4	n/a	4.00	n/a	10.00
Marc	8	3	3.88	6.00	6.06	8.83
Virginia	7	6	2.43	3.83	4.65	5.34
Tommesha	5	5	3.60	4.80	8.28	9.50
Jarrell	5	3	3.00	4.33	7.87	9.61
Aubrey	n/a	2	n/a	5.50	n/a	6.91
Darrius	7	4	4.70	4.75	7.51	7.68
Darrin	6	4	3.00	5.40	6.36	9.00
Felicity	n/a	6	n/a	5.17	n/a	6.87
Aaron	2	3	2.50	5.67	7.67	7.12
Roderick	8	5	4.33	4.40	7.35	8.91
Danielle	2	4	4.00	6.25	7.54	8.24
Demeatric	n/a	4	n/a	3.75	n/a	9.00
Alexander	4	4	3.00	4.25	7.00	7.76
Typical	**6.24**	**4.29**	**3.59**	**4.98**	**6.81**	**7.57**

Name	Sentence Length Range (words; low), Sept.–Nov.	Sentence Length Range (words; high), March–May	Number of Sentences Range (low), Sept.–Nov.	Number of Sentences Range (high), March–May
Larry	3	2	15	16
Shaquilla	3	3	11	23
Christian	3	3	24	19
Jamal	2	3	10	15
Cal	2	3	10	14
Latisha	3	6	9	14
D'Andre	4	3	15	16
Justin	n/a	3	n/a	15
Andre	3	3	15	18
Denise	3	3	17	16
Denel	n/a	6	n/a	24
Marc	3	3	10	17
Virginia	3	2	11	11
Tommesha	3	3	18	23
Jarrell	3	3	14	15
Aubrey	n/a	5	n/a	9
Darrius	4	3	17	19
Darrin	3	4	10	19
Felicity	n/a	3	n/a	12
Aaron	3	3	11	15
Roderick	3	4	12	14
Danielle	4	3	13	14
Demeatric	n/a	3	n/a	13
Alexander	3	3	11	15
Typical	**3.41**	**3.08**	**12.97**	**14.46**

First, we see that the number of submissions for publication has actually gone down. This is not necessarily a bad thing. We've been honing in on quality, intensifying the editing process to include all children, adding numbers of times to edit and re-edit, having students do their own writing, and ultimately having students write their own stories on the computer. The quality of the stories themselves reflects this intensification. We're happy, though, with the larger number of publications earlier in the year since it established our community relationships and helped the children to feel confident in their own abilities to compose and interact with one another in critical situations.

Next, the number of sentences per piece has increased by a factor of approximately 1.40. For a number of students, the increase in this respect has been approximately a doubling of output per sentence since our check in November. We suspect that the increase is reflective of the additional detail students are using in their descriptions, quotes, and sentence connectors.

Additionally, the average number of words per piece has increased by just under a word. That may not seem like much, but we do see far more examples of sentences longer than ten words. The range of sentence length has increased by almost a word and a half, and eight of the children have shown an increase in longest sentences by four words or more. Those students in particular seem to have caught on to the linguistic connectors that have helped them develop more sophisticated descriptions.

Connections and Interdependence

NINA: When I read over the children's stories I realize how open they are about their lives and thoughts. I know my children and they know me. They know I have three sons, and they met my youngest, Derek. They know I have two dogs, and Virginia actually came to my house and met them! I know about their dogs and cats too. I know their little brothers and sisters and have held many of them in my arms. I know their grandmothers, mothers, cousins, aunts, and uncles. We know each other!

Do you notice the line Marc gave me in his story after the chicken burned, "'That's okay. I'm a vegetarian.'" I am a vegetarian and my children know it, and they make sure I have tofu at the picnic. They also make sure there is pizza because they know I love pizza! How incredibly sweet; how incredibly connected we are. Yes, there's that word again: *connection*. And maybe the magic of this classroom is this connection. Yes, all academic material is connected and all written and read work is connected to us, but these secondary connections enable us to make the most important connection—to each other.

Silent Reading and Reading Discussion Groups

NINA: Because children are deciding what pieces they want placed in the anthology, a lot of the material for silent reading and reading discussion are books written and read over the entire school year. While some are choosing to read the newer monthly library books, most are reading their own publications:

Nina: Hi, so what books are you talking about in discussion group?
Cal: I'm reading my book "The Killer Horse."
Nina: Are you going to give that to me to type for our book?

Cal: Yeah.
Nina: Why are you choosing that one?
Cal: I like it and Roderick says he loves it.
Nina: Oh! Why do you like it, Roderick?
Roderick: Because I hate rats and the horse killed the rats.
Nina: Ugh! Now I remember that story. I hate rats too. So I guess we'll
           always get to read it whenever we want once it's in our end-of-the-
           year book. What stories are you going to choose, Roderick?

During reading discussion the children help each other with these decisions and invariably practice reading aloud many if not all of their publications. Remember, their published books are placed in our classroom library
alphabetically so they have easy access to all of their work.

In other classes I sometimes include with the end-of-the-year anthology
an audiotape of each student reading his or her publications. Included on this
tape, too, is the child reciting and singing all of his or her favorite poems and
songs.

Reading Aloud

Just as in April the children dominate most of our reading-aloud time. They
are either reading those red or yellow books, their own publications, or their
favorite library books. They continue to sign up to read and then take comments from the audience using TAG. Many of the same books are read over
and over again by different readers with no complaints from the listening audience. Some of the favorites include: *Are You My Mother?*, *The Berenstain
Bears Picnic*, *One Fish, Two Fish, Red Fish, Blue Fish*, *The Cat in the Hat*, *The Cat
in the Hat Comes Back*, and *The Carrot Seed*.

If I'm lucky I might be able to read aloud once or twice a day. I don't
start another chapter book at this point, but read some of our favorite shorter
pieces of literature. The children often request their favorite parts of the longer chapter books and I willingly comply:

D'Andre: Oh, Dr. Zaragoza, can you read *Charlotte's Web* again?
Nina: Well, we won't have time to read the whole thing again but I could
           read some of it. What part do you want to hear again?
D'Andre: When Charlotte feeds Wilbur a bottle and puts him in a baby car-
           riage.
Nina: Oh! I love that part too. Raise your hand if you like that part. Oh,
           all of you! Great, let's read it, then.

Poetry and Song

NINA: If it were totally up to the children I think they would want to recite poetry all day. Well, maybe with a little reading aloud and writing process sprinkled in! We continue to recite all our poetry and use the class list so that everyone has an equal chance to choose which poems to recite. Many times, too, we go from chart to chart traveling around the room as we read each poem. A child (also chosen in the order of the list) has a pointer and points to each word on the chart as the class reads along and performs the matching physical movements.

On our last day of school we end with our poetry and our goodbye song (Greg and Steve 2003). It is beautiful and bittersweet!

Families and Expectations

Even though we are really approaching the end of the year (the school year ends during the second week of June), I still ask that the families continue to help their children with new word lists and the red and yellow books. As I say in this letter, we want them to have a strong head start in first grade:

May 30, 2000

Dear Families,

Can you believe it's almost June? We have come such a long way. I know you are proud of your children's accomplishments. I am! Our class has excelled in reading, writing, and math. Most children are already reading at a first-grade level. Our math skills are very advanced as well! For kindergartners to be able to add and subtract as quickly as your children is quite amazing. Thank you for all your help with moving them along. All that math homework really did make a difference!

As we close off the year I am focusing on making sure all the children successfully read all of the red books. Most of them are almost there. Please continue to help them every night with these books. Please help them, too, with the new word list I sent home last week. When they master these books and word lists they will have a strong head start in first grade.

I thank you all for working so well with me. We, together, have really made a positive influence in your child's life. Each child already understands the importance of education, being responsible, and working hard to achieve goals. Most important, though, each leaves kindergarten with a true love of learning. Congratulations on a job well done. I urge you to continue to monitor your child's education closely so that they grow to their fullest potential.

I wish you and your family the best. Your children will always be in my heart and prayers,

Nina Zaragoza

My families' help this year is evident in the progress of their children. Our consistent and serious partnership proves to be a crucial part of their children's academic success. I therefore encourage them in this letter to continue to be an active presence in future academic settings. I pray that their children will have teachers that will welcome their presence and understand how a positive, ongoing relationship with families is so critical.

Visitors

Guess who came to visit us in May? Yes! Our pen pals came to visit, and it was so excellent! Guess what we all did together? I think once I tell you you'll say, "Oh, of course!" We did writing process, including TAG, reading aloud, silent reading, and reading discussion groups, and we recited poetry together. Remember I told you that the fourth graders were in a community similar to ours? Well, because of this all the children were comfortably engaged together in the familiar daily schedule and curriculum. What an amazing sight to see tall grown-up fourth graders next to their small, grown-up kindergarten pen pals reciting "Mother to Son," "My People," "The Negro Speaks of Rivers," and other poems! You've read many of the letters from the fourth graders; well, here's a letter from their teacher, Ms. Feria, to her students' families:

Hi Everyone,

I'm writing just a short note about our pen pal adventure with Dr. Zaragoza's kindergarten class. It was quite interesting to observe my fourth-grade students pen pal with the kindergarten class. It was interesting because the classroom learning experiences of all the students were similar. The students in both classes were involved with writing process, silent reading, reading discussion, and poetry. In fact, they know many of the same poems.

The pen pal letters also led to authentic teaching moments within my classroom. Topics included grammar, letter writing skills, and questioning techniques. This consistent letter writing also allowed me to support children as they developed their social abilities more fully.

The most exiting part of this pen pal writing was the children's enthusiasm. They enjoyed receiving and writing letters to each other and waited anxiously for each monthly delivery. Between letters my students would draw pictures for their pen pals, or make them valentines, or think up puzzles and codes for them.

The culminating activity, when the students met each other, was a powerful experience. The children were able to put a face to the name and were able to spend a day engaged in similar activities that they all experienced on a daily basis but in different settings. Our visitation brought the letter writing experience full circle for all of us!

Sincerely, Debbie Feria

Yes, I agree with Debbie that our visit together was a powerful ending to such a rewarding activity. We traveled together in letters for the entire academic year and meeting each other face to face was such a great reward. I think for me this visit was also a "full-circle experience" because I saw Debbie Feria, one of my former university students, as a dedicated, passionate teacher herself!

ERIC: It's the last day of the semester, and I've come to Little River to see the kindergarten students graduate. Nina is directing the students as she usually does:

- Thank you, Latisha, for doing math, but Miss Barnes is talking.
- It still makes me happy to see you do things without the teacher.
- You're focusing on what a beautiful day you're going to have.
- Please don't embarrass yourself or embarrass us during graduation.
- If you talk on stage, you will embarrass yourself and your community.
- Thank you for not talking.
- You look beautiful in the middle.
- If you do that (Nina makes a smiling face), you'll look beautiful. If you do this (Nina scrunches her face, imitating one of the children), you won't look beautiful.
- (Referring to "What a Wonderful World" and "Mother to Son.") Please do it with feeling and love.
- Now you're wasting your free choice time because I won't continue until everyone can see.
- Look at the director. Don't look at her. She doesn't have words on her face.
- You need to listen nicely just as other people listen nicely for you when you're doing this.

Back in October, we looked at Nina's comments. We saw that her comments fit most often into five categories: (1) direction to children to help others in class, (2) assuring that each child is treated as an important community member, (3) a reference to her own modeling of good academic behavior, (4) a reference to the students' own appropriate academic behavior, and (5) a promotion for children's self-approval. Then we saw that from these comments, her sentence lengths most often ranged from four to approximately eight words in length, and each instruction was almost always just a single sentence. You can see just from these nine comments here that the average comment length ranges from five to twenty-four words at an average of just over fifteen words long, and now can be two or three full sentences in length.

As you can see, the development of Nina's instructions also seems to mirror in some respects the linguistic development of the children in their writing.

Just before lunch on my last day of visiting, I conducted a couple of interviews: one with the entire class, and another with students one on one. A number of things stand out for me from these interviews: the students are aware of where they get their ideas, the children's favorite stories are each others' stories, and students named various parts of the class day as their favorites.

First, the students are aware of where they get their ideas. Here are some of the responses to the question "Where do you get your ideas?"

- You think of them.
- From other people's stories.
- Other people read the stories and they get details out of their stories.
- From other books.
- From myself, from my mom, from my sister, from my aunty, from Grandma!
- We read a book and the newspaper.
- I get my ideas from my dog and my cat.
- From a cereal box.

This last answer took Nina and me by surprise:

Nina: Jarrell?
Jarrell: From a cereal box.
Nina: A cereal box! How do you get ideas from that? How do you get ideas from a cereal box? What do you do?
Jarrell: Look at the words in the back and then you read them then you look for the details in the back.
Nina and
Eric: Wow!
Nina: Have any of your stories . . . Can you think of a story that you've used ideas from a cereal box? Which one?
Andre: I read one about the talking giraffe and a mouse.
Nina: Oh my gosh! And that was the story about the talking giraffe. Who remembers that story? So you got that from a cereal box?
Andre: Yeah.
Nina: Wow. That's excellent. Denel?
Denel: Last time when I had a cereal box it had a chicken on it.
Nina: Did that help you with any of your writing or ideas?
Denel: Yeah.
Nina: How?

Denel: Or maybe later today.

Nina: Oh! Okay. Or maybe later today!

The cereal box took Nina and me by surprise, but the class seemed to be nearly unanimous on the idea. Hence, our lesson here is that we aren't yet fully in tune with where all our children's ideas are going to come from. Clearly we need to be ready for them to come from new places, and the children themselves could probably help us generate a list of sources we have never thought of.

Next, the children's favorite stories are each others' stories. They even named a number of stories, either by title or topic, for example, "The Ghost," the monster eating cookies, "Friends," "The Ice Fish," "The Talking Fish," Pokemon and Superman, the flying bird one, "The Loose Lion," "Me and Shaquilla Fishing," "The Cat," the one about the fish, and "The Store." The students could have inadvertently named *James and the Giant Peach* or *Matilda*, but clearly they were able to parse the difference between the read-aloud stories and those of their peers, and capable of naming various peers' stories as well as the reasons why they enjoyed them. Still, perhaps the most telling reason was given by Shaquilla when asked, "Why do you like your friends' stories?" She said firmly, "Because they're better!"

Third, students named various parts of the class day as their favorites. Here are a number of daily events named in the interviews: reading out loud, singing from the chart, reading discussion, TAG, and writing.

You'll note that the schedule of the day is pretty much set, and the routine is easy to follow since it's almost the same each day. However, we do worry sometimes that we as teachers don't reach some students because we'll emphasize one kind of learning and leave another out. For example, since I'm a teacher who works principally with words, am I taking into consideration enough the need for some students to do more kinesthetic learning, even though personally that's not my own learning style? With the variety of answers tapping into various parts of the day, at least with this interview, we can feel like we're able to touch most students' learning styles, even emphasizing their strongest attribute at some point in the day. This conclusion is particularly gratifying, since the initial point of departure is that we treat each student as an author. One might think that we're only going to touch those that have some inclination toward linguistic- or language-oriented talent. Such is indeed an appropriate concern, but at least with respect to the responses from this interview, it looks like we're doing a pretty good job of treating all authors as unique individuals, thereby allowing them to compose in the ways they find most attached to their learning styles and to write about the elements of their lives that most directly touch them.

Finally, I said this to the children: "In the world there are some people that don't know how to read or write. Is this a good thing or a bad thing?" Most children agreed that such a situation was sad. During the group interview, children noted that they appreciated reading so they could progress toward the future, either way down the road or within the next year or so:

Demetric: Bad, bad, bad!
Eric: You think it's a bad thing, Demetric? How come?
Demetric: Because they won't learn nothing.
Eric: They won't learn anything if they're growing up? Andre?
Andre: If they don't learn how to read or write, they can't go to college.
Eric: Okay. Anyone else? And Denise, you had your hand up. Did you want to say something?
Nina: Did you forget the question, honey? Is it good or bad that some children in kindergarten and other places don't know how to read or write? Is that good or bad?
Denise: Bad.
Nina: Why do you think it's bad?
Denise: You need to know how to read.
Nina: What?
Denise: Because you have to know how to read.
Nina: Why is it good to know how to read?
Denise: So we can go to first grade.

However, during the one-on-one interviews, the reasons for knowing how to read were more specific. Here are some of the conclusions children brought:

- Because I wanna be six, and reading makes me six.
- Because I'm big. I'll look older.
- Because if they don't learn how to write, they won't grow up to be a writer. So if they don't grow up to be a writer, they won't get stories and read stories that they wanna read, so I like to be . . . so I like to be grown up and be a writer.

More Letters!

NINA: I think it's quite appropriate to include some letters in this final chapter, don't you? We are definitely a letter writing community. Thank you notes, pen pal letters, letters to families, letters about Brownie and Venus abound.

So here's a letter about these young authors from the principal of Little River Elementary:

August 18, 2003

Dear Nina,

As we begin the new school year I wanted to update you on your kindergarten students that are now entering fourth grade. You would be amazed at how beautiful they are growing academically, physically, and emotionally. You were their first teacher in a school setting and you taught them the joy of learning. They are progressing in a dynamic way!

When they were in second grade, 85% of your students scored at the 99th percentile on the Stanford Achievement Test (SAT), thus allowing them to participate in the gifted program. As third graders, 95% scored levels 3 (grade level) or above on the state assessment tests in reading and math.

I know that their accomplishments are based upon the effective manner in which you taught literacy and your genuine concern for the achievement of all your students. Our students will continue to do well because of the strong foundation you have given them. This has truly made them lifelong learners.

Thank you for being an educator that cares and has high expectations for all students. I pray for your continued success in the lives of your future students. Have a fantastic year!

Sincerely, Gloria P. Barnes

Principal, Little River Elementary School, Miami, Florida

The children's success, of course, is not just due to our kindergarten community, but I do believe our class helped nurture the children's growing love of learning. I also believe that the families of these children were supported and encouraged in our community to build on their children's love of learning. And so, these children hold on to this love and the foundation built in kindergarten as they continue on to first grade.

Eric's Goodbye

I feel like I've been on a long concert tour. The children are the symphony, Nina is its conductor, and I'm the enthusiastic groupie. When the voices all blend together, the result is an awe-inspiring crescendo to a full, bright fortissimo chord. There are times when only a few children are playing, during which I may enjoy a softer ensemble. Occasionally, there are solos, and children are on stage alone, exposing their souls to the world. And like the chords supporting a solo, the children through TAG offer the foundation on which soloists may stand proudly and present their best work. The pieces are composed by the artists themselves; hence, we spend the year remarking on a constant stream of world premieres.

A symphony doesn't need a newspaper review or some numerical or alphabetic value (in other words—a grade) attached to it for its members to understand how well it has performed during a concert. So too is the intrinsic nature of Nina's class. These children don't need grades for them to understand the value of their learning and progress, that learning is most effective when it sprouts from within, and that their assessment of themselves is just as critical as mine would be, perhaps even more so, in spite of their age.

There are occasionally outside influences who act—often inadvertently—to prevent the success of our symphony. In our case, it is the lunch lady who barks at students for not having their food voucher number or the fire marshal who insists on taking all student creations off the wall. There are most likely sound reasons for these adults to act as they do; keeping order in the cafeteria and asserting that the school doesn't burn are indeed acceptable goals, to say the least. However, how these goals are enacted in ways beneficial to the school should be given careful attention. Likewise, the symphony director and its members must respond to these demands, as a community, in creative and dynamic ways. Hence, the good news is that the conductor, in this case Nina, is not alone in dealing with these issues. She appropriately goes to the class and they address them together as a community.

To choose music seems to me a most natural thing to do. To be part of music as a recipient or as a participant is equally inviting. These children demonstrate that to choose learning is equally natural. The good conductor, coach, or teacher makes certain that this initial desire is never squashed, bearing in mind that it is far easier to douse one's motivation to learn than it is to rekindle motivation lost. The best teacher keeps the original motivation afloat and works toward energizing its blossoms. To observe children at the beginning of their educational career, to see their anticipation, and to see them flourish is far more exciting than watching a teacher try to rejuvenate a child's deflated desire. These children came to kindergarten eager, ready, and capable. They walked to class with pride and joy, energy, and a sense of purpose and responsibility.

Throughout the year, I have felt privileged to have spent time with these artists. I have their stories in my head and heart, and I have their faces engraved in my mind forever. I'm honored and grateful that these children are my friends. I wonder what will happen to these people in the future, and that's as it should be. After all, the goal of any good performance is to leave the audience wanting more. Everyone, take a bow!

Final entries for Brownie and Venus

Me and Brownie payd [played] we rad [read] my bak [book]. We Love Brownie we hop [hope] Brownie can kom back. Larry (Written without help.)

Me and Brownie was in my grand mother room leaving [learning] our first grade song love Andre (Written without help.)

Me and Brownie and Venus played with my Nintendo and we watched TV and played school with my brother Anthony. And then we went to bed. Aaron

Brownie and I played ball. Then we watched TV. My mom gave us cookies me and Brownie ate them. After we got a bath and then we had dinner. For dinner we had rice and fish. Then at 7:00 we read. The first book we read was *The Lost Tooth*. It was funny and fun. Next me and Brownie and my big sister talked to Jesus. And we wanted to read a Jesus story. We read how Jesus made things. And we went to bed. Love you forever. We will be friends forever. Brownie you are my best friend. Bye Brownie. I hope I see you next time.

Me and Brownie had got money and we sat down and he said "I love you Denise."

Me and Brownie and Venus went outside to play with my friends. My brother was jumping on the trampoline. He was jumping high. He fell and I said, "Are you okay?" Then we went back in the house and we got some water. It was good and cold. We were playing with my cousin Keyana. She likes Brownie and Venus a lot. She cried when I put them to sleep. I love Brownie. Tommesha

So it's goodbye to Brownie and Venus, goodbye to our fourth-grade pen pals, and goodbye to our dear community. Our community filled with writing, reading, publishing, and sharing with TAG. Our community filled with books and their characters who joined us: Wilbur, Fern, Templeton, Charlotte, James, Stuart, Matilda, Miss Trunchbull, Miss Honey. Goodbye to Langston Hughes, Nikki Giovanni, Shel Silverstein, Gwendolyn Brooks, Eloise Greenfield, and the characters in their poems: the mother and her son, the boa constrictor, the giggler, Harriett Tubman, Lydia and Shirley, Rudolph, and the others. Most of all, goodbye to our community filled with us, all of us: Alex, Demeatric, Danielle, K'Andre, Roderick, Aaron, Felicity, Aubrey, Justin, Darrin, Darrius, Jarrell, Tommesha, Virginia, Marc, Denel, Denise, Cal, D'Andre, Jamal, Andre, Christian, Shaquilla, Damine, and Larry. I know we will never forget each other. Even if we don't remember every name, every poem, or every book written and read, we will all be in each other's hearts. We will always carry the love we have for each other and love we have for learning within us.

Goodbye, dear friends. Thank you for joining us for part of the journey.

References

Berenstain, S., J. Berenstain, and M. Berenstain. (1990). *Berenstain Bears* (series). New York: Random House.

Brooks, G. (1999). *Selected Poems.* New York: HarperCollins.

Brown, H. D. (1994). *Principles of Language Learning and Teaching.* Upper Saddle River, NJ: Pearson Education.

Brown, R. (1973). *A First Language: The Early Stages.* Cambridge, MA: Harvard University Press.

Burgess, A. (1962). *A Clockwork Orange.* London: Heinemann.

Cho, K. S., and S. Krashen. (1995). From *Sweet Valley Kids* to Harlequins in one year. *California English* 1: 18–19.

Cleveland, A., M. Gaye, and R. Benson. (1971). "Mercy, Mercy Me (The Ecology)," recorded on M. Gaye, *What's Going On?* Motown Records.

———. (1971). "What's Going On?" recorded on M. Gaye, *What's Going On?* Motown Records

Collier, V., and W. Thomas. (2001). Reforming schools for english language learners: Achievement gap closure. Presentation at NABE 2001: 30th Annual International Bilingual/Multicultural Education Conference, February 20–24, Phoenix, AZ.

Cummins, J. (1981). *Bilingualism and Minority Language Children.* Toronto: Ontario Institute for Studies in Education.

Dahl, R. (2000). *James and the Giant Peach.* New York: Penguin Group, USA.

———. (1990). *Matilda.* New York: Viking Press.

Deci, E. L. (1975) *Intrinsic Motivation.* New York: Plenum Press.

Eastman, P. D. (1960). *Are You My Mother?* New York: Random House for Young Readers.

Frost, R., and E. C. Lathem (Eds.). (1979). *Poetry of Robert Frost: The Collected Poems, Complete and Unabridged*. New York: Henry Holt and Company.

Geisel, T. ("Dr. Seuss"). (1960). *One Fish, Two Fish, Red Fish, Blue Fish*. New York: Random House for Young Readers.

———. (1958). *The Cat in the Hat Comes Back*. Random House for Young Readers.

———. (1957). *The Cat in the Hat*. New York: Random House for Young Readers.

Giovanni, N. (2003). *Collected Poetry of Nikki Giovanni, 1968–1998*. New York: William Morrow.

Greenfield, E. (1993). Harriet Tubman. In *Pass It On: African-American Poetry for Children*, ed. W. Hudson. New York: Scholastic.

Greg and Steve (2003). *Love Is . . . CD Musictivity Book*. Sayward, BC, Canada: KIDiddles.

Harper, C., and Platt, E. (1998). Full inclusion for secondary school ESOL students: Some concerns from Florida. *TESOL Journal* 7: 5, 30–36.

Herbert, F. (1965). *Dune*. New York: Ace Books.

Hughes, L. (1995). *The Collected Poems of Langston Hughes*. New York: Vintage Books.

Johnson, J. W., and J. R. Johnson. (1899). "Lift Every Voice and Sing." In *Lift Every Voice and Sing*. New York: Walker and Co.

Kelly, R. (1996). "I Believe I Can Fly," recorded on *Space Jam: Music from and Inspired by the Motion Picture*. Atlantic Records.

Kossack, S., L. Martinez-Perez, E. Dwyer, H. Landorf, and C. Alacaci. (2003). Scaffolding expository writing: Text patterns to text skeletons. *International Journal of Learning* http//learningconference.publishersite.com

Krashen, S. (1993). *The Power of Reading: Insights from the Research*. Englewood, CO: Libraries Unlimited.

Krauss, R. (1989). *The Carrot Seed*. New York: Harper Trophy.

Lee, D. (1986). "From African Poems" In *Listen Children: An Anthology of Black Literature*, ed. D. S. Strickland. Toronto: Bantam Books.

Lepper, M. R., and M. Hoddell. (1989). Intrinsic motivation in the classroom. In *Research on Motivation in Education, Vol. 3: Goals and Cognitions*, ed. N. C. Ames and R. Ames. San Diego, CA: Academic Press.

Lewis, M. (Ed.). (2000). *Teaching Collocation: Further Developments in the Lexical Approach*. Hove: Language Teaching Publications.

Marshall, J. (1998). *Goldilocks and the Three Bears*. New York: Puffin Books.

Maslow, A. (1970). *Motivation and Personality*. New York: Harper and Row.

McCloskey, M. (2002). Seven instructional principles for teaching young learners of English. TESOL Institute, November, San Diego, CA.

Nation, P. (2001). Learning vocabulary in lexical sets: Dangers and guidelines. *TESOL Journal* 9, no. 2 (summer): 6–10.

Nettl, B. (1983). *The Study of Ethnomusicology.* Urbana-Champaign: University of Illinois Press.

Ohio Department of Education. (2000). *Academic Content Standards K-12 English Language Arts.* State Board of Education and Ohio Department of Education, Columbus, OH.

Ottolenghi, C. (2001). *Jack and the Beanstalk.* Grand Rapids, MI: McGraw-Hill Children's Publishing.

Pascal, F. (1987). *Sweet Valley High* (series). Toronto: Bantam.

Perrault, C., with G. Dore. (1988). Cinderella. In *Comtes de ma Mere L'Oye.* Poole: Schoenhof's Foreign Books.

Peterson, J. (1993). *The Littles.* New York: Scholastic Books.

Piaget, J. (1970). *Structuralism.* New York: HarperCollins.

Saenz, B. A. (1999). *A Gift from Papa Diego—Un regalo de papa Diego.* El Paso, TX: Cinco Puntos Press.

Salinger, J. D. (1951). *The Catcher in the Rye.* New York: Little Brown and Company.

Schmitt, N. (2000). *Vocabulary in Language Teaching.* Cambridge: Cambridge University Press.

Sendak, M. (1988). *Where the Wild Things Are.* New York: HarperCollins.

Silverstein, S. (1981). *A Light in the Attic.* New York: HarperCollins.

———. (1974). *Where the Sidewalk Ends.* New York: HarperCollins.

Taylor, M. D. (1991). *Roll of Thunder, Hear My Cry.* New York: Puffin Books.

Weiss, G., and B. Thiele. (1968). "What a Wonderful World," recorded on L. Armstrong, *What a Wonderful World.* ABC Records.

White, E. B. (1999 [1952]). *Charlotte's Web.* New York: Harper Trophy.

———. (1974). *Stuart Little.* New York: HarperCollins Juvenile.

Woloshyn, V. E., A. Paivio, and M. Pressley. (1994). Use of elaborative interrogation to help students acquire information consistent with prior knowledge and information inconsistent with prior knowledge. *Journal of Educational Psychology* 86: 79–89.

Zaragoza, N. (1987). Process writing for high-risk and learning disabled students. *Reading Research and Instruction* 26: 290–301.

Zargoza, N. (2002). *Rethinking Language Arts: Passion and Practice.* New York: Taylor & Francis.

Zaragoza, N., and B. Cruz. (2001). Shifting pedagogical responsibility: The use of TAG for self and classroom community assessment. *The Florida Reading Quarterly* 38, no. 2: 19–25.

RETHINKING CHILDHOOD

JOE L. KINCHELOE & JANICE A. JIPSON, *General Editors*

A revolution is occurring regarding the study of childhood. Traditional notions of child development are under attack, as are the methods by which children are studied. At the same time, the nature of childhood itself is changing as children gain access to information once reserved for adults only. Technological innovations, media, and electronic information have narrowed the distinction between adults and children, forcing educators to rethink the world of schooling in this new context.

This series of textbooks and monographs encourages scholarship in all of these areas, eliciting critical investigations in developmental psychology, early childhood education, multicultural education, and cultural studies of childhood.

Proposals and manuscripts may be sent to the general editors:

Joe L. Kincheloe
c/o Peter Lang Publishing, Inc.
275 Seventh Avenue, 28th floor
New York, New York 10001

To order other books in this series, please contact our Customer Service Department at:

(800) 770-LANG (within the U.S.)
(212) 647-7706 (outside the U.S.)
(212) 647-7707 FAX

Or browse online by series at:
www.peterlangusa.com